RONALD BRADLEY

THE TUMULT

and the

SHOUTING DIES

Autobiography of an Old Timer

RONALD BRADLEY

THE TUMULT
and the
SHOUTING DIES
Autobiography of an Old Timer

MEMOIRS

Cirencester

Mereo Books

1A The Wool Market Dyer Street Cirencester Gloucestershire GL7 2PR

An imprint of Memoirs Publishing www.mereobooks.com

The Tumult and the Shouting Dies: Autobiography of an Old Timer

ISBN 978-1-86151-021-1

First published in Great Britain in 2015
by Mereo Books, an imprint of Memoirs Publishing

Ronald Bradley has asserted his right under the Copyright Designs and Patents
A CIP catalogue record for this book is available from the British Library.

The address for Memoirs Publishing Group Limited can be found at
www.memoirspublishing.com

The Memoirs Publishing Group Ltd Reg. No. 7834348

The Memoirs Publishing Group supports both The Forest Stewardship Council®
(FSC®) and the PEFC® leading international forest-certification organisations. Our
books carrying both the FSC label and the PEFC® and are printed on FSC®-certified
paper. FSC® is the only forest-certification scheme supported by the leading
environmental organisations including Greenpeace. Our paper procurement policy can
be found at www.memoirspublishing.com/environment

Typeset in 11/16pt Plantin by Wiltshire Associates Publisher Services Ltd. Printed and
bound in Great Britain by Printondemand-Worldwide, Peterborough PE2 6XD

DEDICATION

For my sister Pauline (Polly Sykes) and husband Pip Sykes who patiently suffered my stories during our long, enjoyable walks together.

And my Grandchildren:

Scott Bradley and Jade Bradley
Parents: Mark and Donna

Kelly Bradley, Samantha Bradley and Jack Bradley
Parents: Paul and Jay

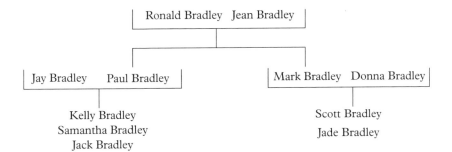

Ronald Bradley   Jean Bradley

Jay Bradley   Paul Bradley

Kelly Bradley
Samantha Bradley
Jack Bradley

Mark Bradley   Donna Bradley

Scott Bradley
Jade Bradley

ACKNOWLEDGEMENTS

The author wishes to acknowledge updated information discovered in the following Bradt Travel Guides since his retirement in 1987:

Bradt Travel Guide - Sierra Leone - Edition 1
Authors: Katrina Manson & James Knight, May, 2009

Bradt Travel Guide - Nigeria - Edition 2
Author: Lizzie Williams, 2008

Bradt Travel Guide - Malawi - Edition 5
Author: Philip Briggs, April, 2010
(See the Summary near the end of the book.)

PHOTOGRAPHIC ACKNOWLEDGEMENTS

I would like to thank my sister Pauline (Polly Sykes) and her husband Pip, who once again listened to my stories and scoured their family albums for suitable photographs from earlier years (1935 to the mid 1950s) for inclusion in this edition, all probably taken with an old and simple Brownie box-type camera which required a visit to the chemists for film development.

My earlier expatriate years followed with photographs taken with a Kodak Instamatic camera which dispensed with the services of the chemist (1955-mid 1970s). The mid-seventies to 2000 saw the advent of more sophisticated equipment (zoom lenses etc) which enabled novices and enthusiasts to produce excellent photographs.

And forward to the experts and professionals:

Mortons Media Group Ltd are renowned for publishing railway magazines. Their archives contain fantastic photographs of various related subjects and I am grateful for their permission to use two images from their recent book *Mallard, The Magnificent Six* by Robin Jones celebrating the 75th anniversary of the introduction of these record-breaking streamlined steam locomotives to our railways in the 1930s and the gathering together at York National Railway Museum of those still in existence.

Brian Sharpe - Mallard at Grantham, 2013.

Robin Jones - Sir Nigel Gresley at York National Railway Museum, 2013.

CONTENTS

EARLY BEGINNINGS AND
THE WAR YEARS

CHAPTER 1

PRIMARY SCHOOLDAYS

1935 TO 1941

Harlaxton Road Primary School

5 Years Miss Sentence
6 Years Miss Rawlings
7 Years Miss Bott
8 Years Miss Imber
Headmistress: Miss Wright

If pupils were under-achieving by the age of seven, Miss Bott took over for a period of special tuition, hoping to get them back into the mainstream before leaving primary at the age of eleven. All other pupils passed this class by and carried on as normal. These underachievers (or backward) children were known throughout the school as 'specials' and their classroom was the 'specials classroom'. All very politically incorrect to us now and I expect disliked by the parents concerned, but I was accepted because their children were receiving necessary tuition in a smaller class with the teacher able to give one-to-one attention to each individual child. It appeared to work well and could possibly have benefits today, but obviously would not be accepted in the modern educational climate.

By the age of six I had become a keen reader and was encouraged by my parents, who kept me supplied with suitable books. My mother and teacher noticed that I held the books really close to my eyes and I was taken for an eye test. The optician informed my parents that my vision was below par and I was lucky not to have been run over by a car.

I received my first spectacles aged six and can still remember that day vividly. They were the best present I had ever received up to that date. Everything was transformed! I naturally thought everyone had difficulty seeing things, but now all was clearer and life was much easier. My parents had to check that I had removed my spectacles when I went to bed as I was liable to keep them on. Even today they are the last thing I remove at night before getting into bed and the first thing I reach for in the morning.

My grandson Scott has a friend of the same age (also Scott) and when they were both around six I asked bespectacled Scott Gilbert how his parents knew he required glasses. "I used to sit with my nose nearly touching the television screen," he replied. (TV, the modern equivalent of the book!) Around the age of six we moved from 7 Cowes Road to 17 Shanklin Drive, on the same estate on the outskirts of town. This was a larger house and garden. Our school was two miles away. Few working-class people owned cars; you walked or biked to your destination. Two young ladies (aged 10) who lived nearby and attended the same school used to take me to and fro and we had to pass under the Harlaxton Road Bridge on our journey. The bridge carried the mainline trains from Scotland to Kings Cross Station in London. Some trains did not stop at Grantham and rattled through at a fair speed, blowing their whistles as they approached the station.

I vividly remember that one afternoon on our way home we were directly underneath this cavernous echoing structure, and so was a tradesman travelling with his horse and cart. The express sped overhead, whistle blowing. The horse bolted and carried the cart and driver 100 yards down the road before the cart overturned, throwing the driver to the ground. I do not know how the horse or driver fared, for we were quickly ushered away by responding adults. It was my first encounter with the more horrific side of life.

In September 1939, war with Germany was declared and times became more menacing. I was nine and used to walking to school and returning home without 'parents or guardians' (to use the modern term). I remember during playtime running across the playground and clinging to the school railings, which were only 100 yards from the main LNER (London North Eastern Railway) line as the new streamlined steam trains Silver Link, Sir Nigel Gresley, Mallard and the earlier Flying Scotsman went hurtling past. The newsagent's premises on Grantham Station platform were securely shuttered before any non-stop express whistle could be heard as it approached the station, enveloping the surrounding area with the smoke from its boiler. The railway line from Grantham to Peterborough was the longest, straightest stretch of track in the country, and locomotives were tested there, breaking many speed records. I witnessed a similar scene in my primary school days (1935-41) from a location to the scene shown here.

Morning playtime also heralded your daily free-of-charge milk allocation, which was delivered in many steel crates. Empty crates from the previous day were collected by the milkman. We eagerly pierced the small centre hole of the securely-fitted cardboard bottle-top, inserted our straws and devoured the contents. There was always at least a one-inch layer of delicious cream on top. Birds of all kinds also appreciated this milk and and if crates were left outside they were liable to peck through the top seal. I use the measurement 1" (one inch) because in those days we measured in inches, feet, yards, miles etc, so today I am happier working in these measurements in preference to millimetres, centimetres and metres.

Classroom windows were taped up to resist breaking and flying glass, should bombs land nearby, which they were soon to do.

'Made in Britain' - how often do you see that sign on the goods now? At that time we could, and did, manufacture anything. In Grantham, population 22,000, we boasted four major engineering works:

Aveling-Barford Ltd	Earthmoving equipment and contractors' plant, plus Bren gun carriers during the war.
Ruston & Hornsby	Diesel Engines
British Marco	Guns and Ammunition
Neals	Mobile Cranes

There were also many airfields on Lincolnshire's flatlands. We were therefore of great interest to the Germans.

Harlaxton Road Primary School appeared to us to be on the direct flight path of the German bombers targeting British Marco, which was situated one mile from our school, and on several afternoons lessons were interrupted as we were subjected to low-level flights over the school with planes swooping, anti-aircraft fire from our ground-based artillery, machine-guns from our attacking fighter planes and exploding bombs from German aircraft falling in the vicinity of Marco.

Whenever the warning sirens were heard we followed a set routine. There was a wide corridor right down the centre of the school from one end to the other with classrooms, storerooms, offices, etc. on either side. We gathered and sat in the corridor adjacent to our classrooms; each child had a large tin box (biscuit tin or similar) which was filled with chocolate bars, biscuits, etc. and tightly sealed with adhesive tape. These had been prepared by the child's parents and were kept in a storeroom and issued to the children by teachers in emergencies as described previously. We sat with these tins on our knees. I assume the idea was that when the school was bombed and we were buried in rubble we miraculously freed our hands and arms, unwrapped the adhesive tape securing the biscuit tin lid and happily devoured the contents until our rescuers arrived and dug us out. I cannot recall anyone questioning the logic of this operation at any time.

During these frightening episodes there was never any great panic among the children or staff that I can remember. Each child collected their gas-mask from the cloakroom in its cardboard container and strap (and knew how to use it if necessary); they then took their places in the corridor. All children carried a gas-mask everywhere at all times and were given regular training during school hours on their use. Training was carried out in special vehicles which would be filled with tear-gas to test the efficiency of their masks and the children would be instructed to insert a finger into the side rubber in order to smell the gas. The finger was hastily removed, as you can imagine.

My Aunt Nelly and Uncle Jack lived near the school and I

conveniently had my lunch with them on schooldays. Uncle Jack was semi-retired; he had worked on the railway operating a breakdown crane for many years but was now our school caretaker. My parents and I often visited them for tea on Sundays, or they visited our house. Other relations would often attend these 'get-togethers'. I can still remember clearly and in detail several pictures of dogs and cats with various other animals that hung on their walls.

CHAPTER 2

SECONDARY SCHOOLDAYS

1941 TO 1945

On reaching the age of eleven I attended the Boys' Central School, a secondary modern establishment. The school uniform consisted of dark brown blazer with yellow piping and crest on the top breast pocket; a tie with matching horizontal yellow and brown stripes completed the mandatory items. Our Headmaster (Mr Thorpe) was a strict disciplinarian, as were his Assistant Headmaster (Mr Speechley), of Science and Maths fame, Mr Redwood (Biology, Music and Athletics), Mr Scudamore (English and Art) and Mr Sewell (Crafts, Woodwork). These were the four main protagonists. I can remember women teachers being around at times but they changed frequently and I cannot remember any of their names. I think these appointments filled vacancies created by male teachers being called up for military service.

You messed around with any of the above at your peril. If you were dispatched to the Headmaster's Study for any misdemeanour you soon discovered that he could wield a cane with some accuracy and force. Day-to-day minor indiscretions by pupils were dealt with by teachers hurling flying missiles such as wooden blackboard wipers and other objects they had at hand on their desks. Stealthily approaching gossiping students from the rear of the classroom and flicking the offender's ear with a 12" wooden rule was another favourite tactic and an emanating howl of pain was always greeted with stifled amusement by the rest of the class.

If a master left the classroom, immediate scuffles would break out between various warring groups; fists and missiles would often be thrown, but there was always a classmate positioned at the door as lookout and on hearing of the master's imminent return the class would quickly regain their seats and fall silent in their studies.

Thinking back to those days, I wonder how you control classes of thirty boys (aged 11 to 15) if you do not approach them with strict discipline? The answer I fear is that if you do not you surely must fail, and this is being borne out in many cases in today's educational establishments housing unruly and undisciplined students.

Mr Thorpe, our Headmaster, reminded us daily that we were ambassadors for the school, saying that people outside would recognise the school uniform and the behaviour of pupils wearing it and judge us accordingly. All the masters kept him fully informed of any misdemeanours they observed in out-of-school hours around the town and at the close of the daily assembly the errant parties would be singled out for a special mention and warning as to the future perils of consuming fish and chips in the street, chewing gum or any similar disgusting habits.

During assembly the teachers sat on chairs on a raised stage at the front of the hall, which also housed the piano on which Mr Redwood played several hymns each morning, our favourite being 'To be a Pilgrim' as we had a classmate who had the surname Pilgrim and the line 'Our first avowed intent, to be a Pilgrim' at the end of each chorus called for measures of self-restraint worthy of Saints (or Pilgrims)!

Mr Speechley (Deputy Head) was over 6ft tall, in his 30s, hair thinning, bespectacled. I never encountered bullying at all from my schoolmates during my schooldays but I did receive a goodly share (usually on a weekly basis) from F.A. Speechley. Being tall, he appeared to gain much pleasure in taunting and humiliating boys of short stature. I stopped growing at the height of 5ft 4½" and therefore would have been shorter than this at that time, which made me the shortest boy in class except for Senescall (I cannot recall his Christian name).

During the early to mid-forties we had no television and the radio was our main source of home entertainment. Variety Theatres were popular and were the means of seeing the top vocalists, comedians, etc. of the day. Every Saturday night from 8 pm to 9 pm a programme called 'Music Hall' was broadcast over the radio and consisted of around six top artists enjoying a 10-minute slot each in which to sing their songs or tell their jokes. Often these performances would be directly broadcast from a variety theatre.

On Monday morning after assembly we would return to our classroom and Mr Speechley would find some excuse to bring Senescall and myself to the front of the class with our chairs and made to stand on them facing the class. Mr Speechley would then regale the class with jokes from the previous Saturday's Music Hall and if they could be re-worked to feature one of us and to our detriment, thus gaining a laugh at our expense, he would be highly delighted at his cleverness. Somehow he believed he was imparting original material and seemed unaware of the fact that several of the boys listened to Music Hall and were also budding comedians and keen to memorise the jokes. My mistake was constantly to spoil his punchline by getting in first, highly satisfactory from my point of view though this inevitably meant standing longer on the chair as punishment!

Mr Sewell held woodworking classes for a two-hour period each week. We commenced by learning the different joints (dovetail etc.) and making them from scale drawings. Obviously these joints in progress could not be completed in one session and therefore the several pieces of unfinished work required taping together securely, boldly named by the proud owner before being consigned to the woodworking storeroom until the next lesson.

Whenever the next lesson arrived I usually found myself scrambling about in the storeroom searching for my missing woodwork items, which had either disappeared completely or were located in parts on various shelves. On informing Mr Sewell of my frustration at these regularly occurring events I received little sympathy, as he dismissed my accusations of foul play (theft by other pupils who needed replacements for their sub-standard work), and he clearly could do without attention being focused on his lack of ability to organise his storeroom. I therefore became a thorn in his side during these classes as I struggled to keep up with classmates, because I regularly had to get more wood and start from scratch. I never really seemed to get anything completed.

When the annual woodworking exam came around we were given adequate time to complete the task in one session without the necessity of storage, and I was always in the top three when the marks were declared. Mr Sewell found it hard to accept that this could happen after my previous lack of progress - an enigma.

On completing our range of joints, each pupil could select items to make, but unfortunately the woodwork continued to disappear and I managed to complete only two items in more than two years; my bookstand took forever before it could be taken home. Not a proud accomplishment, more a feat of endurance. A case of 'The woodworking class is over but the malady lingers on'.

Mr Sewell Senior had a barber's shop, with accommodation above, in Grantham, which I used to frequent whenever it was deemed necessary by my parents. Our teacher, Mr Sewell, and his family lived in the same premises and he would usually arrive home during my time in the barber's chair from which his dad was operating. Opening the door from the street and wheeling his bicycle into the shop past the hat stand, he would notice my school cap and peer towards me. I automatically stiffened and sat to attention. "Hi Dad," he would say, disappearing (with bike) through the door beyond. "Does he give you a hard time?" said Senior. "No, he's okay," I would reply diplomatically, relaxing once again and hoping we could change the subject.

Sport played a key role at the Boys' Central School and the Headmaster seized every opportunity to get everyone involved in various activities. I would not say sport was encouraged - it was demanded. You participated unless you could prove by doctor's note that you had a broken limb or other equally serious impediment.

School was two miles from my home and cycling was my means of transport. Swimming featured prominently on the sports agenda and we attended Wyndham Park Swimming Baths at allocated times. The Baths were quite near the school and a short detour on my morning journey meant that I could cycle through the park and check the board outside the pool which displayed the current day's temperature. Mr Thorpe's law stated that 60 and above meant attendance and submergence with no excuses accepted. I forgot to mention that it was an open-air, unheated pool. Probably some of my life's coldest moments have been spent at that location. 59 meant a sigh of relief and the hope that the sun would not break through until after our swimming period.

At this time I suffered severe thigh pains at various times. They would attack quite suddenly and I can remember cycling along Dysart Road on my way to school when the pain brought me to a halt and I had to push my bike back home unable to cycle further. The doctor asked me where it hurt. I told him and he carried on his conversation with my mother. Suddenly and with no advance warning he struck me sharply with the side of his hand on the spot I had indicated. I crumpled to the floor in pain and he said, "rheumatic fever". I seem to remember my dentist extracting one of my teeth in a similar way around this time.

I used to spend a week in bed on these occasions before I was fit to resume normal activities; I remember it happening a couple of times. The doctor said I should quit swimming for a time and issued me with one of his notes. This doctor's note was one of my proudest possessions at the time and I was able to flourish it with gay abandon whenever Wyndham Park Baths or 60 was mentioned. Since that time I have never suffered further attacks of rheumatism, but I have been cautious about resuming swimming and keep well clear of the activity for fear that it could return.

Cross-country running was my favourite and most successful sport. Every Thursday afternoon the whole school would participate and set off at various intervals. The event was strictly timed and form masters would appear from their hiding places in the bushes along the route ready to castigate anyone walking or taking a breather. The run was approximately three miles and my usual time was around 21 minutes, which placed me among the leaders.

Cricket at school I shall never forget due to a tragic accident. Allan Edwards, fielding, ran to position himself ready to catch a skied big hit; the ball slipped between his cupped hands and hit him on the forehead. He died immediately.

National savings figured prominently during these wartime schooldays, designed to raise money to help the war effort. The scheme became very popular with the general public and many schools played their part by forming savings groups in their local community. Every boy appeared to have his group of savers and I had over 100 members, which entitled me to display a large National Savings Group poster in our front room window.

Every weekend I visited my local members, notebook and savings book in hand, and collected their money. The amount contributed by each individual would be noted and deposited at school on Monday morning, where each form master collected the takings and issued suitable savings stamps of various denominations. After school on Monday I stuck the required stamps in their respective books and returned them to their owners, issuing extra books when required as the pages became full.

Looking back to those days, I realise how trusted we were and what a huge responsibility it was carrying large amounts of stamps and money around at such a young age. It was a great pleasure for me to get to know my members and have a chat about the happenings of the day. They included factory and office workers, a policeman, postman and my favourites, the Beestons, who were father (engine driver) and son (fireman) and worked together on the latest express passenger trains (steam trains in those days). The son was not married and lived with his parents.

Father and son even answered the door together, with mother also making an appearance in due course.

Our paths often crossed, me on my bike going to or from school, father and son in LNER uniform striding to or from their current shift. They were always cheerful, with a shouted "How's it going?" - in unison, of course.

BBC radio featured information regarding National Savings after the main news on Sunday evening and schools achieving outstanding results with their efforts were always mentioned. Our school reached second place nationwide at one period for money collected, and we always hovered around this position throughout the war years.

On reaching £10,000, all the pupils in the school were invited to Grantham Railway Station for a photo-shoot with the blue streamlined steam engine that bore the number 10,000 on the side of its cab. Favoured boys with large savings memberships took positions on the actual locomotive where possible, while the rest formed a group at ground level. I must mention that all boys wore their PT kit (Physical Training). A very enjoyable morning.

Boys were allowed to leave school on reaching the age of fourteen in those days, but you were allowed to stay on for an extra year if required. Our Headmaster arranged tuition in specialised subjects suitable for your career choice (if you had made a decision) during this final year. My father had served an apprenticeship as a turner (machinist) at Ruston & Hornsby, engineers, in Grantham, but on the day he completed this apprenticeship at the age of 21 he was informed that his services were no longer required. It was a form of cheap labour that saved the company paying full tradesman's wages and all apprentices shared the same fate. When I informed him that I wanted to be a fitter he had no objections as long as I did not approach his former employers, as naturally he did not have a high regard for their tactics. He reminded me that as a fitter I would have a broader scope than a turner, who stood at a machine watching the wheels go round all day.

I chose to stay at school until the age of 15 and concentrated on Mathematics, Mechanics and Heat and Engineering Drawing. I also attended evening classes in the same school on the same subjects on three nights (two hours each night) every week.

I was advised to take the Engineering Drawing Examination, purely for experience, which would prove invaluable at a later date when I tried again after starting work and gaining further necessary engineering knowledge. I was not expected to pass the exam as it was stated that they required around 75% efficiency in the actual drawing plus 25% in general practical engineering knowledge, which I lacked. I remember a typical exam question: 'Sketch (freehand) a flexible coupling.' I spent many hours reading engineering books and magazines loaned form the local library (no computers were available to assist in those days) and hoped something would appear in the exam paper that I understood. I passed the exam during my final year at school, which was unusual apparently.

We always had four or five personnel managers from various engineering companies in the town contact our Headmaster each year to enquire if any boys were interested in an interview regarding apprenticeships in various trades. As a result I had an interview and was selected to be an apprentice fitter with Aveling-Barford Ltd, manufacturers of heavy earthmoving equipment and contractors' plant.

Mr Sewell informed Mr Thorpe that he regarded it as a mistake, as in his opinion I was not suited to hands-on practical work as my talent leaned more towards an office, administrative position. Mr Thorpe replied that whatever career I chose to follow I would make progress and be successful in it. I have always appreciated those remarks; after all, I was not intending to be a carpenter.

I hope I have not given the impression that all our masters were tyrants who set out to dominate their pupils and make schooldays an unbearable misery for them; this is far from the truth and I can guarantee that any old boy, if asked, would have nothing but praise for their efforts to impart as much knowledge as possible into our often unreceptive heads. Many of their methods of discipline would be unacceptable today, but we were better for it. No boy arrived home and complained to his parents; it was all accepted as part of school life.

CHAPTER 3

THE WAR YEARS - AFTER SCHOOL HOURS

1941 TO 1946

I have previously covered the war years and how they affected my schooldays and I would now like to expand these memories and explain in some detail how my after-school hours were spent during the same period. Before embarking on these experiences we require more detail regarding my family:

Dad was a fully-skilled turner by trade and had worked at: Ruston & Hornsby, engine manufacturers of Grantham and Ransome & Marles, Bearing Manufacturers of Newark, cycling 14 miles from Grantham to Newark and returning each day after completing his shift (28 miles). He did a regular night shift for seven years 1932 to 1939:

1939 Woolwich Arsenal, London
    Training period working on heavy armaments
    for the war effort.

1939-40 Offered relocation to Canada with family to new armaments factory - declined.

1939 Reserved Occupation at Royal Ordinance Factory, Nottingham machining barrels of 3-7 guns - for battleships, destroyers, etc.

12 hour shifts - 2 weeks days - 2 weeks nights, rotating.

To complete these shifts he walked from home to Grantham Railway Station (2 miles) daily.

Train from Grantham to Nottingham 24 miles.

Walk from Nottingham Station to factory.

After the shift was completed he did the same journey in reverse.

My mother was a typical working-class housewife of the period. Few married women had jobs outside the home and they were expected to stay at home and concentrate on the family.

We lived at 17 Shanklin Drive, which consisted of a row of 22 houses. Dad's friend Jim Streeton, a postman, lived at no 3 with his wife and daughter, who was five years younger than me. Dad and Jim had carried out some detailed research and discovered that the foundations under no 3 lent themselves to development as an air-raid shelter. Work commenced immediately and at a frantic pace, and they soon completed the conversion. I can remember Mother and I going off to no. 3 directly after tea just before the air-raid sirens wailed, usually around 7.30 pm, to herald imminent danger from approaching German bombers. This routine occurred when Dad was on his night shift.

The shelter was entered after lifting the hinged trapdoor and stairs, which led into quite a large area with electricity and sleeping accommodation installed. We would stay there under the house until the all-clear siren sounded and then return home. I am sure we were there when Coventry was blitzed and we routinely heard the enemy bombers passing overhead on their way to various targets with our ground-based guns firing at them and searchlights wandering across the sky trying (often with success) to locate them. The bombs exploding were often heard, especially when Grantham became the target.

There were several types of shelter in use at this time. The Anderson Shelter was a corrugated iron structure designed to be buried below ground in your garden. There were brick shelters above ground at various points in the streets; these were basic as far as protection was concerned, but were useful as a last resort if you were caught outside during an air-raid.

My dad had a Morrison shelter delivered. These were for use inside the house and were of a sturdy steel construction, rather larger than a single bed at the base. Their purpose was for use as a bed, with the top used as a table if required. The four corners consisted of right-angled steel pillars approximately 3 ft. high, topped by a thick sheet of steel; these pieces were all bolted together. All four sides were open, with suitably thick wire-meshed panels that could be easily slotted into position and removed by the person occupying the bed, even from inside.

Our shelter was pushed into the corner of our living-room with three sides of the mesh permanently fitted. It was purchased for me, and I thought it was a terrific piece of furniture. My bed was inside at floor level; a nice piece of thick green material covered the steel top, on which the HMV push-button radio stood, together with my HMV pick-up record player. The Morrison was designed to keep the occupant safe until help arrived, should the house collapse on top of it.

I would place the radio on the floor together with a table-lamp, climb into bed and listen to 60 minutes of late-night dance music before switching everything off and sliding my mesh panel into place. I felt utterly safe in the Morrison.

The German bombing raids continued relentlessly and mother and I would huddle together underneath the stairs in our small cubby-hole when Dad was away on night shift. I vividly remember one night we suffered a particularly heavy air-raid with bombs falling nearby. Suddenly there was a huge explosion, followed every few seconds by other bombs, each one seeming louder and closer than the last. I waited and counted seven, eight, nine, and thought the next would surely be the end of us. The noise stopped and all was silent. I edged towards the front door with my mother urging me to return to her side under the stairs. Opening the door cautiously, I could see nothing ahead or to either side. "Ours is the only house standing," I said. I closed the door and returned inside, shocked. There followed a knock on the door: "Are you okay?" It was Jim Streeton. "Ours is the only house standing," I repeated. "No, the estate's still there - have a look now the dust's settled," he said. He was right.

Mr Patman had a large orchard near the estate and his lorry displayed in bold letters the message MY BUSINESS IS GROWING, which I always thought was quite clever. A stick of nine bombs had straddled his orchard and were travelling towards our houses; another three bombs would have seen many casualties. There was also a large unexploded landmine among the craters and early the following morning we were told to stay indoors where possible until the bomb disposal team had done their work. Shortly afterwards we were given the all clear.

Our smallest bedroom had suffered damage to the ceiling and lumps of plaster had fallen onto the bed. Nobody was occupying it at the time. During the heavy bombing raids on our towns and cities, many civilian lives were lost. Grantham had several raids and suffered casualties as a result.

One day the elder brother of one of my friends, who was around 18 years of age, decided to visit one of the town's four cinemas, which were all located in the same area approximately two miles from his house. His route took him onto the main London road, which was a wide, busy road with a pavement on either side. One pavement ran directly along the side of Ruston & Hornsby's factory wall, the opposite pavement passing shops - a newsagent's, etc. After passing this factory area he was virtually only a half mile from the town centre and the cinema of his choice. It was around 7 pm when he left the house.

The air-raid sirens wailed around 7.10 pm to signal that enemy aircraft were in the vicinity, and almost immediately afterwards the imminent danger siren followed, which meant aircraft overhead. Several bombs exploded on either side of London Road adjacent to the factory, and one left a large, deep crater where the pavement had previously been alongside the factory wall. Many people were either killed or injured on that dark winter's night. My friend's brother never returned home - he was never accounted for. It was not difficult to retrace his steps, coupled with the timings of the explosions, to place him near the scene of that factory-wall bomb.

My years at the Boy's Central School coincided with interesting and alarming war years (1941-45). I, like many other boys, preferred to cycle home for lunch before returning for afternoon lessons. On one such day I was cycling home up Dysart

Road when the sirens sounded and I was amazed to look up and see what must have been a squadron of German bombers directly overhead and flying quite low. None of our ground gun batteries or fighter aircraft were in action; it appeared quite deserted on the ground - no people, no vehicles. Being only five minutes from home I decided to press on the pedals somewhat harder and continue towards my destination. The German airmen were obviously of the same opinion, as they passed low overhead heading towards Nottingham (24 miles) or Newark (14 miles). As I reached home the sound of bombs could be heard as they attacked Ransome & Marles' bearing factory in Newark.

Dysart Road was the scene of a further incident, and the result could be seen clearly the following morning. During the previous night there had been a mid-air collision which involved one of our aircraft on a training flight and a German bomber. Incidents like this were quickly dealt with by the relevant authorities and as little information as possible allowed to circulate. The messages 'Walls have Ears', 'Be like Dad - Keep Mum' etc. were all around on buildings and transport.

Rumour circulated that our unarmed Anson training aircraft deliberately rammed into the German bomber, which had appeared in its flight path. I never did see or hear where our plane landed, but the mangled remnants of the German bomber lay in a field just beside the road and appeared to verify this story; one of its engines was missing, and was found about 200 yards further along the opposite side of the road embedded firmly in the front lawn of a large house, the engine's closest point being approximately two feet from the drawing-room bay window.

Needless to say, both sites were being cleared as quickly as possible as dawn broke. The German aircraft had obviously dropped its bombs and was on the return journey.

The footnote to this story is that two retired ladies lived in the house and were sitting in their room just a few feet from where the engine dropped outside. Shortly afterwards the ladies moved to 18 Shanklin Drive and became our neighbours and friends.

The rear of our house overlooked the long back garden, which was filled with various vegetables cultivated by my dad, who was a keen gardener. My favourites were the peas, and I often sat between the rows shelling them and consuming more than I should, with the resultant stomach ache. Following on from our garden was a large area of allotments, of which my Dad had one; he had always loved gardening, vegetables and flowers, and did not need to be told to 'Dig for Victory'. He could be seen busily tending his potatoes, etc. whenever he had a few daylight hours away from work.

After the allotments were two farmers' fields on which cattle usually roamed; these fields led to Barrowby High Road, the main route from Grantham to Nottingham, and the vehicles could be seen moving along the road in the distance from our house.

My bedroom overlooked this scene and on several early morning occasions as dawn was breaking I saw one of our bomber aircraft hedge-hopping and flying as low as possible limping back to base or the nearest airfield, obviously with some damage or mechanical fault. There were many books on aircraft recognition circulating at this time, British, American, German, etc., pictured in silhouette form from various angles, this being the usual format, and most boys were very proficient at the time at aircraft recognition and would frequently test each other. Another schoolboy occupation was collecting shrapnel, and the most rewarding time for scouring the area was early morning after anti-aircraft gunfire had been heard the previous night. Pieces of incendiary bombs were also highly prized.

There were other desirable collections around at this time. Smoking was a very popular habit with adults and was part of the social scene. It was not frowned upon as it is today; it is now seen by doctors and health officials as an expensive health hazard, so it has rapidly declined and is completely banned in most social areas. The realistic films of the period, black and white or Technicolor, all show actors smoking in smoke-filled surroundings depicting various ways of lighting a cigarette, smoking it and passing the smoke through the nostrils, all in close-up and in glorious Technicolor.

Schoolboys were extremely interested in these adult smokers wherever they were, because each packet of cigarettes carried one numbered card with a picture of a footballer, cricket or other sports personality or subject. Others carried ships, aeroplanes or other subjects. A complete set usually consisted of 50 cards and each manufacturer had their own sets of cards printed. Collecting complete sets of 50 cards was a schoolboy endeavour. Unfortunately their circle of smoking friends would often purchase packets which contained cards you already possessed (there was no way of knowing which card would be inside the packet). Duplicates could often be swapped during school hours and albums for them could be purchased separately.

Every home had its accessories, 'knick-knacks', ornaments etc and at that time an ash tray of some kind in ornamental glass or metal was always featured prominently as these were essential to accommodate the needs of friends or visitors who smoked even in the occupants did not. Silver table lighters were also on display and a Ronsonn table lighter priced at £5 would often be purchased as a wedding present. Cigar and pipe smokers had their own accessories.

CHAPTER 4

THE WARTIME GRANTHAM SCENE

RELATIVES

Auntie Nelly & Uncle Jack Pearson

I have touched on this relationship earlier with regard to my primary school days. Auntie Nelly was a relation on my mother's side of the family, although I do not know her title.

Uncle Jack had spent many years working on the railway as a breakdown crane operator and after retirement he became caretaker at Harlaxton Road School, so we often met briefly during school hours. They often visited us on Sundays, arriving in the afternoon for tea and staying for a gossip and drinks in the evening. I had acquired the usual schoolboy 'jokes' such as the imitation cigarette, spilt ink, the sauce bottle that emitted a bang on removing the cap, etc. But my favourite and most treasured was a marvellously lifelike pint glass of Guinness, complete with a thick layer of froth on top. Uncle Jack's favoured drink was

Guinness, and after pouring a very small amount of the real thing on top of the froth on my fake I would serve everyone with their drinks on a tray. Uncle Jack would select his Guinness and would cause much amusement for a few seconds before he solved the problem. I caught him several times before he became wise to the event. Fond memories of a favourite uncle and aunt.

Aunt Dolly & Uncle Syd Branson

Aunt Dolly was again related to my mother's side of the family, but I do not know her title.

Uncle Syd was manager of the Furniture Department in the Co-Operative Store in Grantham. He was a tall elegant man, always smartly dressed in a suit and tie, and we would cross paths in the morning, I on my way to school and he en route to his work at the Co-Op. I remember he always carried a pair of white gloves in one hand, but I never saw him wear them. His immaculate appearance stood out from the crowd at a time when men dressed more smartly than they do today.

Although married, his general demeanour was slightly effeminate or 'camp', as it would probably be called now, and this was highlighted by a lisp during conversation. Uncle Syd was called up and disappeared from the scene for some time serving with the RAF (in Belgium I believe) in some form of communications work. He would visit us whenever he came home on leave. I do not recall him gaining any promotion during his service career; it was definitely not his lifestyle choice and he made no secret of his desire to return to his job at the Co-Op as soon as possible.

Mention must be made regarding his ability to 'tell jokes'; these were risqué or 'saucy jokes'. When he visited on leave he would interject the conversation with frequent "Have you heard this one, Alf?" or "Have you heard this one Else (Elsie)?" The 'Else' was delivered with his customary lisp. He was quite amusing, and such a nice chap you could not take offence.

This story has a happy ending: after demobilisation he resumed his position as manager of the furniture department at the Co-Op.

Uncle Twilley & Aunt Annie

Aunt Annie was again related to my mother's family, but once again I must plead guilty to ignorance of title. They lived in College Street, in a house whose front room had been converted into a shop which traded in groceries, bread, milk and most other consumables - a General Store.

'Twilley' - he was always referred to as 'Twilley' by family, customers and friends - was a rather unkempt person with a small Hitler moustache and a flat cap, plus waistcoat which he never appeared to remove inside the house or outside. When in town I would often be out walking with my best friend Joe Hall and remark, "Here comes my Uncle Twilley." Casting our eyes up the road, we easily recognised him astride his three-wheeled milk cycle advancing towards us. The unusual form of transport was not the only giveaway, as unfortunately he had what my fad termed "ten-to two feet", with reference to a clock face, which was also a contributing factor to recognition.

Twilley used to deliver milk to his customers daily around that area of Grantham. The milk cycle had two large front wheels and a smaller rear wheel over which the saddle was placed and you pedalled for propulsion. How much milk the large square container carried I do not know, but I imagine it was an excellent form of exercise, especially when encountering gradients. I must not omit the milk ladles which were attached to the side of the container.

It was common knowledge among lady relations visiting the College Street premises that whenever Twilley invited them to view the home-made wines which he manufactured and stored in the cellar you politely declined. The reason was never divulged to this curious schoolboy.

Uncle Vic Vale & Aunt Gert

Aunt Gert was Dad's sister. (You thought I didn't know?) Uncle Vic and Aunt Gert lived further along Dysart Road than we did. We were about two miles from town and they were two and a half.

Uncle Vic had been in the Navy in the First World War and served in the submarines, losing one eye in the process. (This had been replaced by a glass eye.) They had three children living at home (two boys and one girl), Vic Junior, Glen and... (I knew you would catch me out again eventually!)

Mother and I would often walk into town at various times on Saturdays and I would assist her with the shopping. We alternated our setting-off times for a reason which was not always successful. "Here's your Uncle Vic coming! Cross over to the other side of the road quickly and he may not see us," she would say. The staggering figure of Uncle Vic using the whole width of a very wide pavement could be seen moving slowly towards us. "Hello you two!" he would call across the road. "Hello Vic," we would reply, leaving out the 'Uncle' to avoid further embarrassment. The plan had failed miserably once again, and we crossed over to his side of the road before he attempted the operation and became our latest road fatality.

Uncle Vic enjoyed his beer, but he was a lovely man when sober. His eldest son, Vic Junior, was a chip off the old block and was eventually called up for war service and, you've guessed it, he served in the Navy in submarines. When he came home on leave the remarks were amended to "Here's your Uncle Vic and Vic Jr coming - cross over to the other side of the road quickly and they may not see us!"

Uncle Ernie Coulson & Aunt Flo

Aunt Flo was Dad's sister. Uncle Ernie had been a career sailor as a stoker on the old steamships, and the walls of their house in George Street were covered with pictures of ships and battle scenes. 'The Fleet at Scapa Flow' was a scene I remember. His muscular arms were covered in tattoos and I was fascinated by the intricate designs.

After completing his naval service he was employed by the electricity board and worked in a large building which housed the generators supplying Grantham and the surrounding area with electricity. On my Sunday morning visits with Dad he would sometimes be on standby duty and the three of us would go to his workplace and watch him operate a switchover of generators, starting up the recently serviced standby generator before shutting down the operating one for servicing. The coloured button-pressing and switch-throwing in this noisy atmosphere had me enthralled, and I was always disappointed when we visited and he was not required for these duties.

He regaled me with stories of his experiences in far-off lands across the sea, and I admired and respected him immensely, a true hero. He died shortly afterwards.

Aunt Peg & Husband

Aunt Peg was Dad's sister; her husband's name I cannot

remember. We did not see them very often - in fact I can only remember the one occasion when they visited.

Aunt Peg was a small woman with a small round face and a small pug nose. She always wore a fur coat with a fox fur draped around her neck, the fox's face hanging down one side of her body and its tail hanging down the opposite side. These fur items were very fashionable at this time. As an added accessory she always carried a Pekinese dog (alive) under her arm. I can remember seeing them approaching our house as my parents and I stood at our front room window. "Guess which is Peg and which is the dog?" said Dad.

Granddad & Grandma Bradley

Granddad was a Master Plumber and was self-employed. He was well connected and usually worked in the larger houses and estates. I remember being told that he carried out work in Belvoir Castle, near Grantham, when required.

Dad would regularly suggest that we paid them a morning visit to allow my mother to prepare Sunday lunch unhindered. Smartly dressed in my 'Sunday suit' we would walk the two miles into town.

They lived in a small house in Welby Gardens and had reared thirteen children there, and even though the ages of the children were spread over many years and they gradually moved out on attaining adulthood, it still left a large occupancy at all times. It was hard to imagine how they managed, but Dad informed me that they were all well-fed and clothed, although they did have a tendency to form small groups of partnerships of boys and girls with a senior member supervising the daily washing and dressing routines.

There was a small garden along the side of the house and the front opened onto a large paved yard. A telegraph pole dominated a corner of this area and I was attracted to it and its iron rungs, which were affixed at intervals until they culminated at the top. I wondered what height I would be able to achieve given the opportunity, and when the adults were deep in conversation I seized my chance, crept out of the house and started my ascent. I had reached the halfway mark when... "Hi, come down here!" shouted Dad from base camp. Granddad was standing beside him. I made my descent and on reaching ground level Dad remarked, "Your mother will shoot me if you mucky that suit!"

"Alf, he's heir to the Bradley millions," said Granddad, patting me on the head.

"He'll have to work for his money like the rest of us," Dad replied.

We moved back inside the house; the suit seemed okay, I thought, after careful examination. Granddad died soon afterwards.

Grandma Bradley

Grandma was a very short woman who always appeared to dress in black. After Granddad's death we visited Grandma more regularly each Sunday. The three of us would sit around the fireplace with our drinks. Grandma liked her glass of stout and Dad had the same, whilst I enjoyed my Tizer or lemonade. I was always fascinated by the china figurines on the mantelpiece and the ornaments occupying the hearth, my favourite being the silver rampant horse.

Dad and Grandma would be discussing the previous week's events - she enjoyed her cinema visits. "Been to the pictures this week Ma?" Dad would enquire. "Yes, I saw a beautiful picture; can't remember what it was called but Mary Pigsfeet [Mary

Pickford] and Various Dugbanks [Douglas Fairbanks] were in it." This statement lived on and became a family joke.

Dad would recount to mother and me how Grandma would play jokes on the children, on one occasion placing a wooden chair on top of the stairs with a length of string attached to one of the chair legs and leading downstairs to where she was sitting. She would then gather the children around her and recount the story of a pirate with one leg who died years ago but his ghost could still be heard pacing the corridors. With the children sitting around in rapt attention, the string would be firmly pulled and the chair would come rattling down the stairs. Startled, children would dash out into the night, leaving Grandma chuckling with mirth. Not the actions that would be applauded in today's child welfare climate, but times and attitudes were very different then.

Before leaving Grandma after each Sunday visit, she would escort us around her small garden where she still grew flowers and vegetables. Dad would always press a pound note into her hand, saying, "Buy yourself a drink, Ma." "You are good to me, Alf," she would reply. Sadly, her death was soon to deprive us of these much enjoyed visits.

NOTE: A tradesman's standard wage was £6 per week at that time, and they were pound notes, not coins.

Welby Gardens has now been demolished and replaced by a large supermarket belonging to one of our largest national chains. I have visited this store and located the spot where the house would previously have stood. After carefully roaming the aisles to determine the precise position, I thought 'Granddad and Grandma's front room was here'. Nostalgically I stood and looked around at the bustling scene. Shoppers skirted around me with their trolleys and small children, all intent on securing the best bargains. This was no place for nostalgia, and I departed hurriedly.

Uncle John Meredith & Aunt Ida

Uncle John was my mother's brother. A career soldier in the Leicestershire Regiment, he had attained the rank of RSM (Regimental Sergeant Major). He had married in England and was later posted to India, where he spent many years of his service life with his wife Ida. When the war with Germany started the regiment was relocated to Singapore but their wives stayed behind in India. When Japan entered the war as an ally of Germany they invaded Malaya and overran our meagre defences in Singapore. Uncle John spent the rest of the war as a prisoner of the Japanese; many in the regiment lost their lives in the fighting that ensued there.

At home in England we received very little information regarding John's welfare over the years that followed. Ida, in India, was unable to forward any detailed news; a couple of standard, brief air mail messages stating that he was okay, censored and probably dictated by his Japanese captors, were all that we received.

Shortly after John travelled to Singapore with the regiment, Ida gave birth to their first child, Christopher, and they lived alone together during his first formative years. Eventually Ida and Christopher returned to England and lived with us in Shanklin Drive. The war with Germany had ended in 1945, and 1946 saw the surrender of Japan and the release of their prisoners of war.

John came home to us and joined his family, which consisted of a wife he had not seen in years and a son aged five who was resentful towards this stranger who had suddenly appeared and come between him and his mother and imposing forms of discipline on him that he was not accustomed to.

The Japanese were renowned for treating their prisoners badly; overworked, often beaten and underfed, many died of starvation or illness during their captivity. John resembled a living skeleton, ill, weak and with a troubled mind that constantly relived the cruelty he had witnessed and the resultant death of many of his men. He spent many days and weeks just sitting on our sofa staring blankly ahead, saying little and never mentioning the war. On a bad day he would sit with head in hands covering tearful eyes. One day I entered the room inadvertently; his shirt was removed and Ida was dressing raw lash marks that ran across his back. I apologised for the intrusion and departed hurriedly.

Time healed differences between father and son and normal family life resumed. John regained his strength, moved nearer the barracks in Leicester and resumed his rank and career organising young entrants joining his beloved Leicestershire Regiment. He died in the 1960s.

Sister Pauline

Pauline was born in 1941. I have omitted this event until late into the war years because there is very little you can say about babies except refer to their usual routine of doing most things in abundance and at random, which includes eating, sleeping, crying and generally messing-up your days and nights! It was a joyous occasion for all the family of course, and I have always loved her dearly.

When she was three years of age, to say we were inseparable was probably the understatement of the year, and whenever I sat down she usually took up position on my knee. Going to the toilet was a difficult operation as far as I was concerned, as she would insist on following me, and after I firmly locked the door she would take up a position outside and refuse to move until I came out. Not an ideal situation.

Pauline attended my old Harlaxton Road School on reaching the age of five.

Pauline had her own small doll's pram which she would push around with various occupants, and Dad possessed his own toolbox, which would be required when my bicycle brakes needed adjusting, punctures needed repairing or lights were checked for efficiency and correct operation. Other work requiring tools and his attention around the house appeared at regular intervals and Pauline would be in attendance watching proceedings closely on these occasions. Dad trainedher as his apprentice and in time she became conversant with the names and uses of the tools, even being able to recognise spanner sizes when they were requested. This mechanical aptitude was soon apparent, as when left alone she would dismantle her doll's pram and three-wheel pedal cycle and then search around for any wooden fence or gate capable of receiving a hammered-in nail, successfully accomplished or otherwise. All toolboxes were securely locked whenever they were not being personally supervised.

My mother had a set ritual which was performed every night just before our bedtime, and it has followed me down the years for as long as I can remember. Pauline was no exception to the rule and it soon became part of her nightly routine as well. A large brown jar would be removed from the cupboard, then dessert spoons would be issued and pushed into the sticky, gluey, brown substance inside. Spoons were then removed and rotated skilfully to enable the mixture to be contained before the contents were pushed into a wide-open mouth. According to my mother, cod liver oil and malt cured all ills and supplied all necessary vitamins.

Wartime Lodgers

During the war people were transferred from one area of the country to another based on their employers' requirements and to fill vacancies. This applied particularly to young female employees who often filled vacancies left by young men who had been conscripted into the Forces. Women were serving in the three services in maintenance jobs and other essential back-up work. They replaced serving men in the munitions factories and absent farm workers by joining the Women's Land Army. Incidentally I always thought the Land Army girl's motto 'Backs to the Land' was highly inappropriate and a PR disaster, but the girls did not appear to object, a case of taking it in their stride I suppose.

For some reason I cannot explain, Grantham Inland Revenue Offices appeared to be a main centre of attraction for qualified ladies in the field of tax collecting. The Office Manager lived in Shanklin Drive and was a friend of the family. The Government was busy pushing the message that citizens should open up their homes to this type of worker; therefore we assisted the war effort by answering the call.

Betty

I cannot remember Betty's surname, but she was transferred to Grantham Tax Office from the Sheffield Branch. Betty fitted in nicely with our family and was a very homely, single young lady with a long-time boyfriend and therefore did not savour the delights of fraternising with off-duty, live-for-today servicemen from bases in the area who roamed the streets and frequented the bars of night-time Grantham during the week looking for a good time. As soon as the week's work was completed Betty was aboard the train to Sheffield to spend the weekend with her boyfriend, where they indulged in their favourite pastime of roaming the hills and dales of Yorkshire until her return on Sunday evening. Betty was only with us for a few months.

Mary the First

I cannot remember Mary's surname, but she quickly replaced Betty in the tax office and in our home. Her home town was Warrington in Lancashire. A short, pretty young woman around twenty-one years of age, she soon became a much-liked addition to our family. Mary was very sociable and unlike Betty was not inclined towards wasting evenings sitting at home when good times beckoned around town.

As previously stated, the Morrison shelter in the front room served as my bed during the bombing years and after everyone was upstairs in bed I had the room to myself. I was then able to relax and enjoy my nightly dose of the current dance bands broadcasting over the radio: Geraldo, Joe Loss, Carroll Gibbons, Lou Preagar, Maurice Winnick, etc. etc. Around midnight I would switch off the radio and be dropping off to sleep when, often, the front door would be opened quietly and gently closed, after which Mary and Johnny would spend time in hushed intermittent conversation in the hall saying their goodnights. "Shush, Ron's in there, he'll hear us," Mary would say in whispered tones. Johnny rarely said anything in reply. After five or ten minutes Johnny would leave the hall through a quietly-opened front door and disappear into the night. Mary would close the door as quietly as possible and creep silently up the stairs, shoes in hand, to her bedroom.

Johnny was an American GI from Wisconsin and was welcomed into our house whenever he called for Mary or brought her home after a date. I had many interesting conversations with Johnny and he always supplied me with copious amounts of chewing-gum and sweets ('candy') whenever he visited. I like to think he was not trying to buy my silence!

Mary and Johnny were married from our house and they asked Dad to be best man. He was proud to accept.

Mary the Second

Mary the second then became part of the family for quite a long time. She also came from Warrington Tax Office on transfer to Grantham and replaced Mary the first after she married and departed the scene.

Mary the second was a strikingly beautiful young lady in her early twenties, and with her dark flowing hair and good figure she could turn heads and easily pass as a model or film star of the times. There was not a trace of a Lancashire accent and she spoke perfect English, leading everyone to believe she came from a good family background, but later during her stay with us she would divulge humbler beginnings. Mary did not crave the bars, clubs and bright lights and was happy to spend evenings at home with us and also the weekends, having no desire to travel to her home town of Warrington. Occasionally she would go out on a date with a serviceman, but it was usually officer material; no squaddies for Mary - she was a class act!

We had similar musical tastes (jazz, dance bands), listened to music on the radio and played my ever-increasing record collection. I was very fond of Mary. I liked her very much - but you knew that already, didn't you?

CHAPTER 5

THE WARTIME GRANTHAM SCENE (2)

A TRIP AROUND GRANTHAM TOWN, 1941 TO 1945

The Cobbler

One of my favourite errands, and the one I always volunteered for, was a visit to the cobbler's on Dysart Road to take any of the family's shoes for repair. Dad would supply the money required and off I would go to Mr Sharp's house. Unlike today's easily disposable culture of wear to destruction and throw away we repaired the same pair of shoes many times over whenever the soles or heels wore down.

Knocking on Mr Sharp's front door, I would wait eagerly for the cobbler to appear. "Dad says will you sole and heel these?" I would say, handing him the bag and turning to return home.

"Hang on lad, your Dad will need these repairing quickly," he would reply. "Go down the passage and meet me at the back door."

These were the magic words I had been hoping to hear. In the rear garden stood a large wooden workshop which housed the machinery and tools; the lights would be switched on, he would don his apron and with the command "Sit yourself down lad", he would point to the chair. Then the machinery hummed into life and the operation would commence. I would watch entranced as he deftly cut the leather to shape and tacked it to the shoe. The smell of the leather being trimmed was an added bonus, and after polishing the shoes on his machine they would look like new, and all completed in a few minutes.

The Farrier

Baxter the Farrier had premises near the Market Place, and the large workshop doors were always wide open during working hours, allowing passers-by to gaze inside and witness the horses being shod. Many Shire Horses were still being used by the breweries, etc., to transport heavy loads and to watch this operation with new horse-shoes being shaped under intense heat and then fitted was always worth a few minutes' stop.

Burgess & Coulson

During 1944 jazz music suddenly burst on my scene, and I vividly recall the exact afternoon when, returning from school, I switched on the radio and heard 'Body & Soul' being played by Coleman Hawkins on the tenor saxophone. I was transfixed by the beauty of his interpretation and to this day I never tire of listening to it. I purchased the record immediately and learned as much as I could about the history of jazz music, the improvisations on popular songs and the talented musicians performing past and present.

Burgess & Coulson was the best record store in town and in those days there were only 10" shellac records available, which if left in hot direct sunlight would warp and become unplayable. Each side had a maximum three-minute duration and when each side was finished required turning over to hear a further three minutes approximately on the opposite side. This time limit was a severe restriction on musicians who desired to expand their ideas and stretch out their improvised passages of music. Sometimes an extended piece of six minutes duration became parts 1 & 2 of the record, but this interval during the flip-over spoilt the whole effect. Later came the 12" long-playing record, which revolutionised the jazz and opera music scene and allowed 20 minutes' music on each side.

At the beginning of every month the record companies such as HMV, Parlophone, Decca, Columbia, Rex, etc. would make their brochures available in record stores. Eagerly awaited, these detailed, free of charge pamphlets were full of photographs and information on all types of music from opera to jazz and new releases. The following Saturday morning, armed with my jazz list, I would enter Burgess & Coulson's and hand it to the Manager, who would then place my desired selection on the counter. Being a regular customer, he was always anxious to assist, safe in the knowledge that there would be a guaranteed sale in due course. There were two soundproof booths where the records could be played prior to purchase and the Manager always made sure I was undisturbed during my occupation of one of them. Sheer bliss - a big-band bonanza. HMV and Parlophone usually had the top jazz artists assigned to their labels and a 10" record cost 5 shillings and 4½ pence. Other labels were slightly cheaper.

Before departing the shop you wold probably require new needles for the pick-up arm on which to play your treasured vinyl records, and you will note that I have not used the modern names of tone arm, cartridge and stylus because there is little comparison apart from their position on the record deck. The old arms were heavy and bulky and you purchasedthe best needles available at that time. Steel needles in packs of 10, manufactured by HMV or Columbia, were recommended and each had to be discarded after a very few playings. The needles were crudely screwed into the pick-up arm. The thorn needle followed; this was at least lightweight, but useless after you had played a few sides. The modern dynamically-balanced tone arms, cartridge and stylus are far superior. They are long-lasting and give excellent sound quality.

The radio was a great source of dance-band music and programmes devoted to jazz. It was the era of the big-bands, usually consisting of 13 instrument-playing personnel who travelled the country (be it America or the United Kingdom) from one end to the other, mostly on one-night engagements. Some bands were fortunate in having resident status, eg Carroll Gibbons and his Savoy Hotel (London) Orpheans, Lou Preager from the Hammersmith Palais (London) and Henry Hall and his BBC Orchestra. There were also the smaller groups - the sextets, quartets and trios. The armed services had excellent outfits such as the Squadronaires (RAF) and all the bands had resident male and female vocalists. There were bands in their hundreds and most of them were excellent, but eventually they became unsustainable due to costs and the closing down of venues, and most of them were disbanded as the years passed.

'Tripey' Alice

Dad loved his sea food, cockles, mussels, shrimps, whelks, winkles, etc., and always regarded them as a special treat whenever these dishes were placed before him after my mother had meticulously prepared them. Another favourite dish was tripe, and I was introduced to this at a very early age when Dad and I would devour large platefuls of it together - and I am not referring to 'tripe and onions', just plain tripe covered with a plentiful coating of vinegar. I can consume it in this way even today.

Whenever I was in town with Dad, we would always end our day with a special ritual before returning home: "Let us go and see Tripey Alice," he would say. The lady specialised in all of the aforementioned and many other delicacies. Her name was obviously Alice and she was quite elderly, but Dad had known her and the shop for many years and she appeared to be known as 'Tripey' by all and sundry. Alice knew of the nickname (I cannot recall her true name) but appeared to have no objection, whereas today it would be sexist, politically incorrect, probably libellous, etc. etc.

The Circus

Dysart Road ran from Barrowby, a village on the outskirts, into Grantham, a distance of three miles. One mile from Grantham lay open fields on either side of the road, and a visiting circus would occupy these fields on their annual visit to the town. Elephants would take their positions near the boundary fence awaiting oncoming pedestrians who they knew would keep them well supplied with buns, bread and other treats, even though food was still strictly rationed. This was probably a cunning method of supplementing huge elephant appetites, devised by the circus owner and employees. The elephants were always quite friendly and appreciated these donations from both adults and children.

The Cinemas

Grantham boasted four cinemas - the State, the Picture House, Empire Cinema and the Central Cinema. The State cinema was the most lavish and the programmes ran for the whole week, consisting of the Pathé News followed by a cartoon; then came the second-rated (or B) movie and finally the main feature (or A) film. In between these films came a fifteen to twenty-minute interval which usually featured a Compton organ rising from below ground level and being played by Lewis Gerard. The organ was constantly illuminated from its interior by coloured lights; the words of the tunes being played appeared on the cinema screen, with a bouncing ball hopping from word to word and denoting when to sing the word in the ensuing singalong. As you can imagine, a cinema visit would be of three hours' duration minimum and as it was a rolling programme, once seated you could remain there throughout the afternoon and evening.

Lewis Gerard was a Grantham police constable and an excellent organist with a regular radio contract with the BBC.

The other three cinemas changed their programme mid-week; remember, these were the days before television.

The Market Square - Woolworths' store

Woolworths' store seemed to dominate this area and its well-kown name in large gold lettering on a red background covered the entire width of the building and was set high above the entrance doors. Long uninterrupted counters set conveniently at eye level ran deep into the length of the shop and carried a vast array of objects, all for sixpence or less. 'NOTHING OVER SIXPENCE' was the bold statement directly under the Woolworth's name outside.

Piper's Penny Bazaar

This establishment stood next to Woolworths. Whether they claimed to sell everything at this price I cannot remember, but it must have been around this figure as it was highly popular among schoolchildren with pocket money to spend on their way home from classes around 4 pm.

Needham's wool shop

Whenever my mother found time from her housework, her knitting holdall would appear and be placed carefully at the side of her chair, after which she would seek out the latest knitting pattern. The sound of clicking needles would then form the background to any radio programme being broadcast, or any conversation.

Needhams' Knitting Shop in the town kept her busy, supplying patterns and wool from which she rapidly produced the latest styles in knitwear. These jumpers, cardigans, gloves, scarves etc were then displayed in the shop, and needless to say family, relations and friends were well supplied with requested items. Fairisle jumpers were very popular at this time and I was very pleased with mine, as were Liam and several of my friends as we wandered around together like a special clan.

I was often given the task of holding skeins of wool in outstretched arms while Mother rolled the wool into balls, manoeuvring my thumbs adroitly to allow the wool to escape. "That's a good job done" she would remark as the last of the wool disappeared. I stretched my aching arms and rapidly retired from the scene before a change of mind resulted in the appearance of more wool from the holdall.

Catlins & the Co-Op

Regularly on Saturday morning I would accompany my mother into town in order to assist her by carrying the shopping she inevitably accumulated. Although I found being dragged around on these excursions quite boring, I had the incentive of knowing that on the expedition's completion we would retire to Catlins for refreshment.

Catlins was situated on the main London road and on the ground floor it sold cakes of all shapes and sizes, varieties of bread, exotic blends of tea, etc. Ignoring the temptations around us, we would take the stairs to the first floor and enter the charming restaurant, bedecked with oak beams. This was the habitat of ladies who lunched, a beacon that shone in the austere times we lived in. Tea and cakes would be ordered and a waitress in full uniform would deliver the silver tea-service and tiered stand holding a variety of cakes. I enjoyed it immensely and so did my mother. Eventually, after I had consumed most of the cakes, we would depart and head towards the bus station. We had walked into town but always convinced ourselves that shopping bags merited the bus journey home.

On reaching the bus station my mother would say, "Before we go home let's visit your Uncle Syd at the Co-Op." The Co-Op was situated on the opposite side of the road from the bus station. The Furniture Department covered the whole area of the first-floor and on entering Uncle Syd would usually be found in the presence of ladies, usually one but often more. Peals of laughter would be heard at regular intervals and we always assumed he was inserting one of his riskier jokes into his salesmanship patter.

I always imagined his repertoire of jokes had been categorised into sections bearing various star-ratings - three for mild, four for risqué and five for highly volatile. He was a good reader of people's reactions and after carefully scrutinising a new customer would insert a three-star item. On further acquaintance it could be upgraded to four-star, etc. He never seemed to offend or to receive a slapped face; in fact, the ladies appeared to keep coming back for more (furniture, of course).

The Hornby Train

Watergate, and the toy shop situated on that street, commanded my attention one Christmas time whenever I was in town. The whole shop window consisted of a large wooden base with a complete railway model display with tracks, a station, tunnel, fields with model animals, railwaymen, travellers and other relative pieces. Along the rails the model of the locomotive Sir Nigel Gresley travelled incessantly, pulling its passenger carriages around until the shop closed in the late evening.

I told Dad everything about this wondrous display and on our next trip into town together we both pressed our noses to the window and returned home very impressed with everything we had seen.

On Christmas morning I came downstairs to discover that complete Hornby train layout dominating the room, with Sir Nigel Gresley still on its journey.

Grantham Hospital

A few days before Christmas, probably 1944, my cousin Liam,

who was around 13 at the time, was making a cup of tea when he proceeded to scald himself on the arm with boiling water from the kettle, consequently being admitted to Grantham Hospital for treatment.

A favourite medical operation of the times was the removal of tonsils and adenoids if you had trouble from a constant sore throat, and a few days after this particular Christmas I also found myself in hospital for the removal of my tonsils, which only entailed a four or five-day stay.

This situation would be of little interest, except for a few odd facts. Cousin Liam occupied the far end ward, and his was a corner bed. From my neighbouring ward I could see him through the large open archway, and noticed he was constantly occupied manufacturing green felt rabbits of various sizes, cutting felt pieces and sewing and stuffing these objects throughout the daylight hours. I do not know which member of the hospital staff taught him this skill and on my frequent visits to his bedside (he was not allowed out of bed) I was secretly envious of his newly-acquired talents as the green felt family of rabbits grew larger with the passing days.

He was the only child in his ward, the remaining beds being occupied by wounded RAF personnel who all appeared to be nearing the end of their tenure and wandered freely around from ward to ward without hindrance, the only exception being Matron's impending visits when they would rapidly return to base.

I was the only child in my ward, but in my case I was surrounded by injured Italian POWs. They were quite friendly, their only thoughts at this time revolving around how soon the war would end and how they had allowed themselves as a nation to get embroiled in the war in the first place. The Italians never appeared to have any heart for the fight throughout their alliance with Germany, and surrendered to our troops whenever they had the chance.

I never did discover the fate of the green felt rabbit family, although I suspect they all hopped off to some hospital charity organisation. I had learnt however that the old adage was correct: 'Put two rabbits together and...'

The Lincolnshire Poachers

Dad had a friend called Mick Foster. Mick had a ferreting friend (whose name eludes me) and they would arrange to meet very early on dark Saturday or Sunday mornings whenever Dad was available and not working. I was eventually accepted into this fraternity after suitable rigorous training and accepting vows of silence.

It was 3 am and the knock on my bedroom door with Dad's hushed "Ready?" told me it was time for action. The three of us, plus a ferret whose head was peering from Mick's coat pocket, would quietly slip into the darkness, through the allotments and out onto the fields ahead. In the hedgerows we would seek out the rabbit holes, quietly set our nets and dispatch the ferret into the warrens below ground. There would be much scuffling, and it was at that point that my precision training came to fruition. As rabbits hurtled from the ground escaping the marauding enemy and they became entangled in our nets, I would deliver one sharp, quick blow with the side of my hand to the back of the rabbit's neck - mission accomplished.

We would return home after catching around eight rabbits. There were always rabbits surplus to our requirements (no refrigerators at that time) and when dawn broke I would knock on neighbours' doors and enquire, "Dad says do you want a rabbit? Freshly killed this morning." The answer was always an ecstatic "Yes, tell your dad thanks a lot!" as the grateful housewife whisked the rabbit into her kitchen and prepared for action. Basing the following on my mother's actions, it was easy to imagine the lady recipients in Shanklin Drive all participating in the same operation around the same time, hunched over the kitchen sink skinning a rabbit, removing and separating entrails, pieces you can eat and others that you cannot, thoroughly washing before cooking, etc. I can still vividly recall this task - the bloodied sink and mother's splattered apron. All housewives were capable of this task at that time; meat was rationed, and rabbit was tasty and had been popular for many years prior to the war. How many women would be capable of preparing this meal today?

Homing Pigeons

Adjacent to my Dad's allotment was the allotment of Gordon Drake, who had little interest in "Digging for Victory" but believed more in embracing the RAF motto 'Per Ardua Ad Astra' (Through Hardship to the Skies). Gordon had constructed on his site a large pigeon loft which I believed was the best loft for miles around, painted on the outside with green and white vertical stripes.

Gordon was a young man of around twenty-six and why he was not serving in the forces I do not know, probably medical reasons. We became friends whilst watching his pigeons flying around the area on long summer evenings. I was officially allowed to throw small pebbles near them whenever they landed on a rooftop or the loft roof for a rest, and thus dissuade them from this practice, which was anathema to him and could remove the 'racing' from racing pigeon. I noticed that this 'taking a breather' usually occurred when Gordon went home for a meal, rather like schoolboys misbehaving when the master left the classroom.

On Friday evenings Gordon would take his selected pigeons into headquarters in Grantham, where they would be officially ringed on one leg and dispatched in their baskets on trains to various parts of the country where a race was to start; they would then be released to embark on their journey home.

My mother would look out of her kitchen window across the allotments to the left approximately 50 yards away. "Gordon spends more time in that loft than he does at home," she would remark to anyone around at the time. On a Saturday afternoon around 6 pm Gordon and I would take up positions adjacent to the loft entrance; our portable radio would be switched off and the tension would mount as we scanned the sky for our first arrival. As our pigeons returned home there would be efforts to clock the birds with their arrival times on their ringed legs as quickly as possible, as the race could be won or lost in this vital period.

Gordon fared quite well in his race placings and whenever he met my mother would remark, "I'm going to set your lad up with a few pigeons when he gets older."

"Oh no, you're not - that's never going to happen!" she would reply.

Gordon and his wife started divorce proceedings shortly afterwards - I believe racing pigeons were cited.

Jehovah's Witness

Gordon's brother also lived on the estate. He was a Jehovah's Witness and as such refused to join the military. He would attend court to plead his case and be sentenced to six months' imprisonment. After serving his sentence he would once again appear on the scene, until after a few weeks' respite he was once again served with his call-up papers. Refusing conscription meant a further six months in prison and the merry-go-round continued. In the interim periods of freedom he would volunteer for fire-watching roster duties with the men who were past call-up age.

Walks with Tony

Throughout my earlier years I enjoyed the freedom of long country walks with our dog Tony, a Field Spaniel. We would wander across the fields and walk miles along the canal path and Tony would occasionally take to the water for a swim.

On summer days when Dad travelled to Nottingham on his day shift, he would arrive back at Grantham railway station at around 8.30 pm. The distance to our house from the station was approximately three miles, and Tony and I would leave the house and time our walk so that we would meet Dad around the halfway mark. Tony was usually first to see Dad approaching and would hurtle along the pavement, breaking all spaniel speed records. We would head for home with a tail-wagging Tony while I recounted my day's adventures.

Sometimes Tony accompanied mother and me into town, and on these occasions we would place a pair of gloves or a folded newspaper in his mouth for him to carry. He accepted this task readily, as the object was the urban equivalent of a pheasant, I suppose. We knew his concentration would centre solely on delivering gloves or newspaper safely to the final destination. He steadfastly refused to acknowledge other dogs he met on his journey and would not deviate from the pavement, however crowded it might become, until he finally dropped the article on the carpet dry and unmarked after returning home.

Whichever member of the family awoke earliest every morning would have the task of opening the front door to enable Tony to greet the outside world. It was imperative that this duty was completed before the postman (or woman) arrived around 8 am. (Yes, mail was delivered before I departed for school and there was an afternoon delivery as well). If the postman inadvertently managed to open the front gate and push the letters through the letterbox, he would be in big trouble, because on turning around he would discover a menacing, snarling Tony refusing to allow him through the gate onto the street; he would be a prisoner in our front garden. Being a Field Spaniel of some repute, Tony was under the impression that his mouth was a better and safer way of delivering mail than any letterbox.

We therefore had to be certain that all postal staff were fully informed, and as Tony always waited for their arrival at the gate they should push all letters containing money-orders, tax returns and other vitally-important documents into his eagerly-awaiting mouth, whereupon with wagging tail he would deliver the correspondence to one of the occupants. The occupants would take full responsibility for any damaged or missing items.

There may be a PS here: "If you are changing delivery personnel, please inform them of the situation immediately." The operation always appeared to work perfectly and some of Tony's greatest friends were postmen (and women).

The many basic brick-built air raid shelters located in close proximity in streets around our towns and cities were designed to give people some form of protection if they were caught outside during an unexpected attack from enemy aircraft. We had one positioned directly opposite our front room window on the far side of the road, and it became the sports centre for our local street gang.

One end of the shelter would serve as the football goalposts, after the correct dimensions had been meticulously marked with chalk. We did not have a 'regular' goalkeeper but we rotated the occupancy of this position quite frequently, as over-zealous boys attempted full-length saves and landed on the tarmac surface of the road quite heavily, sustaining various degrees of injury to arms and legs. Limping, bandaged and plastered players were a common sight, and all the footballers' mothers had well-stocked first-aid boxes.

The opposite end of the shelter was devoted to cricket. Stumps and bails were drawn with chalk, which meant that you could dispense with the wicket-keeper and reposition him in the field (or tarmac). In fact there was little action behind the batsman due to the brickwork. There were heart-stopping moments when balls headed towards gardens or windows, but the occupants of the neighbouring properties never complained and all windows in the area remained intact despite the over-enthusiasm of the sporting schoolboys. It was the enemy airmen who ruined the gardens and smashed the windows.

Dustmen, coalmen, milkmen and postmen

Dustmen were a hard-working group who were not then known by fancy titles such as refuse collectors, disposal operatives etc. They also lacked hydraulically-operated refuse lorries to lift and tip wheeled rubbish bin contents into waiting rotary crushers after the householder had sorted the items into various categories and placed the bins in a convenient location on the pavement, thus enabling the refuse collectors to do their work with the minimum of inconvenience.

The old-style dustmen wore jackets with large leather patches across the shoulders and around the elbows. They opened the front gate, walked down the side of the house and into the back garden, where heavy galvanized bins (cast iron coated with zinc to prevent rust) with separate lids would stand. These bins, with mixed contents, would be lifted onto heavily-padded shoulders and carried to the dustcart, where once again the contents would be manually deposited before the bin was returned to its rightful place in the garden and the front gate was carefully closed on departure.

Dustmen and coalmen operated in similar ways. Coal houses were usually brick built and included with the property, before central heating became commonplace and gradually replaced the coal fire.

The first house I purchased new, in 1956, had coal fires, and the coal was stored behind a locked door in the outside wall of the house. This storage space was directly under the stairs and there was naturally no access to it from inside the house. I had central heating installed soon after I moved in, but many houses on the estate relied on coal for several years after this.

Cleaning out the fire grates early on cold mornings ready for lighting the fires once again was usually the housewife's task as her husband prepared for work. Instead of depositing the ash and cinders in the dustbin, many households used them for laying pathways around their gardens and allotments. Eventually these well-trodden areas became hard, weatherproof, inexpensive walkways.

Rolled-up sheets of newspaper were used as a base on which to lay small sticks of firewood before striking a match to light the newspaper and start your fire. Coal was then added in stages through the day as required.

Postmen and postwomen featured prominently in our daily lives, and morning and afternoon deliveries of letters would be awaited eagerly. Telegram boys in uniform would speed around on their bicycles, although they were not so eagerly awaited as they were usually the bearers of bad news. A telegram was more costly than a letter and was just a brief, basic message which had to be delivered as quickly as possible.

Milkmen delivered daily, and usually left the required amount in bottles near the front doorstep, at the same time collecting empty bottles from the previous day's delivery. A note left under a bottle would advise if the quantity required changing. In the days before every kitchen housed a refrigerator, daily deliveries were essential.

All these delivery men received their monetary rewards (tips) at Christmas from grateful householders, and I often had to chase along the street in pursuit of their transport after hearing my mother shout, "Quick! I've missed the milkman / postman / coalman / dustman), here's some money, go and run after them!" On catching up with the man in question I would tell him breathlessly, "That's from number 17". "Thanks lad," the driver would reply as he placed his money in the communal tin or tins in his cab. "Merry Christmas" he would say as I walked away.

Service Personnel

There were many airfields in the Grantham area and dotted around the flatlands of Lincolnshire. Some were occupied by American airmen and others by British, Dutch or Polish flyers; I can even recall a Canadian aerodrome. This mixed bunch of nationalities could cause its own problems when off-duty personnel descended on the town, and military policemen were always in attendance should arguments occur over girls or too much consumption of drinks from the local brewery or other outlets. Throw into the mix an added shot of various Army personnel and you had a volatile cocktail.

Various service authorities would consult together to ensure the mix was segregated and watered down as much as possible during these periods of off duty, but it was an impossible task, especially considering that most airmen were bomber crews with a notoriously short operational lifespan and with a 'Live for Today, Tomorrow May Never Come' attitude.

The Tide Was Turning

Hitler, Goering and his Luftwaffe had attacked our ally Russia and discovered that they had bitten off more than they could chew. Apart from daring low-level daylight raids on Germany by British and Allied airmen plus the American Air Force, we were now able to increase our night bombing capacity, and the thousand-bomber raids were born.

During the long daylight hours of the summer months, around 7 pm nightly we would hear the faint drone of fully-laden bombers approaching. It was a sound that had become familiar to us during the German blitz - but now there was a difference, they were our boys.

The squadron would approach quite low and when directly overhead they would begin to circle around. Within minutes a further squadron would approach from a different angle and join this gruesome merry-go-round. Further bombers converged in the sky above us and the air filled with their menacing, throbbing engines as they manoeuvred into their planned formation, after which they would all strike out in one direction - towards Germany. These were the thousand-bomber raids.

Neighbours would gather in their gardens to watch this spectacle. "It seems morally wrong," said one. "The Germans started it!" came the reply.

CHAPTER 6

APPRENTICESHIP & NATIONAL SERVICE

1945 TO 1951

Reporting to Mr Watson, Apprentice Supervisor, I was ushered into his office, where one complete wall was taken up with a board denoting the names of the 100 apprentices working at Aveling-Barford Ltd at that time. The headings on the board were split into sections: Craftsmanship, Discipline, Timekeeping and a percentage box for each month of your six-year apprenticeship, which was shaded in the appropriate percentage colour you had achieved. There was no place to hide from the system, and you fervently hoped you could attain those red colours proclaiming 80 to 100 per cent.

Four of us lads started on the same day. The other three reported to the Stores, which was the usual procedure, as it was a crash course of three months which enabled you to recognise machine tools and the names of various spare parts before taking the next step working as a machinist or fitter. I bypassed the Stores and was introduced to the foreman of the Inspection Department, which was unusual, as it was regarded as an apprentice-free zone. Had my Certificate in Engineering Drawing & Design influenced this decision? I never asked.

The department consisted of Foreman, Chargehand (who both shared the office), and two Inspectors who were approaching the retirement age of 65 and could usually be discovered in the Machine Shop checking the first items of a batch of manufactured parts before giving approval to the turner or miller to go ahead. Bert, the Lister truck driver, would then transport the batches of completed parts from the Machine Shop to the Inspection Department for complete and final checks. This complete and final check was performed by six beautiful young ladies, age range 21 to 25, who sat around a large table and performed their measuring magic taking into account various tolerances allowed. I was thrust into this hotbed of activity by our Chargehand, who thought Ada could teach me a few things about part-numbering. Ada was around 21, dark haired, and around my height of 5ft 5 ins. She was the seventh lady in the department and her job was to operate a small machine which accepted small parts and stamped their part numbers in suitable places. Individual numbers could be inserted into a rotary wheel which clamped into the machine; the rotary wheel was then lowered onto any flat part and the wheel then moved along the surface under suitable pressure, thus permanently stamping on the number. The opposite ensued when stamping a round surface; the individual numbers were then inserted into a flat-surfaced holder.

Apparently I was a quick learner, and this allowed me to take over this operation and enabled Ada to rejoin her table of friends and once again discuss intimate matters of the utmost importance.

I missed the close proximity of Ada as we shuffled around our machine, adjusting the pressure to suit the various parts.

These girls were allowed to prepare for lunch and closing time ten minutes prior to the factory siren sounding at 12 noon and 5 pm. The ladies' room was outside the Machine Shop in the yard beyond the main door and entailed a 100-yard walk down the centre aisle with the machinists on either side giving them their full attention until they disappeared through the door. I admired these girls immensely, as unfazed they treated the aisle as their catwalk, on which they were displaying the latest designer wear in blue boiler suits, tightly belted around trim waists; hips swaying, they could all have been mistaken for fashion models. A smile from one of these ladies to a machinist acquaintance on passing would draw ribald comments from his workmates nearby.

Male employees were allowed four minutes to cover their grimy hands with Swarfega from suspended containers fixed above a long row of adjoining washbasins, rinse and towel before clocking off and dashing madly to the bicycle shed or canteen as the siren sounded. Cycles would be quickly grabbed and hundreds of workers would speed towards the main factory gate and onto Houghton Road, where mothers would whisk up young children and escort them to safety.

There were two 10-minute tea and snack breaks mid-morning and mid-afternoon during which the Inspection girls could discuss the previous evening's romantic events and focus on the interludes that could happen that very night. On starting work in the Department I enjoyed my breaks in solitude at a table some distance away from this giggling bunch, but this situation was not allowed to continue, as they eagerly requested my presence at their table and refused to take 'no' for an answer. Being thrust into this cauldron of hot gossip and girl talk was quite embarrassing at first, and I'm sure they enjoyed seeing my face redden at frequent intervals during their more intimate revelations. Thanks girls, for broadening my engineering knowledge and also for enabling me to take forward steps, then leaps and bounds along the path of understanding the complex, complicated fairer sex!

When I left the Department the Foreman presented me with an envelope containing a large amount of cash donated by the employees. An unexpected gift, and greatly appreciated. The Inspection girls were the remaining few of a large number of women who worked at Aveling-Barford during the war years replacing so many skilled men who were called into the Services. The factory switched to producing Bren gun carriers during this period.

Prior to my next move to the Fitting Shop I was told to report to the Apprentice Supervisor's office, where I received my briefing before reporting to Cyril Shields, the Fitting Shop Foreman. Mr Watson pointed to my name on the wall chart, which was now showing three red sections, denoting that my first three months' endeavours had earned me the excellent 80%-100% category. I was told to keep up the good work and left his office quite pleased with myself.

The Fitting Shop was on the opposite side of a large open paved area to the Machine Shop, the size of two football pitches, where the completed machines were fuelled, oiled and greased by the Testing Department on the third side of the yard prior to road tests outside the factory area. The remaining side of the yard contained a large, airy, wide-windowed office complex which housed the Drawing Office with draughtsmen in regimented rows seated at their drawing-boards with their T-squares and drawing instruments detailing and recording every single item from all angles that were manufactured by Aveling-Barford. This was a highly regarded occupation at that time, but advancing computer technology over the years has made the draughtsman a dying breed.

Climbing the outside staircase to Cyril Shield's domain, I nervously reported in, hoping to receive further instructions regarding my future. The office was designed to afford panoramic views on all four sides through large windows and was set high above floor level on the first floor. The ground floor housed the office of four chargehands, and next to them were the timekeepers. I was rapidly collected by a chargehand and deposited at a bench with my first batch of work and a drawing showing the parts and instructing the recipient on how to achieve the desired results. This introduction to 'hard manual labour' was normal for a newcomer; you worked alone and it was designed in order to discover your capabilities as quickly as possible. You received work assembling small sub-assemblies used in various machines, the kind of tasks others shied away from and rejected if possible, entailing riveting, which required much hammering, drilling and grinding and testing the arm muscles. A batch of this work could consist of 100 completed items with a piecework time allocation of five minutes per item; you therefore arrived home after work with blisters on the palms of your hands and aching arm muscles.

Every job was based on the piecework system, and if the work was completed on or before time there was a bonus above your normal wage to be added to your pay packet at the end of the week. On commencing your apprenticeship at 15 years of age, your weekly wage was approximately 15 shillings, and this increased year by year until on reaching the age of 20 you were earning £2.10 shillings. On completing your apprenticeship and on your 21st birthday you became a fully-skilled tradesman and your wages leapt to £6 plus per week.

These figures must be taken in context with today's monetary values. In 1950 a fully-skilled tradesman received approximately £6 per week and a top manager would command £20 per week.

Aveling-Barford manufactured contractors' plant and earthmoving equipment of various types and sizes: dumpers from 1yd to 9yd cubic capacity; diesel road rollers from 1 to 14 tons; graders, trench-cutting machines and calfdozers. Usually these machines were being assembled in batches of five. There were also sub-assemblies such as gearboxes and transmissions being prepared separately, ready to be installed in these machines.

After a few weeks working at the bench I progressed to my next step on the assembly team of 1yd dumpers. This same team also built the calfdozers. One fitter was in charge of one senior apprentice completing his final year and three younger apprentices.

'Ninck' Schofield

The senior apprentice was 'Ninck' Schofield. I never knew his Christian name and I doubt if many other people did apart from his parents! Ninck was highly respected among the apprentice fraternity, not so much for his knowledge and skill but his extraordinary prowess at spitting long distances with effortless ease, which left us marvelling at this natural talent. I imagine that if he had lived in America his ability would have been discovered by the film industry and he would have been whisked away to Hollywood, where he would have enjoyed a prosperous career appearing in cowboy films. The saloon doors would suddenly swing open to reveal Ninck, who would look around the room before projecting from his mouth a chewing-tobacco missile that would enter the centre of a spittoon some distance away.

Ninck lived on the same estate, and at midday and 5 pm we would cycle together on our journey to and from work. The Dysart Road home journey covered a steep gradient and we regarded it as a test of stamina to surmount the obstacle as rapidly as possible. Other Barford workers covered the same route but declined to join us, preferring a more leisurely pace.

Alf Garnham

Alf Garnham had a reputation as one of the most skilled tradesmen in the Fitting Shop, so I was pleased to be placed under his wing assembling 10-ton road roller gearboxes. Alf was a tall, bald, thin man in his forties with the ability to recount risqué jokes, rhymes and songs throughout the day, and I remember very few being repeated. As the weeks progressed and I became ever more proficient in the complexities of the gearbox it was noticeable that Alf was absent from work on a regular basis, and I found myself gradually able to complete the work without assistance. On completion the gearbox was removed to a nearby test-bed where it was operated for several hours; gear teeth were painted with blue dye which, when in operation, showed if they were meshing together correctly, and the various gears were selected before finally being passed for installation in the roller by a chargehand inspector. Alf would often return to work to discover he had a passed gearbox already clocked off and I was progressing nicely with another. He would then sing his ribald songs more loudly than usual. Some said he suffered from an oft-occurring illness, while others ventured the opinion that he was quite wealthy and could afford to take time off.

Ted Tattershall

Ted was our neighbour, also assembling the same type of gearbox, with an apprentice called Humphries (I forget his Christian name as he was always referred to as Humphries). Ted was in his mid-forties and always wore a flat cap. He also gave a unique kind of whistle through his teeth whenever an 'S' appeared in a word, so even the briefest conversation would be punctuated by these strange whistles. Humphries had a short attention span and often felt the need to go walkabout and enjoy a gossip with friends, sometimes disappearing completely for long periods. Ted would walk over to me: "'Ave you seen young 'Umphries?" he would enquire.

"Saw him about 30 minutes ago," I would reply.

"If 'e keeps skivin' off I'll report him to Cyril Shields. I'll soon need a selection of gaskets stamping out for this gearbox."

Some tradesmen were employed by Aveling-Barford for the duration of their working lives and when the company moved from Rochester to Grantham, many families uprooted and came with them. There was a father and son fitter combination with a younger son serving an apprenticeship in fitting.

I was growing in confidence as the months passed in the Fitting Shop and I began to realise that I could perform my duties as well as anyone around me and better than most in many instances. This was borne out during the second year of my apprenticeship. Each year the top two apprentices were offered a three-month period working at our Sydenham Repair Depot in South-East London as an incentive and reward for past efforts. David Chambers and I were good friends and pleased to accept the invitation.

Mr Watson, our Apprentice Supervisor, informed us that our lodgings would be paid by the company and we would be allowed one return rail ticket per month from Grantham to Sydenham via King's Cross to spend a long weekend with our families. This travel allowance would also be paid by the company. We would be free to travel home from Sydenham after finishing work on Friday and return by rail on Monday morning ready to commence work at 1 pm.

My wall chart entries were looking good with continuous monthly red sections, I had noticed - so let the next adventure begin.

1947

The Sydenham Repair Depot was in south-east London and specialised in the overhaul and repair of the company's products. It was also the base for travelling service engineers who attended breakdowns across the south of England. I was particularly keen to work at the depot because they also repaired the various engines that were installed in the machines, whereas at Grantham we received the engines new from the manufacturers and assembled them as a unit into our earthmoving equipment.

Our lodgings were situated on Sydenham High Street above Sainsbury's and were reached from a side street off the main shopping area. Climbing a long flight of stairs, you reached the first floor where Mr & Mrs Chalker occupied a large living and dining area to the rear, their central bedroom and bathroom plus very large front living room overlooking the busy High Street. We were the Chalkers' lodgers and we lived on this floor, where Mrs Chalker prepared our excellent meals and treated us as family members.

On the second floor lived Cissie, the landlady's daughter, and her husband Jim. They occupied a similar flat but with two bedrooms. Dave and I were installed in one of these bedrooms and used the bathroom and toilet facilities on this floor. Complicated, but it worked well. Cissie worked below in Sainsbury's and Jim was a carpenter employed by Lewisham Council.

Mr Jack Chalker, our landlord, I would guess was well over 65 years old and cycled to and from his workplace daily, where he was employed as a Janitor. He would arrive home from work and haul his bicycle up the long, steep flight of stairs, get washed and changed, enjoy his evening meal and retire to his favourite corner chair. Smoking his pipe, which would often fall from his mouth when he dozed off, he would watch the black and white television programmes. Mrs Chalker would severely reprimand him for falling asleep, which he always denied vehemently. (There was of course no colour television at that time.)

The three months were coming to an end. Dave Chambers was homesick and eager to return home, but I had enjoyed my visit both from the work and leisure perspective and was sorry to be leaving. Mr Clarke, the Depot Manager, called me into his office and asked me if I would like to continue working there. I eagerly accepted the chance and Mr Clarke made the necessary arrangements.

My work now entailed stripping down engines that required repairs and cleaning and ordering new parts where required; when these items were received the engines were assembled and tested. All this was done under the supervision of skilled fitters. When the service engineers were involved with heavy work and required assistance they would often ask the Manager if I could accompany them. Sometimes the work would be completed in one day, but often it would entail staying at the location for several days and we would stay at a local hotel. I found the whole travelling experience very rewarding.

In my leisure time on Saturday morning I would board a no. 12 London Transport double decker bus at Cobb's Corner in Sydenham and travel the 12 miles to Oxford Circus. On each trip I would plan to visit a different venue, and by following this procedure I found my way around London quite well. I also visited any football ground in the London area whenever the team I supported (Leicester City) was playing there. I would also walk around and explore my local Sydenham area of Lewisham, Catford and Penge.

Speedway was a popular sport at this time and the top teams attracted large crowds on race evenings. I became a keen New Cross Speedway supporter and proudly wore my badge (Maltese Cross) with hanging pendants denoting the years of support. I was also fortunate because most of the speedway venues used our smaller rollers for track maintenance and when travelling with a service engineer in their locality we would call in on a 'courtesy visit' to enquire about the wellbeing of their roller. I would casually mention my speedway interests, and as a result I found myself with a constant supply of complimentary tickets to New Cross, Haringey, Wimbledon, etc.

I had started playing tennis since coming to Sydenham; Jim and I played most weekends. We also supported Crystal Palace football team whenever they played their home games at Selhurst Park.

1949

During 1949 I received my call-up letter for National Service. Since the war ended every male on reaching the age of eighteen had had to serve a period in one of the armed services unless they were unfit, and medical examinations were carried out to determine your level of fitness.

On attending my medical I was shocked to be informed that I had a weak heart and I would be referred to a specialist for further checks. Having played various sports throughout my life and being now actively engaged in tennis, plus the fact that my work entailed strenuous manual labour, I was mystified that this condition had not shown itself in shortage of breath, tiredness, etc. Further examination by a heart specialist proved to be reassuring and I was informed that everything was in order. Apparently I have a fluctuating heart rate which evens itself out in due course and my previous doctor must have checked at the wrong moment. I was told to inform any future doctor of this condition, especially if undergoing a medical for insurance purpose.

CHAPTER 7

NATIONAL SERVICE

Padgate: Basic Training

I chose the Royal Air Force for my 18-month period of National Service and was relieved when my selection was confirmed and I was instructed to report to Padgate in Lancashire for my basic training.

On arrival at the Camp we were met (not welcomed) by four drill corporals who proceeded to shout orders ("Stand up straight and to attention!"), their demeanour being quite hostile and cynical. We were soon to discover that this attitude would continue relentlessly for the next eight weeks. Each corporal was in charge of a billet (or wooden hut) consisting of approximately 24 men and would be responsible for your drill and rifle training plus general discipline.

We were issued with a full kit of clothing, bedding, eating and drinking utensils plus a rifle and bayonet. Then followed instructions on how to fold blankets and sheets to the correct width and how they should be presented on the bed for daily inspection. Black shoes were to be highly polished, as were all buttons on tunics together with belt buckles. We were pursued relentlessly day and night by corporals and asergeants whose whole object was to create some degree of order and discipline from this rabble they had been unfortunate enough to have thrust upon them.

If anyone asks me if I am right or left-handed I have to reply, "As in what situation?" I truthfully do not know myself until I have checked it out - I am ambidextrous. In most sports I am left-handed or left-footed, but I write right-handed. I mention this now because it forms such a large part of your military career and when we stood on the parade ground for our first lesson in rifle drill I realised in horror that everything was alien to me and the command 'Shoulder arms' would result in the rifle resting on the wrong shoulder. I had to concentrate hard at all times to ensure I was not the odd one out in the tightly-drilled ranks. The situation was compounded on the rifle range when I automatically tucked the rifle into the wrong shoulder, closed the wrong eye and had to reach over for the bolt, which for me was fitted on the wrong side. This did not bode well on the command 'rapid fire!' as I fumbled and reached around a mechanism designed for the other 99% of the population. Our corporal naturally went berserk, ballistic, and appeared towering over me shouting, "Not another @*##*!"

My career Regimental Sergeant Major uncle, on later hearing of my misfortune, informed me that had I been a long-serving military man they would have persevered and eventually 'persuaded' me to change my ways. 'Rome wasn't built in a day,' stated the old adage, but changing riflemen in eight weeks was obviously too much to expect.

After morning parade had ended and before dismissal we all

waited expectantly for the ritual that followed and obviously gave our corporals huge delight. The letters from home would be shared between them after which they would loudly call out the names of the recipients, adding, "Oh look, they are all air mail" and hurlimg them to all corners of the parade ground. The mayhem that followed as airmen scurried after their letters afforded them much amusement.

Whenever we lined up on various occasions the formation was dictated by surname and, being Bradley, I came second to an Armstrong who shared life with us at that time. We rarely escaped unscathed as our Corporal asked for three or four volunteers, immediately followed by "You, you and you", pointing to the hapless Armstrong, Bradley and whoever was next in line. I picked up many unsavoury tasks in this way. Wilson and Young were always amused.

In the latter weeks of our basic training we were given a choice of jobs open to us and told the percentage marks we would need to acquire if we were to secure our selection. Aptitude tests were then supervised by training officers. Designed to highlight your mechanical or clerical capabilities, these tests comprised assembling various components, mental arithmetic, problem solving, etc., and were all set with time limits. I had selected Engine Assistant, which meant working on aircraft engines and thus continuing my civilian occupation as a fitter. I was extremely worried about the RAF's selection procedures as several of my friends had approached the career officers with the desire to be drivers and, equipped with the utmost confidence, had approached with a wide smile and civilian driving licence only to be turned down immediately and told there were plenty of vacancies for cooks. Apparently the RAF preferred to train drivers their way and did not appreciate cocky eighteen-year-olds approaching their driving instructors with driving licences and know-it-all attitudes. More a life-change than a gear-change I suppose.

It was with a huge sense of relief that I learned I had been accepted as an engine assistant and to report to Cosford near Wolverhampton for trade training.

Our passing-out parade was duly performed, after which we were invited for a night out with our drill sergeants and corporals, to discover that they were human after all.

Cosford: Trade Trading

Cosford near Wolverhampton was a technical training airfield, and we were soon introduced to the world of aircraft engines. This new intake of aircraftsmen all appeared to have technical backgrounds, and I suppose this was one area where the RAF appreciated some prior knowledge of machinery with engines being a welcome bonus.

We started in the workshop almost immediately and were issued with a technical drawing of a five-pointed star, which we had to cut-out of a piece of ¼" thick steel sheet. We were not allowed to use any electrically-driven machinery or tools to assist us in this procedure, all drilling being done with manually-operated hand-drills, cutting by hand-saw and smoothly finished off by filing. After completing the star, our next task was to cut out the star shape in ¼" thick steel sheet, again with no mechanical assistance. Our steel star was then required to fit smoothly into the cut-out star shape and able to be rotated around each of its five points. Marks were awarded accordingly.

We attended classes on the internal combustion engine, with theory and practical tests following. An aircraft's internal batteries should only be used in an emergency to ensure they are always fully charged and ready for that emergency should it arise; hence the aircraft's engines are started by external means whenever possible. We were taken outside to a small single-engined aircraft and given instruction in the procedure of swinging the propeller by hand to start the engine. This procedure was re-enacted constantly by each one of us standing in front of the propeller and going through the motions before commencing on the real thing. Forage cap removed from head and tucked into tunic, pull the prop down, tucking arm away quickly and move away as rapidly as possible. Finally the pilot took his seat in the cockpit and we proceeded with the real thing. It felt very satisfying when the engine kicked into life and I think I moved away more rapidly than anyone else.

Wolverhampton Wanderers Football Club was nearby and I was privileged to see the Wolves play several of their home games at Molyneux at a time when they were enjoying enormous success with their captain Billy Wright and great forwards, Mullen, Hancocks and Jesse Pye.

During my time at Cosford my dad had taken a job in Leicester. My Aunt Hannah and my cousins Liam and Freda were already living in Leicester and my aunt was employed by a doctor and his partners, who had a surgery there. My aunt and cousins lived in accommodation above the surgery, and as it was a large house, my dad, mother and sister Pauline also moved to the same address.

Our training concluded, we were all issued with details of our next posting, which would be our working environment probably for the rest of our National Service. Some received their news with excitement, especially those with an overseas posting. I just wandered around with a puzzled expression asking everyone the same question and getting the same negative answer until approaching one of our corporals I enquired, "Where is North Luffenham?"

He replied, "Where do you live?"

"Leicester," I said.

"Well, it's about 20 miles down the road from there."

North Luffenham

North Luffenham in Rutland was part of Transport Command, and on arrival I found it to be a hive of activity. Our living accommodation was good, brick buildings consisting of four large rooms on the ground floor, each housing twenty airmen with a Corporal's single separate room adjacent to each one. The first floor had exactly the same layout. Our block contained airmen employed on the airfield.

I was taken to the airfield and introduced to our Flight Sergeant and various sergeants and corporals who specialised in maintaining aircraft engines, airframes and radar equipment, etc. It did not take long for our Flight Sergeant to inform me that North Luffenham held the trophy for being the most accident-free airfield in Transport Command and had been for several years; he therefore did not expect my arrival to jeopardise this happy situation in any way in the future. I felt it futile to reply that I would do my best to maintain the status quo, as this was obviously not what was required; improvement was the only acceptable way forward.

F700 (or Form 700)

The Flight Sergeant then introduced me to a large blue book approximately 2ft x 1ft titled the F700. Each aircraft had an F700 and it was virtually the history of that aircraft from its first day of operational duties. Every single piece of work carried out on that aircraft, no matter how small, was recorded and signed for by the tradesman responsible; even the refuelling and oil checks were noted. An aircraft could not take off until all tradesmen had signed for the completion of their check; therefore any missing signatures were easily noticeable. When the pilot entered the Flight Office he was able to scrutinise the F700 applicable to his aircraft and ascertain details of work completed since the previous flight, and when fully satisfied he would sign before take-off.

On the airfield we worked shiftwork, as aircraft were flying day and night. Our shift pattern was crazy to say the least, as we worked a different shift each day for three days and the fourth day was a day off. I cannot remember the shift hours, except that after completing a Thursday night shift at 7 am you were allowed Friday, Saturday and Sunday leave before reporting for work on the Monday morning. This enabled me to spend long weekends at home in Leicester quite frequently.

We had a variety of aircraft in service including Dakotas, Valettas, Ansons and Doves. It was a training ground for pilots and aircrew and each aircraft became a flying classroom. Pilots were coming fresh from single-engine aircraft and learning to fly twin-engined Dakotas, etc. The aircrew consisted of freshly-qualified navigators, all supervised by experienced aircrew. We as ground staff were always given prior warning when fresh batches of fliers were due to arrive and commence their courses. Most of them appeared ignorant of basic airfield procedures, however, which could lead to tension between the two parties. Marshalling was something we had to be proficient at as we directed planes travelling along the ground but unfortunately at night and using our marshalling wands (or torches) there was sometimes a lack of trust and the pilot would switch on his Aldis lamp (or searchlight) to scan the ground ahead, thus blinding the hapless marshaller. On these occasions we were instructed to throw our wands high in the air, walk away and leave the pilot to his own devices before reporting said pilot.

The Crew Room was a large wooden hut and a haven for airmen (AC1, AC2 and LACs) who had completed any work allotted and signed their applicable F700 to verify this task. The F700s were housed in the Flight Office next door, the domain of our Flight Sergeant.

Marshalling wands were plentiful, and they were housed in a large plywood crate in a corner of the Crew Room. There was a table and a few chairs, but these were not as popular as the single mattresses scattered around the floor, which were used by airmen taking a quick nap during a night shift after completing pre-flight checks, safe in the knowledge that their aircraft were on long cross-country flights and not due to return until 3 am, when they would have to complete their checks once again and carry out any resultant minor maintenance work required.

The phrase 'marshalling wands' could conjure up an air of panic in the unwary and unprepared, and I always walked around the airfield at dusk making a mental note of which dispersal points housed parked aircraft and which were vacant and capable of receiving any future landings. The Crew Room door being thrown open at 2.30 am and the figure of a Flight Sergeant bawling "Aircraft landing!" was followed by dozy figures hastily grabbing wands and dashing onto the pitch-black airfield. Not to be recommended. Dakotas were landing in quick succession and converging down the perimeter track chasing airmen who were anxious to locate the nearest dispersal point and finally place the aircraft with its nose facing into any prevailing wind, the rear or tail end being light and susceptible to lift. Adverse weather meant lashing down the plane at the wingtips with ropes and attaching them to a heavy weight (a concrete block) on the ground. Frequent weather changes meant aircraft might have to be repositioned at any moment, a case of 'all hands on deck'.

Pilots were not allowed to start their engines from their internal batteries as these were to be kept fully charged and only used for emergencies, so two ground staff attended each starting procedure. One took the ground trolley containing batteries underneath the fuselage of the plane and connected it to an electrical socket. The second member of the team gave instructions to the pilot via marshalling wands on how this operation was progressing, when to start engines, when the trolley was being disconnected, when the trolley was clear of the aircraft and finally when it was clear for the aircraft to proceed. Unfortunately lack of 'swatting up' on basic procedures by the pilot often resulted in the trolley being dragged along underneath the aircraft with trolley-operator rapidly running clear of an advancing tail wheel and marshaller frantically running ahead of the aircraft signalling 'emergency stop' with crossed wands.

Our group of engine mechanics were discovering that we were responsible for many additional duties apart from the routine. We had to fill up the aircraft fuel tanks before and after flights, check oil-levels and replenish before and after flights, plus:

Single Engine Landings or Circuits and Bumps

The pilots were trained to take the aircraft into the air, switch off one engine and continue flying for a given period before bringing the plane in to land on that one engine. For reasons previously explained, an external battery trolley was then required to start the engine. Unfortunately this task fell to the engine mechanics, who based themselves at the end of the runway where a wide, white line had been painted right across the tarmac where the wheels of the aircraft would stop if the operation proceeded according to plan. These single engine landings continued through the day and night; daytime landings could be dangerous and night-time landings could be highly dangerous. (See above, 'swatting up on basic procedures'.) These runway duties lasted for four-hour periods.

After a few months I was promoted from AC2 to AC1 - Aircraftsman Second-Class to Aircraftsman First-Class. I was getting myself recognised by our staff pilots due to my name appearing regularly in the F700 with regard to various engine repairs, and often they would ask me if I fancied a flight after noticing my signature against a repair of some importance. This was probably done to test my confidence rather than get me some respite from our Flight Sergeant. After gaining his permission I would depart on a 'cross country' night flight in one of our Dakota flying classrooms. These cross-county training flights would usually be around four hours' duration and maybe flying across to France or flying over other European countries.

I would sit in those Dakotas with their basic facilities and look out into the night sky and try to imagine what the Bomber Command crews' lives had been like five years previously flying through enemy gunfire and being attacked by German fighter planes, most of the crew being around 18 to 20 years old. I admired their courage and wondered if I could have been as brave as those men in the same circumstances.

Being airfield shift workers, we were treated leniently regarding discipline on camp and on the occasions we were stopped by the RAF Police for a slovenly appearance, we only had to show our airfield passes to be sent on our way without further hindrance. Tuesday nights were camp 'bull' nights when rooms had to be cleaned, dusted, floors polished, kit laid out correctly etc. before inspection the following morning. We were often working on Tuesday nights and sleeping throughout most of the following inspection period the next day. A notice reading "Shift Workers" placed outside on the door was sufficient, and a quick glance from the doorway at the snoring occupants was enough to satisfy the inspecting officer.

Periodically the notice board would display a request for volunteers to serve in various postings abroad, and I would volunteer for them all. I would be called before the Commanding Officer, who would inform me of his views: "Terrible place Bradley - request denied, carry on." Unfortunately it all centred on our 'Most accident-free airfield in Transport Command' trophy and was a case of 'If your face fits...' If you worked efficiently they held on to you, and if you did not you were soon posted elsewhere.

The Berlin Airlift was operating Dakota aircraft on its mission supplying food and clothing to Germany and required engine mechanics for servicing and repairs to these aircraft. I volunteered. I stood before the Commanding Officer. "Terrible place Bradley - horrible conditions, request denied - carry on." Shortly afterwards I was promoted from AC1 to LAC - Aircraftsman First-Class to Leading Aircraftsman. I was pleased to receive my LAC 'propellers' and sew them on my uniform.

At North Luffenham accidents did happen occasionally, to spread an air of apprehension. Our worst incident occurred shortly before our shift ended at 5 pm one afternoon when our Sergeant approached and told us that an extra flight was required that night. Some work had just been completed on a Dakota in the hangar and this was to be the aircraft used after we had installed it in a dispersal area outside. There were suggestions that as we were only a few minutes away from the end of our shift, the ground crew taking over should have this task. Our Sergeant rejected this suggestion.

Moving immobile aircraft such as a Dakota on the ground meant fixing a long steering bar onto the tail wheel of the aircraft to enable the bar to be moved from side to side, thus moving the tail wheel, which in turn steers the aircraft. A second person is required in the cockpit to operate the brakes; this person is looking skywards and cannot see the ground directly in front due to the angle of the plane when on the ground, and he must rely on directions from a further two airmen on the ground based forward of each wing-tip, where they can be seen. Two or three airmen on the trailing edge of each wing and pushing their weight are now sufficient to get the plane in motion.

The crew were a little irked to get this duty at this late stage of their shift and galvanized into action and with shouts of "let's get this show on the road!" the brakeman dashed into the cockpit and hastily took up position; two wing-tip men positioned themselves ready for action and the airman designated to fix and operate the steering bar was ready to go. So many men had appeared along the trailing edge of each wing that not all volunteers could be accommodated. "Let's go - push!" saw the aircraft rapidly gain speed along the ground towards the hangar doors. Oh yes, I forgot to mention the hangar doors previously: two large doors on rollers which should be opened to their full width to allow planes in and out for repairs. Unfortunately our hangar door operators did not respond quickly enough to the rapidly-approaching Dakota and with last-second panicking shouts of "brakes!" and "stop-pushing!" plus a tail-wheel operator veering from side to side and losing control due to excessive speed, the wing-tip hit the hanger door and was crushed.

We had a written-off Dakota on the airfield and its wings were serviceable. Our shift was told that if we removed the wing required from the write-off and used this to replace our damaged wing before shift commenced the following morning we would hear nothing more about the incident. With this ultimatum we continued working through the night, removing the two wings and swapping them around before refitting them. Believe me, there are hundreds of nuts and bolts closely situated around the roots of those wings where they join the fuselage.

As previously stated, the engine mechanics had several extra duties, and I now found myself with another task which I was keen to perform. I was given instructions and a test on starting and operating Dakota and Valetta engines whilst the aircraft are stationary; we were forbidden to move them. This was useful for engine tests after repairs and also entailed assisting radar mechanics as they required engines running for their checks. It gave me great pleasure day or night to select two airmen to operate the trolley batteries and signal the necessary instructions. I could act the role of pilot if only for a few minutes. "Whoever heard of a stationary pilot?" I can imagine you are saying.

Demobilisation was drawing nearer and I was offered the chance of promotion to Engine Fitter 2nd Class (or Fitter 2) if I signed on for five years. I must admit that I enjoyed my term of National Service in the Royal Air Force; it had been hard work, but I liked the life. As regards the RAF as a career, it was a case of waiting for dead men's shoes - promotion was very slow. Our Flight Sergeant knew everything there was to know about aircraft engines and was nearing 21 years of service. My Corporal was a Fitter 1st Class with 12 years' service, so there was little chance of promotion on the horizon.

I played football for the station team and from my position on the left-wing would notice our Commanding Officer among the spectators at various matches.

So it was the end of the RAF career of 2407821 Leading Aircraftsman, Engine Assistant R. Bradley. My Demobilisation Book was issued and I quickly turned to the final page for the Commanding Officer's reference: "A very keen and enthusiastic footballer" was the brief statement. Not very encouraging for showing to Aveling-Barford Ltd, manufacturers of heavy earthmoving equipment & contractors' plant. They did not have a football team.

CHAPTER 8

THE SERVICE ENGINEER YEARS

LONDON, LEICESTER, NEWCASTLE & SOUTH WALES
1950 TO 1955

1950

After demobilisation I contacted Aveling-Barford in Grantham and also Mr Clarke, the Sydenham Depot Manager, regarding resuming my apprenticeship there. This was duly arranged and I found myself in familiar surroundings workwise and with my previous landlady Mrs Chalker and family.

I had received £25 demobilisation money and I wandered around my local shopping area of Catford and Lewisham and bought a new tennis racket for £5, a new green and white check sports jacket for £5 and new light grey sports trousers for £5, which left me with £10 in my pocket, all I possessed moneywise until my next payday in two weeks' time (we were paid a week in arrears). I vowed never to be in that situation again. The sports jacket was a direct reaction against the drab blue uniformity of RAF-issue clothing over the last 18 months. A few weeks after these purchases I visited Alexandre the Tailor's in Leicester and was measured for a semi-draped suit, which was the latest style and in a plain sky-blue colour. The price was £20.

The old routine soon fell into place - the fortnightly trips on Saturday afternoon with Jim to support Crystal Palace Football Club at Selhurst Park and playing in the Sunday morning tennis matches. Lewisham Hippodrome was a well-known variety theatre when these establishments were still drawing packed houses on both evening performances and before television was to bring about their demise. Mrs Chalker's friend had a large house round the corner from our address and she had a standing contract with Lewisham Hippodrome to supply board and lodging to two of their visiting variety artists each week. This lady knew that I visited the theatre regularly and supplied me with a complimentary ticket for a seat at the second performance every Tuesday night, so I was privileged to see the headline acts of that period. Penge Theatre had an excellent amateur dramatic company which performed a different play each week. Jim had little interest, so Cissie and I would usually attend weekly.

Work was continuing nicely and it was satisfying to see a machine that had been completely stripped down for a complete overhaul being positioned on a low-loader after re-assembly, freshly painted and ready for transportation to its base.

There were several characters at the depot, some old faces, some new. An old fitter friend, Reg, was a Charlton Athletic Football Club supporter and we would sometimes attend a home game at the Valley, standing on the embankment behind one of the goals, in the days before mass seating and when attendances topped 60,000. The service engineers driving around in their Austin A40 saloon cars were virtually the same personnel, and I envied them as they proceeded to destinations I had heard about and always wanted to visit, although I was lucky in the fact that whenever they required an extra pair of hands they put my name forward to the Manager. Although it may have no relevance, I must mention that chrome items had a very poor coating at this time which peeled away shortly after the product was manufactured, which gave me immense disappointment when cleaning chromework on my machines or vehicles.

There was one odd character who had appeared during my time away on National Service, a refined, debonair, well-spoken gentleman of around 35 years of age. He had a red Morgan sports car and would arrive at the Depot in the morning in his sharp suit, park the car and nonchalantly walk to an office, where he would change into a boiler suit ready for the day ahead. He informed anyone who enquired that he was preparing to be a service engineer. The general consensus of the working personnel was that he was more likely to be a forthcoming manager of the Service Division. He was not mechanically minded and did not appear to have seen a tool-box before, and he definitely had little idea of how to use the items inside it. We were therefore very guarded in our dealings with him, regarding him as some kind of spy planted by senior management.

After a non-productive day he would meticulously wash and change into his suit before starting the car and driving though the suburbs towards (we imagined) the heart of London and his luxury penthouse in Chelsea or Mayfair - although we could never persuade him to divulge any of his private life, except that he was married. He certainly did not wear his boiler-suit like a badge of honour as we all did at that time; we were quite prepared to walk along the street displaying our oil and grease patches like hard-earned medals.

At the 10-minute break times in the morning and afternoon, peals of laughter would be forthcoming from men recounting experiences and telling ribald jokes. Our suave gentleman would also participate in this raucous badinage, but like himself his jokes and rhymes were more subtle and sophisticated than the average contributions:

> *A young lady from Barking Creek*
> *Had her periods once a week,*
> *Her friend from Woking said "How provoking,*
> *Not much poking, - so to speak?"*

After only a few weeks he disappeared in the red Morgan, never to return.

1951

I was informed by Aveling-Barford that as I had followed my trade as a fitter my term of service with the RAF would be included as part of my apprenticeship, and no further time would need to be served. On the 11th May 1951 I received my Apprenticeship Certificate, which showed my months of service with the company all in the colour red for excellent, and on that date my wages increased from approximately £2.10 shillings per week to a fitter's basic rate of over £6 weekly.

Looking back over the ten-year period from the age of 11 to 21 we were always subject to a life of overriding discipline with a strong work ethic:

11 years to 15 years	Secondary Education	Headmaster & Masters
15 years to 18 years	Apprenticeship	Foreman, Chargehands & Fitters
18 years to 20 years	R.A.F	Flight Sergeants, Sergeants & Corporals
20 years to 21 years	Apprenticeship	Manager, Foreman & Fitters

Between 21 and 25 years of age a man was most likely to marry (in those days) and with marriage came the further responsibility of supporting a wife (few women were employed outside the home at that time) and probably soon afterwards there would be children, and so the strong work ethic was continued. Today, unfortunately, young people often gravitate towards a college degree which is worthless and crave a nice, comfortable, clean existence, preferably starting at the top as a manager. Engineering apprenticeships are few and far between as our manufacturing capabilities have been lost to companies overseas and the dirty, hard-working apprenticeships are shunned as fit only for second-class citizens. Discipline and job satisfaction have in most instances disappeared.

The Festival of Britain took place in Central London during the year and I visited the site frequently. The Festival Hall was a new building planned and erected for this occasion; its modern facilities and acoustics were built with a long-term future in mind and I have attended several jazz concerts there. It remains a top venue for concerts today and is the only surviving exhibit of the Festival. Battersea Park in London also enjoyed many visitors during this same period when a large funfair in the Park was also part of the Festival of Britain.

1952

From my lodgings in Sydenham High Street to the Aveling-Barford Depot was approximately 1½ miles. I had been walking the route for over three years and was very familiar with the surroundings: straight up the High Street and past Sydenham Railway Station on the opposite side of the road, over the railway bridge and onto Cobb's Corner before turning right and along a busy road for three quarters of a mile before crossing the road and approaching Mill Lane and the depot. I have had to cross the road only once on my journey.

There was a period of two to three weeks during the winter when darkness fell around 4 pm after a heavy smog descended over London. It was named 'smog' because it was a mixture of fog and sooty smoke which came from the coal fires (central heating was not available) and rose into the air before descending later. On leaving work at 5 pm everything on the roads had come to a standstill; the London Transport double-decker buses had been abandoned on the roads by drivers and passengers. Pedestrians were groping their way to their destinations, fumbling along the sides of buildings, stumbling up and down pavements. Even the brightly-lit shops on the High Street could only be recognised when you were adjacent to them. My journey would become an obstacle course as I groped along in this hostile environment. Inside the house you were unable to shut out the smoky, sooty smell and whenever the word 'smog' is mentioned that smell is there in my nostrils. The smog caused the deaths of thousands of people who suffered from lung problems such as asthma.

I was approached by our Depot Manager, who asked if I was interested in becoming a service engineer. This had been my goal since first arriving at the Depot, so I accepted the chance readily.

I was conversant with the Aveling-Barford products and they were powered with engines manufactured by several other companies, so it was arranged that I should attend crash courses with these engine manufacturers before embarking on my service engineer career. It was envisaged that my training period would last around six months.

It was made clear to me that taking up the role of service engineer meant I would be on call-out 24 hours a day and be ready to assist customers with machine breakdowns night or day. On completion of training I could also be posted to any part of the country to cover that particular area.

My training began at Rustons in Lincoln. We fitted their engines in many of our heavier diesel road rollers and two weeks on the factory floor working with their fitters was educational and informative. Petters' Engines in Loughborough was my next stop, followed by a course with Dormans' Engines at Stafford. A trip to Glasgow followed, where I attended a course with Cummins Engines. We used the Leyland 600 diesel engine in our graders. I eventually arrived in Leyland, Lancashire, where I spent a week in the factory followed by a second week in the classroom.

Our teacher was an old retired (or nearing retirement) Leyland fitter who the company thought (I presume) would be more usefully employed imparting his Leyland engine knowledge to customers rather than sitting on the park bench with his dog. He enjoyed the morning and afternoon tea breaks when two ladies would appear through the classroom door manoeuvring a tea-trolley laden with Banbury and Eccles cakes, which appeared to be the staple diet of folk in that area. He would then engage in conversation with the ladies and classroom at large and much merriment would ensue, assisted in no small measure by the partaking of said nourishment.

Serious business would be resumed as we studied the matter in hand and our teacher pointed to the wall chart before commencing in a broad Lancashire accent: "If you're walkin' along approachin' a Leyland six 'undred engine and you 'ear it a 'untin' and a hoscillatin'..." The class would endeavour to keep a straight face until we had heard the remedial treatment for this malfunction but unfortunately "a 'untin' and a hoscillatin'" would be repeated several times, and we found this virtually impossible. Whenever I was in Grantham or the Sydenham premises of Aveling-Barford I would pass a stationary grader with engine running and remark to the attendant fitter or operator, "I know what's wrong with that engine, it's a 'untin' and a hoscillatin'." Remarkably, the story and catchphrase spread like wildfire and very soon it did not need to be said as the fitter or operator would jump in first with a "I know, it's a 'untin' and a hoscillatin'".

Aveling-Barford's main factory was in Grantham, but in recent years they had opened another manufacturing outlet in Newcastle on the Scotswood Road. After completing my engine training I was instructed to familiarise myself with this part of the company and it would also be an opportunity to work on machines I had not covered in the Grantham Fitting Shop.

Grantham was easy-going with regard to trade union membership; you joined the engineering union or you stayed out - your choice. Newcastle was strictly all union and I questioned the logic of my impending visit, especially as I was a non-union man; also, union membership was discouraged in the Service Department because our necessarily longer working weeks surpassed the 44-hour maximum plus the unsociable working hours. It was decided that I should give it a try without causing any trouble or walk-outs, etc., and if I came up against any obstacle I was to return to Grantham immediately.

I arrived at the Scotswood Road factory and the first question I was asked concerned union membership. I informed them that I had no intention of joining the union. Serious faces were all around me as I was transported to my lodgings. On arrival the following morning the Foreman suggested I use his office until the union representative could sort out my membership. I informed him that I would not be joining and would have a general look around before leaving as soon as possible. I wandered around the Fitting Shop and it was apparent that word had spread rapidly and I was experiencing being 'sent to Coventry' or, to be precise, ignored by all and sundry.

In an effort to pass away some time I wandered into the Stores, where large metal containers each held the component parts to assemble a 10-ton road roller gearbox. I signalled to the overhead crane operator that I required one of the containers to be moved. Luckily he co-operated, perhaps because we did not speak to each other or maybe it was curiosity about what I intended to do next. There was a vacant space on the gearbox assembly line which I claimed and quickly commenced work.

Eyes followed my every move as I toiled in my own private world. Chargehands, fitters and their apprentices all passed by silently, avoiding face-to-face confrontation. After a few days my gearbox stood completed and then I had it lifted onto the testbed, where I let it run smoothly and efficiently for several hours before summoning an inspector to give it his blessing. He was unable to fault it and signed my time card ready to be clocked-off. The gearbox had been completed well within its allotted piecework time and was therefore worth quite a few pounds.

I was not on piecework, so I presented the card to my gearbox neighbour with the remark "It's no good to me", and suddenly the whole Fitting Shop personnel were anxious to make my acquaintance. I had three very happy months there and made many friends. Union membership was never mentioned again.

It was Friday night, and with the weekend ahead I intended to commence my exploration of Newcastle the next day. There was a knock on the door, which I duly opened. "Come on, bonnie lad, get yourself ready, we're going for a night out!" said a familiar Fitting Shop face. And so my introduction to the Newcastle weekend culture began. "Has he got a front door key?" enquired my friend to the landlady who replied in the affirmative. "He'll see you in due course," said my friend. "Howay," said the landlady knowingly.

We joined other men from the Fitting Shop, some with their wives and girlfriends, and so the weekend would begin, with Newcastle Brown Ale in abundance and night turning into day. Back to the lodgings for a clean-up and change of clothes before leaving once more to watch the Newcastle United football team led by Jackie Milburn, their centre-forward hero - that's if they were playing at home. Wonderful times with marvellous people.

It never failed to amaze me how different the two Fitting Shop personnel were. The Grantham crowd worked by the book; absenteeism and any time off would probably be the result of illness, whereas many Newcastle fitters had installed their own radios on the workbench and the afternoons would prove most interesting as they listened to the horse-racing. Suddenly a fitter would reach for his coat. "Where are you going?" I would ask. "I've just won on the horses and I am off to the bookies to collect my winnings!" he would reply as he headed for the clocking-off machine, with no intention of returning that day. Everyone knew it was bookies first stop, followed by a few pints of Newcastle Brown Ale afterwards to celebrate.

Working with a fitter friend on a trench cutting machine one day, I was concentrating on the steering mechanism. There was a large vertical steering shaft of approximately 6" diameter and I needed to fit a large brass steering worm (wheel) onto the shaft. To ensure a smooth fit I had removed (filed off) any rough edges on the shaft and wormwheel. The second stage of this operation would be to fit a key in the shaft and then lower the worm gently down the shaft, line-up the worm keyway with the shaft key and tap into position hoping for a nice tight fit. I was still on the first part of the operation and had slid the wormwheel down the shaft where two separate oil-covered, machined surfaces met (wormwheel and end of shaft). The oil on the two machined surfaces acted like a glue and wrapping my fingers underneath each side of the wormwheel I tried to snatch it back up the shaft. I was standing on the machine with legs straddled across the steering mechanism about 6ft above the ground level when I felt a searing pain from the end of my right-hand middle finger. Blood poured everywhere as I climbed down and hurried to the Ambulance Room for treatment. Apparently my workmate had noticed my difficulty and walked up behind me with a long steel crowbar, which he placed between my legs and under the wormwheel and quickly with a jolting movement aimed at releasing the wheel, but in doing so he had accidentally caught my finger.

I was explaining the incident to the nurse in the Ambulance room when two fitters entered carrying my workmate. "Place him on the bed," said the furse. He had fainted after witnessing his handiwork.

I was of no great assistance to anyone directly afterwards, and I required my finger dressing regularly, so I contacted my doctor in Leicester, who had a surgery in the same building at my home address, and he recommended I return and he would continue the necessary treatment. Aveling-Barford Service Division in Grantham were also in agreement, as my time in Newcastle was concluding.

Pete Turner was a fitter at the Sydenham Depot, and we often visited London together during the Festival of Britain and its Battersea Park attractions. Pete had a sister who held a senior position in the administration of Hatfield House near London and he spent many weekends there on visits. He approached me one Monday after one of these visits with news that he had met a very nice young lady at Hatfield House who had come over from Holland with one of her girlfriends for a short time in order to get a better grasp of the English language; this meant being employed at Hatfield House as domestic workers. Pete had asked the young lady for a date but unfortunately the two girls had vowed to go everywhere together during their stay in this country, so he was asking me to form a foursome. I was not too keen on this blind date arrangement, mainly because I always dreaded being in the company of a girl taller than myself. It would have been easy at the time to enquire the height of these ladies and why I did not I cannot understand, unless the fact that Pete was the same height as myself reassured me. I went along with the arrangement.

Hatfield to King's Cross Railway Station was only a short journey, and it was arranged we meet them there. Pete made it clear to me that I would follow his lead regarding introductions. The girl he approached first was the one he was interested in, and I would be left to fend for myself thereafter. I comforted myself during the journey to London with the consolation that the date would be over in a few hours and that would be the end of the story.

Pete and I stood on the platform at King's Cross as the train from Hatfield arrived. "There they are!" he said, and my heart sank as the girls approached us. One was my height and very attractive, while the other was 6ft tall at least. I naturally assumed he would head straight for the short and attractive one, and I was quickly working out the hours I would have to endure before the end of our date. I could not believe my eyes when Pete attached himself to the tall lady!

Ali Bosman and her tall friend came from Rotterdam, Holland, and their English was already quite good. Ali and I quickly became good friends and the four of us would meet at King's Cross on Saturday mornings and enjoy our days together visiting the tourist attractions until it was time to see them safely on the last train to Hatfield. The Lyons Corner Houses were great restaurants at that time and we frequently enjoyed meals there. We would usually book tickets for a theatre show every week and I always enjoyed my days with Ali immensely.

I was never very keen on the foursome idea of togetherness and after a few weeks I was sure Ali was in the same frame of mind. As the other two were quite happy with the arrangement I suggested my plan to Ali; it was quite simple to carry out - London is a very crowded place and as we hung back in the London Underground's passages we slipped away and mingled with the crowds until the coast was clear. This meant the end of the inconvenient foursome and after this Pete and I met the girls at King's Cross, after which both couples followed their own agenda until either meeting up at a theatre where four tickets had been booked together or eventually meeting at King's Cross for that last train to Hatfield.

Ali's parents had only wanted her to spend three months in England, but when this period approached she persuaded them to agree to a further three months; her friend also stayed for the extended period. Ali's father owned three butchers' shops in Rotterdam; he managed one, his wife managed the second and a manager was employed in the third. Ali stayed at home and acted as housekeeper. The girls returned home reluctantly after their six-month stay at Hatfield House.

One day I was summoned to Grantham Service Department and met with our Service Manager to discuss my future arrangements. He was of the opinion that Leicester was a very convenient location as a base to push further into the heart of the Midlands and South Wales, and if I wished to work from home it would meet with their approval. There was a service engineer already based in Dudley, Staffordshire, and we could liaise when convenient for both parties.

Grantham had approximately five service engineers working directly from the factory and covering a wide area. Leicester is 32 miles from Grantham and would be in easy reach if I needed to collect spare parts. Most of the service engineers were married men, and although they were fully aware of their 24-hour commitments to our customers they preferred going home to their families at 5 pm rather than preparing for an overnight breakdown in some distant location, so news of my posting was welcomed by the Grantham personnel. The news was also welcomed by our man in Dudley (also married), who informed me of his frequent visits to South Wales - signs of things to come.

Working from home in Leicester would prove to be a very rewarding and enjoyable time. I had left home in Grantham when 17 years of age and now after five years it seemed strange at first to be resuming family life after this long period away. The fifties were among my favourite years and although life was still austere after the war years, I still look back and remember joyful weekends with a packed agenda of my favourite things to do and see. My cousin Liam, his mother and sister Freda had an apartment in the same house, enabling Liam and me to attend the same events together, a favourite being the Saturday afternoon football fixture where we supported our favourite team, Leicester City, who seemed to alternate between the First and Second Division of the Football League on a regular promotion and relegation basis. I believe I have supported them through at least two seasons of promotion football and always maintain that if you have supported your favourite team throughout a promotion season you have witnessed and been rewarded with some wonderful entertainment.

We had two or three close friends who Liam had known throughout his preceding years living in Leicester, and on Saturday night they would arrive at our house to join us before we all proceeded into the city for a few beers at the Manchester (yes, it was Manchester) Working Men's Club, followed by a few more at other Working Men's Clubs. These clubs abounded at that time and were lavish establishments that provided entertainment from artists starting out on their careers and others who had been on the circuit for many years. Our friends would always eagerly ask if my dad would be coming with us and I would convey their message to him with a "Hi Dad, the lads want to know if you're coming for a drink with us?"

"Just give me a few minutes to get ready," he would reply, his face breaking into a beaming smile.

He always appreciated the fact that the younger generation regarded him as 'one of the lads', and I had been aware of this in recent years as I came to regard him more as a brother than a dad, and I was never reluctant to ask his advice on any matters of concern as I learned how to surmount life's various obstacles. I respected his wisdom greatly.

Sunday evening provided top class live entertainment at the De Montfort Hall in Leicester, which was almost opposite our house in Regent Road. The artists appearing for just the one Sunday performance would often be appearing at the London Palladium on the Monday and throughout that week. Top American recording artists of the day - Guy Mitchell, All Martino, Les Paul, etc - would have big-band backing from British musicians Ted Heath, Johnny Dankworth and many more. Often the bands would feature their own vocalists, and Ted Heath was always a sell-out concert with extra seats arranged on stage directly behind the band which I have occupied with Dad and Liam on two occasions. Yes, Dad always enjoyed the De Montfort concerts.

A Ted Heath concert at the De Montfort Hall was always a highlight for me and an event which was eagerly anticipated. 'The Hawk Talks' was a musical arrangement which was popular at this time and the band's version was top of the charts, with the record selling in vast numbers. The climax to this piece would see Ted Heath cease conducting, collect his trombone from the side of the stage and join his trombone section. The musicians stood in line with all arms working their trombone slides in perfect unison and with the crescendo building as they brought the chorus to a finale amid a standing ovation from the rapturous audience. It was an experience that truly raised the hairs on the back of your neck!

There is a similarly outstanding passage of music in the Woody Herman version of 'Caledonia', where the notes from the trumpet section soar higher and higher as they bring the arrangement to a pulsating conclusion.

A favourite remark of Woody Herman regarding his vocalists and instrumentalists was "Light them up and make them a star". He certainly knew how to do that. Magical musical moments, never to be forgotten.

A subject worth mentioning at this stage is the way everyone dressed in the fifties. Smart attire was the norm throughout the age groups, and men's casual uniform of blue jeans and open-necked shirt whatever the occasion had yet to dominate the scene. Young men arrived home from work, discarded their boiler suits, cleaned themselves up thoroughly and donned a clean shirt, tie, suit and polished shoes ready for an evening out. What background you came from did not matter in the slightest - you all dressed smartly in a nice suit and felt (and looked) a million dollars. Note the black and white films of the period: everyone wore a suit (even the gangsters) or sports attire. Many young men watching the cinema screen would see their favourite film star appear and make a mental note of that semi-draped suit before visiting Alexandre the Tailor the following Saturday and thumbing through the cloth samples, knowing exactly what style and colour (the Technicolor films helped) they required. You may also have selected (from Humphrey Bogart's latest epic) a fawn raincoat with leather buttons, tightly belted at the waist and the length only a few inches above ground level. I know I did.

The young ladies looked fabulous in their mini-skirts and latest fashions.

Working from home in Leicester was keeping me busy, especially with referrals from the Grantham Service Department and customers now realising I was in the area and easily accessible. My married service engineer friend in Dudley and I were covering the same Midlands and South Wales area, so we kept in constant contact regarding work. South Wales kept him busy, as there were many open-cast coal sites around there at that time and also many councils who held contracts with Aveling-Barford to have their machines inspected annually by a company representative. I took over a large number of these inspections whenever I could. These were the days before we had constructed our motorways and I would plan to leave our house in Leicester around 3 am on the Monday, which would mean arriving in Merthyr Tydfil at approximately 7:30 ready to commence work in their council depot. I would use Merthyr Tydfil as my base for the week and stayed in an excellent hotel there. Two days in Merthyr would see my inspections completed and I could then branch out to other inspections in Port Talbot, Neath, Aberdare, etc., before heading home for the weekend on Friday evening. I always kept abreast of the weather forecasts during the winter months getaway route through the mountains between Merthyr Tydfil and Abergavenny which could easily be cut off by heavy snowfalls. It never happened to me, but there were frequent close calls.

1953

Ali in Rotterdam invited me over to Holland for two weeks during the holiday and I gladly accepted her invitation. Her friend did not invite Peter. For the duration of my visit Ali's father had hired a car so that I could see as much of the country as possible, and he was anxious to know if I had any special request. Arnhem immediately came to mind and was top of my visiting list, as the British and our Allies had fought one of our deadliest battles there during the war. The war graves cemetery was beautifully maintained and it was sobering to read the inscriptions on the rows of white crosses of men killed in action. Arnhem had been a large-scale battle with parachutists dropping into the zone from gliders towed mostly to their destination by Dakotas and the parachutists dropped from their gliders directly before and after they were released by the Dakotas over the target. Many men were killed by the enemy before they dropped to the ground. Gliders and aircraft were destroyed in large numbers.

The crosses bore the details of these courageous men, pilots and aircrew, mostly between 18 and 20 years old. The Dutch people were very friendly; the war had ended only a few years previously. I was impressed by the large number of Dutch people who could speak English, and Ali was anxious to ensure that those within earshot knew I was English. We were then included in many conversations during our travels, and during a sightseeing trip by tourist bus the courier requested information regarding nationalities of the tourists. Several responded - Germans, Austrians, Belgians and French; then Ali loudly proclaimed that I was English, whereupon the lady courier came and sat nearby, directing most of her attention to us and ensuring we saw and understood everything of interest around us.

Rotterdam had large areas that had been rebuilt after suffering war damage and we spent many hours visiting the many excellent art galleries. I enjoyed rowing along the rivers and became quite proficient during my visit. Soon after I returned home I invited Ali to spend some time with me and my family in Leicester, and we visited the usual tourist attractions and travelled to the nearby cities of Coventry, Birmingham and Nottingham, plus theatre and De Montfort shows.

We spent a wonderful few days together, but unfortunately she had family demands in Rotterdam and I had company demands in the Midlands and South Wales. A case of what might have been.

1955

Our Service Department in Grantham was headed by a Service Manager who had held a high rank in the REME (Royal Electrical & Mechanical Engineers) during the war. He had brought into the Department several of his junior staff (sergeants) who worked with him during this period and who were now service engineers who appeared to have the monopoly when much-sought-after overseas visits were awarded to service personnel. I was anxious to take advantage of this perk and made my views known over the years, stressing that I as a single man did work many unsociable hours away from home, whilst many Grantham personnel appeared to work a 9 am to 5 pm regular routine and rarely spent a night away from family and home. Obviously I rocked several boats, causing waves to lap against the office walls of the Department. Our Service Manager assured me that my opportunity would come and I felt a sense of *déjà vu*, as if I was in the presence of my Commanding Officer in the RAF once again.

Another annoying occurrence which irritated me every time I opened my wage packet was the fact that I as a single man working many hours of overtime was paying a large percentage of these wages in income tax. I longed to escape this drain on my finances and had always harboured a desire to work abroad, but was under the impression that you required at least ten years' experience following your trade before being eligible for overseas positions. It was a culmination of these two factors which led me to answer a job vacancy for a Heavy Equipment Workshop Foreman on an iron ore mine in Sierra Leone, West Africa. I forwarded my application without expecting much success, as I thought I was lacking experience and too young for the job at twenty-five. I was pleasantly surprised to be called to London for an interview which was conducted by six senior directors and managers of the company, who after conferring informed me that the position was mine. I accepted gratefully.

I was due my two weeks' holiday and had booked a trip to Paris with Liam the following week. My new company would arrange my departure for Sierra Leone a couple of weeks after that at a date convenient for me.

I returned home and continued tidying up various jobs locally, intending to terminate my employment with Aveling-Barford after returning from holiday. On returning home on Friday afternoon from work completed locally, I received a telephone call from Grantham Service Division requesting that I drive my car immediately to Grantham, where it would be serviced during my absence on holiday. I informed them that this instruction could and should have been conveyed earlier as I was now officially on holiday and leaving for Paris early the following morning and would leave my car in my garage with keys and ready for collection at any time. This arrangement I was told was unacceptable and I must comply with the aforementioned request. I placed the telephone down firmly and embarked for Paris.

On my return from holiday my car was still in the garage and my mother informed me that there had been no response from the company regarding collection. I headed towards Grantham, Aveling-Barford Ltd, and the Service Manager's office. He told his secretary that he was ready to see me and as I entered he started his reprimand.

"Read this first," I said, thrusting the envelope across his desk. He read the enclosed letter of resignation and pushed it back towards me.

"I can't accept that, you're an Aveling-Barford man through and through," he said.

"Maybe that's the reason I was taken for granted, if you were under that impression," I replied. "Here are the car keys, it needs a service," I remarked as I departed the office.

After a brief period he called me back and asked what my future plans were. I informed him of my Sierra Leone job. A few minutes afterwards I was told the Service Director wanted to see me in his office in the main administration block. He requested the full story and my reasons for leaving. I informed him he was presiding over a small clique of former REME personnel and of my desire to be part of any company visits abroad, which was being routinely thwarted. The Director offered me an immediate six-month visit to India, travelling around the country and visiting our customers - a courtesy visit with all expenses paid and my company wages paid into my bank account during my absence. I thanked him for his offer and said it was months too late coming. "If you require your job back at any time, contact me personally," he said as I departed.

It was the start of a new direction in my life which would shape my future.

THE EXPATRIATE YEARS

1955 – 1987

CHAPTER 9

THE BACHELOR YEARS IN WEST AFRICA

SIERRA LEONE 1955-57

Airwork and Hunting Clan were two airlines which catered for the expatriate community in the mid-fifties, and it should be remembered that 1955 was many years before cheap air travel for the masses opened up Europe and the rest of the world to the tourists of later years. Flying was then an adventure approached with excitement, and as I have mentioned previously, you would be dressed in smart attire from top to toe. Gentlemen outnumbered the ladies around three to one, as males were usually business executives on short trips or expatriates on contract travelling to and from leave in their countries of origin.

Travelling to Sierra Leone and West Africa in general became a four-day experience that would live in your memory forever, especially if you were flying there for the first time, unlike the latest sojourns, which are quickly forgotten unless you have the misfortune of missing luggage or airport delays. The journey commenced by afternoon train from Leicester to St Pancras Station and onwards by the London Underground to Gatwick or Heathrow, where a hotel room had been reserved by the company. The following morning we boarded the aircraft for an early start and were greeted by the crew and stewardesses. The Viking was a twin-engined propeller aircraft (jet engines were not in commercial use at this time) and all flying was completed during daylight hours. Drinks and light refreshments were served after take-off and the stewardesses could carry out their duties at a far more leisurely pace than today's hectic trolley-dolly routine.

Around midday we landed at Las Palmas airport in the Canary Islands and were transported to a luxury hotel by the beach for lunch. The flight crew and stewardesses mixed in with the passengers at all times and everyone became quite friendly as the journey progressed. After a leisurely meal we boarded the aircraft and took to the air once again. During the afternoon flight we landed in some remote spot in the desert where the plane was refuelled by French Foreign Legion personnel who were assigned to these duties as punishment for various crimes or discipline lapses. It was not a regular airport and consisted of a few basic facilities, all operations being supervised by trained officers of the Legion.

We landed in Tangiers and were transported to a hotel for the evening meal; it was also to be our accommodation for the night. The flight crew were also staying at the hotel, but before going our separate ways we were given strict instructions by the stewardess that it would be an early take-off the following day and we must be ready to depart the hotel by 6.30 am. Sampling the nightlife of Tangiers was not to be missed and after a shower and meal most of the flight passengers soon departed the hotel, keen to sample the delights of Tangiers.

The following morning revealed that many of our flight were feeling the worse for wear and many remained unseen. The stewardesses had obviously experienced this situation many times previously and were prepared for the worst; it was a case of all hands to the plough as we all dashed around knocking on the doors of missing occupants until all were awake and making a move. It eventually reached a point where the stewardesses had one or two passengers running behind schedule and with the query "Are you decent?" would enter their room and assist with hurriedly packing cases and generally herding them to awaiting airport busses. You do not witness those scenes when travelling today.

After take-off, another leisurely day would begin with intermittent drinks and light meals. The stewardesses were not overly rushed in their duties and would sit and spend time with their passengers; they would stand in the aisle and participate whilst group photographs were taken.

Bathurst, Gambia, would be our next overnight stop with accommodation at a top hotel. The aircrew would join the passengers for a meal and drinks as this would be a last get-together before reaching our final destination of Freetown, Sierra Leone, the following day.

On arrival I was taken to the company's Freetown office, where a driver and car were waiting to transport me to the site at Marampa, my home and workplace for the next 15 months of my contract. We arrived at the mine and the Personnel Manager dropped me off at my bungalow and said he would give me a couple of hours to get unpacked, cleaned up and acclimatised, after which he would collect me for dinner at his bungalow, where his wife was preparing a meal. Later we would visit the mine clubhouse, where many of the staff were guaranteed to be in attendance and introductions could be made.

After ablutions were completed and I had the chance to survey my accommodation, I was pleasantly surprised at the standard of furniture and furnishings together with kitchen utensils, bedding, towels, etc. It appeared well stocked. The bungalow was built above ground on supporting stilts and the space underneath could be used as a garage for your transport, as there was sufficient headroom to accommodate most vehicles. This plan obviously required a flight of steps from ground level to the front door. My attention was drawn to the two main windows in the living room, which had a large box-shaped area the size of the windows attached to the outside wall and covered with mosquito netting, except for the base, which was sturdily built and offered a nice perch for reading etc when the windows were opened. The view from the windows was uninterrupted by any buildings and looked out onto open plains. I could wait no longer and threw open one of the windows. With my whole body resting on the perch, I looked out over the plain as darkness began to fall.

Suddenly the sky had become overcast and the heavens opened to a torrential downpour. I closed the windows rapidly as bolts of lightning hit the ground with the deafening sound of thunderclaps happening simultaneously. You could not describe the lightning as forked, as it did not deviate on its journey earthwards. It was not bolts of lightning but shafts, thick shafts that you could see hitting the ground on the plain and the thunderclaps happening simultaneously with the lightning strikes. You did not need to count the seconds between the lightning and thunder to ascertain how many miles away the storm was; you witnessed the visual impact and knew you were in the centre of it.

The rain lashed through the mosquito netting of the two window boxes, which were now acting as water containers directly outside the closed windows. The rain settled on the porch, gradually built up until it reached the lower edge of the window and finally seeping through, dripping down the inner wall of the living-room and onto the concrete floor.

Looking around the room, several things became quite clear: (a) The walls directly under the windows had a gloss paint finish, as opposed to a matt paint finish. (b) There were no carpets on the gloss finished concrete floor - only a few rush mats.

The rainwater was now covering most of the floor area. Luckily the rain had stopped and the storm had abated. I sat in a chair surveying my living room and reliving the last thirty minutes. I had never witnessed a storm like that before. The events had been quite harrowing. Welcome to Sierra Leone, West Africa. Welcome to Marampa. There was a car horn sounding outside...

The following morning I met my cook/houseboy, who was busily sweeping the previous evening's rainwater through the open front door, where it cascaded down the steps to the ground below. The rush mats were draped over the steps' handrails to dry out and there was a general air of routine rainy season procedures prevailing. I have already mentioned the view from my front windows which consisted of a palm-tree dotted plain as far as the eye could see. I was now looking from the rear of the bungalow, where a large mountain dominated the skyline. This mountain was named Masaboin and contained rich deposits of high-grade iron ore; it was where the Sierra Leone Development Company (SLDC) had concentrated its activities since 1930. It was now 1955 and apart from evening out the peak and constructing winding access roads cut into the mountainside and leading to the summit, Masaboin looked as though it would be yielding its precious mineral for many years to come. Masaboin and I would grow to know each other over the following 15 months in what was to become a love/hate relationship.

Food and any supplies required were ordered weekly from Freetown, where your individual order would be followed through and processed by the local office staff and debited to your account. There was a small food store on the mine which stocked essential items likely to be required. The clubhouse was a very popular destination for bachelor staff, with little to occupy their leisure time in this remote location, and vast quantities of beer and spirits were consumed. This often resulted in vehicles being discovered damaged, having left the road after being driven by staff who were worse for wear. Senior management overlooked the majority of these misdemeanours (in some instances being involved themselves).

There were only four or five married couples on the site and on rare occasions a lady had been known to forward a complaint against some bachelor member of staff, whereupon the General Manager would draw attention to the fact that if he made a habit of reprimanding the transgressors, they, being single, unattached and carefree, would probably resign or leave at the first opportunity, and he did not desire that outcome.

Our cook/houseboys were our own responsibility and we paid their wages. Staff members lost no time advising me to watch them closely and keep a daily check on my food stocks, as they were liable to diminish rapidly if ignored. Small amounts of tea, sugar, rice, etc would disappear frequently, and opened bottles of spirits would gradually diminish in content. Gradual thieving was inevitable, and tolerated as long as it remained within reason.

Most companies operating abroad in tropical climates set a retiring age of 55, and SLDC followed this policy. Two of our staff were nearing this milestone and I thought at the time how wonderful it would be if I were in a position to retire at such an early age whilst still active, healthy, and able to pursue hobbies - I decided to make this my eventual goal. These men would also be retiring on a good pension as they joined the company prior to 1939 before the Second World War. Anyone working at the mine at this time was classified as having a reserved occupation and valuable to the war effort; they were also unable to travel to the United Kingdom on leave as the journey by sea or air was fraught with danger from enemy aircraft or submarines, warships, etc.

The tractor workshop was always busy repairing caterpillar tractors, scrapers and various heavy earthmoving equipment, especially in the wet season when their working site on Masaboin resembled a swamp of grinding paste, the wetness and iron ore forming a deadly mixture which caused rapid wear to all components it came in contact with, especially the tracked machines constantly churning through this damaging erosive area. The workshop housed a long roller-conveyored machine (or track-repairing machine) on which a caterpillar track could be fully laid out and the worn track pins pushed out by a hydraulic press which was installed on and part of the machine. The track shoes would also be worn, so new shoes and pins would be laid on the roller conveyor and assembled by pushing in the new tight-fitting pins through the shoes and assembling a new track with the aid of the hydraulic press. Old worn pins and shoes could be rebuilt for further use by a process of welding and machining.

I was always wary of this machine, or to be more specific, its African operatives. The Africans seemed to find it difficult to carry out linear tasks, ie lining-up by eye a track pin that required a straight entry into the hole of the track shoe before applying a hydraulic press to the pin. Frequently I witnessed a misaligned pin travelling some distance across the workshop. In direct contrast to this I have stood fascinated by their skill as they formed radial objects by eye, ie pulleys, where they would cut out the width and length required from a sheet of tin or steel and tap away with a hammer until they had formed a circle with the material. On checking with a measuring instrument it would usually be close to perfect.

Driving the Land Rover from the workshop up the spiralling road on our ascent to the top of Masaboin, we observe a scene of constant activity, dominated by Caterpillar D8 tractors pulling caterpillar scrapers which are scraping along the ground digging up the layers of Masaboin which contain the iron ore into their large scraper buckets; the material is then transported to a large grid near the edge of the mountain, where it is released and travels by conveyor belt down the mountainside to the mill, where it will be processed. During the dry season the iron ore particles can be seen glinting in the sun underfoot as you walk around. Routine maintenance is constantly underway in a large hangar on site, where oil and tyres are changed and minor adjustments and repairs made.

The mill processes the material extracted from Masaboin and delivers the pure high grade iron ore urgently required by many industries. The highly complex machinery is serviced by a skilled team of tradesmen. Pure iron ore is then transported from Marampa to the port of Pepel by the company's private railway system, which is operated and maintained entirely by company personnel, all with a railway background or training. Pepel was a loading point for the large iron ore carrying ships which arrived there for loading from accumulated stockpiles. Company personnel were based here to operate and maintain the conveyor belts, cranes and other loading machinery.

There were two American diesel engines each capable of pulling 100 wagons fully loaded with iron ore which travelled daily along a stretch of railway track 100 miles long. Directly behind the diesel engine was a carriage designed for any company staff who needed to travel to or from Pepel, and it had been made as comfortable as possible, with large armchairs and tables. This railway track was patrolled by a manned inspection vehicle between deliveries as the line was open to sabotage by Africans along the route usually placing large trees or other obstacles across the track.

A few weeks after arriving at Marampa, I received a carton from home which contained all my collection of 10" Ted Heath 78 rpm vinyl records. (This was before the 12" long-playing records.) Luckily they had survived the journey and were all intact. I ordered a record player from Freetown and was able to enjoy my favourite big band music once again.

There was an excellent tennis court at Marampa and I spent many enjoyable off-duty hours playing in single and doubles matches there.

I mention the following because I have no reasonable explanation for it: the bungalow was above ground on stilts, with steps leading up to the front door. You entered the front door and were in the living room. Standing in the living room by the door you could see directly across the room into the bedroom; if the bedroom door has been left open you could also see the bed. I was just dropping-off to sleep after retiring to my bed around midnight when I heard a Land Rover draw to a stop on the road outside my bungalow. This was unusual at this late hour and I listened intently. The door of the Land Rover slammed and I heard footsteps mounting the stairs, and when they reached the top I heard a key being inserted in the lock; the door was thrust open and a male figure in dark attire and wearing a white dog-collar purposefully strode across the room towards me, sat on the side of the bed, swung his legs onto the bed and superimposed himself on top of me. At this point I, in the same movement, sat bolt upright shouting in horror. It had all been a nightmare. I made myself a drink and eventually returned to bed.

In the workshop the staff would gather together at morning tea break to exchange gossip and news gleaned from various sources. The previous evening's nightmare had been so dramatic that I risked being ridiculed, but I broached the subject of dreams and their meaning. I recounted my story and was amazed when it was greeted with furtive glances and a seriousness I had not expected. Several longer serving employees immediately said "It's the Vicar". He explained that one of the European office staff (a timekeeper) had been highly religious and had been nicknamed 'the Vicar' by staff members. Apparently he was a keen cricketer and played in the Marampa team. I was told his name but it did not stick in my memory. Oh yes - one detail I forgot to mention: he lived in my bungalow!

The working hours at the mine were 7.30 am to 5.30 pm, except for the actual business of removing or extracting the iron ore from Masaboin, where an around-the-clock operation of three eight-hour shifts, seven days a week was the schedule. I worked a normal day shift, but being responsible for the repair and maintenance of the machinery on the mountain that was extracting the mineral I was on call if required during the other two shifts. Call-outs were a frequent occurrence; often the problem could be solved within an hour where my opinion or permission was required, but many times they were more complex and ran into several hours, sleep being interrupted as a result. Over a period of time I suppose my health suffered and I became thoroughly run-down.

During the eleventh month of my fifteen-month contract I started sweating and shivering coupled with lethargy and aching limbs. We had a company doctor and small hospital at Marampa, and when I paid him a visit he informed me I had malaria and should return to my bungalow, then prepare myself for an immediate trip to Hill Station Hospital, Freetown, where facilities were better; in the meantime he would arrange my transport and driver.

I had always complied with health instructions regarding malaria. Paludrine tablets (not 100% effective) were taken daily, with long trousers and long-sleeved shirts worn in the evening, and insect repellent was used frequently. Unfortunately I worked in areas you were warned to beware of; the wet season on Masaboin was a breeding ground for mosquitoes that lurked in the water-collecting insides of new and discarded tyres; pools of water lay stagnant all around and when I was called out during the night mosquitoes could be clearly seen around my office walls. "It's only a matter of time," I would say to myself. Apparently I was right.

The female mosquito flies around near ground level between dusk and dawn and carries the malaria parasite in its saliva. When you are bitten the parasite enters the bloodstream, causing infection to blood, liver and eventually the brain as it multiplies.

The journey to Freetown I cannot recall. Apparently I was in a serious condition for the first three days. I can vividly remember regaining consciousness for a few minutes and feeling cheated, extremely annoyed and angry at the situation I found myself in. "This cannot happen, I must not die, I refuse to die so young. I have so much still to do, so much to achieve; my life is incomplete, I refuse to die." An added thought: "What will my parents say?" I drifted into unconsciousness once again.

Health care was sponsored by the company, so I enjoyed the privacy of my own room. After a few days the situation improved, although I was very weak and had difficulty walking more than a few steps. The doctor told me to walk a few steps around the corridors daily and gradually increase the distance every time. On departure he left instructions that I was to receive a bottle of Guinness with each evening meal. I was anxious to make a rapid recovery, so I exercised as much as possible, completing many trips around the corridors of the hospital each day. After one week my improvement was noticeable, and the doctor suggested a return to Marampa, providing I could have light duties until the end of my tour. I informed him that this would not be possible as light duties did not enter into any part of my work. He then offered to discuss with the company the possibility of cutting my contract short so that I could return to the UK and take my leave before returning to Marampa and completing a further contract plus my missing time from this tour. This last suggestion was definitely unacceptable, as I intended to give SLDC my necessary three months' termination notice on my return to the mine. I stayed a further week in hospital before returning to duty at Marampa.

The last three months of my tour passed by without any serious incident, and I regained my health rapidly and was able to play tennis once again. I made many good friends during my tour, and it was always interesting to listen to their stories, especially those experiences recounted by the hardened expatriates who had spent many years working in various countries around the world. Many retained small notebooks with the addresses of companies where they had been employed, with 'for and against' notes alongside each one, and these were exchanged whenever a new face appeared on the scene.

The Club was a popular rendezvous for the expatriates; they organised the activities and volunteered for the duties entailed. The bar was no exception; there were no definite closing hours and if someone was drinking it stayed open for business.

Enjoyable evenings were spent in my bungalow, sometimes with friends, often alone, air-conditioning fully on and with the whirr of the ceiling-fan and oscillating portable fan (yes, I had both) being drowned by the big-band music of Ted Heath. I was in Marampa heaven. I think it's time for another beer.

CHAPTER 10

THE BACHELOR YEARS IN WEST AFRICA (2)

NORTHERN NIGERIA, 1957-58

I returned to Leicester after completing a fifteen-month tour of work in Sierra Leone and was now due three months' paid leave. My salary had been £1,000 per annum (or approximately £20 per week); remember, that at this time, 1955, a tradesman's wage in the United Kingdom was £6 per week (approximately £300 per annum). I had also received a bonus of 15% based on my 15 months' total pay. My total savings for the tour in Sierra Leone were £650.

I walked around Leicester shopping and viewing the passing scene when my attention was drawn to the large showroom window of Colmore Cars. There in all its glory was a brand new shiny red MG Midget Sports Car, and the price was - £650. Yet although it was high on my 'most wanted' list, I did not succumb to temptation. I intended to work abroad again as soon as possible and it would have proved a waste of money at that time as my attention was focused in another direction. Prior to working in Sierra Leone I had often travelled by road from Leicester to Coventry and noticed a very pleasant area of green fields on the outskirts of the green belt, approximately five miles from Leicester and just before the turn-off to the small village of Narborough. If ever they built houses there, that would be my ideal area in which to live, I would always say to myself. And the building of a small estate was now in progress.

I parked the car and wandered around to the usual showhouse, a detached, three-bedroom home with a kitchen, living and separate dining room with a detached brick-built garage alongside. There were also semi-detached and bungalow styles on view. I was very impressed with the showhouse and also the fact that the row of detached properties were not built in a rigid straight line but staggered on their various plots of land so that some enjoyed large front gardens and smaller rear gardens and vice versa. Walking down the road, I picked out a well-advanced property sited well to the front of its plot, which meant that it had a long rear garden leading to a copse, which was protected as a small nature reserve with the River Soar beyond.

I was paying particular attention to this well advanced but deserted house (as I thought) when the Foreman and two workers appeared form its interior and we engaged in conversation.

"Don't forget that you can have a brick-built garage with a full concrete driveway leading up to it anywhere down the side of the house for £150," the Foreman remarked.

"Anywhere?" I said.

"Just say the word."

"Got a stick of chalk?" I enquired.

I took the chalk and walked down the side of the house, and

with deliberate steps passed the end of the house and kept walking the length of two average cars before chalking a line across the would-be driveway. I turned and looked directly at the Foreman.

"That's where I want the garage door to be," I said, expecting a laugh followed by a suitable derisory comment.

"Yes, that's okay," he said, sticking a few wooden markers across my chalkline. The two workmen dutifully hammered the markers into the ground.

The showhouse sales team were delighted with my selection, as I informed them I was definitely going ahead with the purchase. I was supplied with brightly coloured brochures which basically read: *Detached three-bedroom house £2,140 plus detached brick-built garage £150.* I returned home to Leicester and told my mother we were going out for a short drive. We returned to the site and I showed her the house and informed her I was going to purchase the property as an investment, and I wanted her and Dad with sister Pauline to move in and look after it for me. I would pay all the bills and expenses incurred. Everyone was delighted, and we began planning our move.

The *Construction News* and *Daily Telegraph* were good sources of information regarding jobs overseas at this time, and before my three months' paid leave was completed I was once again called to London for an interview, which proved successful. A position as Workshop Supervisor had been offered at Amalgamated Tin Mines of Nigeria, Bukuru near Jos, Northern Nigeria, and the contract was good, so I readily accepted.

We had moved to 65 Abbey Road, Narborough, Near Leicester and I had been able to assist in the settling-in process of decorating and painting, etc. I had secured a mortgage on the house with a deposit of £650 (my Sierra Leone savings) plus an extra £150 which paid for the garage. The total cost of the house was £2,140 minus £650, which left a mortgage of £1,490, but in 1956 it was very difficult to borrow money; banks and mortgage lenders held vigorous interviews before parting with any money:

"Where do you work?"

"Nigeria, West Africa," I replied.

"Nigeria has an expatriate lifespan of 50 years of age," I was informed. "What is your occupation?"

"Workshop Foreman, tin mining."

"Mining is high on our list of most dangerous occupations," he commented. "How many years do you intend to work in under-developed third-world countries?"

"Just long enough to clear my mortgage," I lied.

"Underground or opencast mining?"

"Opencast," I answered.

If I had worked underground I would probably have come up with all the wrong answers. Surely opencast would earn me a point or two?

The meeting was obviously not progressing smoothly, so I added that I hoped to clear the mortgage in five years. They remained unimpressed.

"The opencast answer as opposed to underground is the one redeeming feature to a succession of worst-case scenarios in a most dangerous, possibly short lifespan. Why should we lend you money?" was his brief summary. I replied that I was a bachelor earning good money who did not intend to marry in the next five years, by which time I would have cleared the mortgage. It was explained to me that they had to base their findings on a married man with two children and bachelor status meant nothing to them. I reasoned that not many men aged twenty-six could put down a deposit of that size unless they were a rock and roll or pop star, and prepared to depart. They relented and I secured my mortgage.

Before flying out on my next contract I measured up my front of house plot width together with my side area leading to my (soon to be built) garage and ordered a smart set of wrought-iron panelwork which would be set into a soon-to-be-built low brick wall with brick supporting columns. I also ordered a pair of wrought-iron front gates each 6ft wide which would open onto my 12ft wide concrete driveway. The site bricklayers arrived and rapidly completed the garage at the spot I had stipulated. Before leaving they emphasised that this garage was the only one to date that had a window fitted at the rear. The day after they completed their work I noticed a large sack of nails, two trestles and two long planks had been left behind. I notified them and they replied, "If we've left them we don't need them." The trestles and planks were used in DIY decorating for many years afterwards.

The floor area of the garage would be laid together with the driveway. The rear garden had a gradual slope from the back door to the end of the garden, which meant the garage floor would require some material in the foundation to fill it up to a level surface. That material duly arrived in a small 1yd capacity dumper whose driver tipped the contents into my garage and departed. He would obviously return, as the load had made little impression on the area, and on closer inspection I found the load had been complete bags of cement, which had a minor crust of 1" approximately due to dampness. I quickly summoned Dad and the neighbours on either side of us. "Anyone require some decent bags of cement?" I shouted, knocking on doors and hurrying into action. Dad, two neighbours and I quickly removed the bags and spirited them away before returning to the scene once again. "The Dumper's coming back!" was the cry as we all disappeared out of sight.

The second load was tipped in, and when the lorry left, 'Operation Cement Removal' resumed. The dumper driver did not appear to notice anything untoward as he delivered many loads of cement-bag seconds. Maybe he disappeared round the corner before stopping with a puzzled expression as he scratched his head and wondered. It resembled one of those scenes when ships hit the coastal rocks and local inhabitants would plunder the shipwrecked cargo. I believe many households in Abbey Road benefited from the three large hidden stockpiles of cement in the vicinity.

The driveway and garage were completed, my wrought-iron panels had arrived and so had the bricklayer contractors I had engaged to work on my planned drawing of the boundary wall. The bricklayers were making good progress as I prepared to leave for Nigeria, so I left the supervision in the capable hands of my dad. A parcel arrived containing two house numbers (number 65 in silver on a black background) plus two house nameplates for fixing in the brick columns supporting the gates; these matched the number plates.

I handed the parcel to the bricklayers. They looked at the nameplates and said, "What's Masaboin mean?"

"It's the name of a mountain I used to work on in Sierra Leone and it enabled me to earn the money to buy this house." Maybe our relationship was not love or hate; maybe it was respect.

My journey to the Amalgamated Tin Mines of Nigeria would be in two stages. Kano in Northern Nigeria was the regular route by air, and then an internal flight to Jos airport would follow. An employee of ATMN would pick me up at Jos and we would then travel the 12 miles to Bukuru, the administrative area of the mines. It had been arranged prior to my flight that I would stay overnight in Kano as a guest of our Office Manager, who was resident there.

My flight was relaxing and uneventful, arriving after dark, and I was met at the airport and driven to the Manager's bungalow, where he apologised for a certain amount of untidiness and chaos, explaining that he had just moved from bachelor accommodation to this sizeable bungalow as his wife would be arriving from England in a few days' time to join him here in Kano for her first visit to Africa. The bungalow had required quite a lot of work over the last few weeks—decorating and complete rewiring had been essential. Carpets, curtains, kitchen utensils and furniture had been installed and final electrical work had now been completed, allowing the workmen to move out that very day. All that remained now was a thorough clean and tidy-up, he proudly announced.

The meal was excellent, and after drinks we talked generally. As my flight departed early the following morning, he showed me to the guest bedroom where I would be sleeping. I stared intently at my luggage and decided against excess unpacking, as I was unfamiliar with the routine that would follow in the morning; early morning travel can develop into early morning panic. I groped around for everything necessary for a smooth start the following day—washing and shaving kit, clean shirt etc. All other items were left in my suitcase ready for a quick getaway. And so to bed.

It could not have been more than one hour later when I awoke to the smell of smoke and turmoil in the bungalow and as I quickly opened the bedroom door I could see a fire had started in the roof above the lounge. The Manager was shouting and busily removing what he could from the interior to a safe distance outside. I dressed rapidly, threw my few unpacked items into the suitcase and deposited my belongings outside. The Manager and I then worked together dumping items in the garden, running backwards and forwards as quickly as we could. During this hectic period we were fully aware that the fire was taking hold and the fire-ravaged ceiling was liable to fall on us at any moment. We completed as many trips as we dared until, abandoning all further efforts, we retreated to the safety of the garden.

We stood outside on the lawn and watched as the bungalow burned, during which time a gas cylinder housed in the kitchen took off vertically in a red ball of flame which disappeared over Kano, the remnants landing I know not where. The second incident occurred virtually at the same time as we gazed open-mouthed at the fire engine, lights flashing, siren sounding, disappear down the road only 100 yards away. On final arrival the crew apologised and informed us that they could see the fire but could not ascertain which route to take to reach it. We all watched helplessly as the structure crumbled. I cannot recall any other person assisting us at any time during this crisis; my memory may be playing tricks, but I doubt it.

The Manager and I retired to his office, where we stayed until the break of dawn. Later we surveyed a concrete base and the smouldering remains of a home which in a few more days should have witnessed a joyful reunion. We continued on our way to the airport.

On arrival at Jos I was met by the Personnel Manager and we travelled by road through to Bukuru, approximately 12 miles from Jos, and on a further two miles to Rayfield Village, the hub of

ATMN, where the Administrative Centre was located. Jos Plateau is around 1,250m above sea level, an area of scrub plains and rocky plateaus with mud-brick bungalows and houses in sandy fields. It has developed as the tin-mining centre since its inception in 1904 and was known as a place to make money, a boom town. 10,000 tons per year were mined around World War One. Jos enjoys a relatively comfortable climate ranging from 20 C and 25 C and many expatriates take their local leave in the area.

ATMN was split into two working locations, the Northern Section being the larger community, while approximately 10 miles further along the main road the Southern Section operated. The tin mines were generally found on this plateau, which ran from Jos to Bukuru, the main mining town on the Kano-Bauchi-Jos-Bukuru main road. Our workshops and many of the expatriate houses were straddled along either side of this road for about five miles in the Northern Area, with many dirt or laterite roads branching off from the main road and leading to more remote accommodation. After leaving Bukuru the road forked and you proceeded to either Abuja or Makurdi, with the general layout described previously; it will be clear that the community was spread over a wide area, as were the many tin mines operated by the company.

After being officially received at Rayfield I was driven to my workplace and introduced to the expatriate staff. The Heavy Equipment (or Plant) Workshops were situated just off the busy main road; the main gates were literally only a few yards from them and much concentration was required when entering or leaving this compound. This industrial area was shared with the Transport Department, which was a separate entity and had its own expatriate staff operating from their workshops on one side whilst we operated from the other side of the compound. Our main mining equipment consisted of approximately 30 Caterpillar D8 and D6 tractors scattered around the plateau at various locations, and these were serviced full-time by an expatriate service engineer and his African team of fitters and welders, who travelled around the area constantly maintaining and repairing the machinery on the many small mining operations dotting the area.

The other large operation was concentrated around the Rayfield area, where large deposits of tin were located and rich seams were to be found. Twenty Euclid bottom dumpers operated in two teams of ten, constantly following two Euclid belt loaders which were powered and towed by two Allis Chalmers HD21 tractors digging deep trenches of earth, which the machine then dispatched along its own angled conveyor belt into the waiting dumpers below. These then transported the earth to the mill nearby before releasing the load and returning to the belt loader. This constant operational cycle continued throughout the working day and required attention by an expatriate Service Engineer with his team—adjusting conveyor belts, clutches, etc., and completing servicing schedules from their site workshop.

The workshop tour duly completed, I was transported to my new residence, which was situated two miles further along the road under a high rocky outcrop around 100ft at the highest point; here a dusty track led off the road to three bungalows set some distance apart. My bungalow was furthest from the main road and the track terminated at that point. I was fascinated to see an elaborate brick fireplace which was serviceable, complete with chimney and signs of recent use. At that moment I realised that advanced information received was correct; the dry season from November to March resulted in cooler temperatures and chaotic dry north-east winds which the locals called the

Harmattan. It blew sands from the Sahara right across the country.

A cook/houseboy was installed, whose wages I would pay, so I could terminate his employment if I was not satisfied with his efforts. Most household requirements, food etc could be obtained in the local African or Indian shops in Bukuru, and vegetables could be purchased cheaply and in abundance from the African Market, where cook/houseboys would congregate daily, needing only the slightest excuse to enable a visit (we need potatoes, etc etc) and exchange the latest gossip and information regarding their European employers. This news was imparted in a kindly, friendly way, a kind of one-upmanship over the other cooks ('My master's got a new car, or whatever') and in the case of European families I would often learn from my cook which madam was pregnant, which in disbelief I would deny, to be eventually proved wrong.

There was a pleasant veranda to the rear of my bungalow which looked out over the plain to a Hausa village in the near distance. Some Hausa people are very primitive and wander around the local areas and towns virtually naked. The company supplied each European bungalow with a night security guard; mine would arrive as darkness fell around 6 pm daily and take up position on the veranda, which had electric lighting which was kept on throughout the night. He would be armed with two spears and a shield at least, plus blankets for warmth. It was common expatriate knowledge that when the bungalow occupants turned off the lights and retired to bed the watchman would probably do the same. I gained much delight and amusement from my encounters with the watchman, and whenever I returned late from a social evening at the ATMN Club I would look out onto the veranda with the sleeping night-guard, stealthily open the refrigerator door and slam it shut with a resounding bang. Spears would fly haphazardly around the veranda, accompanied by startled shouts. "It's only me!" I would say as we grinned at each other. Retiring to bed, I wondered who would fall asleep first!

The mine's working hours were quite civilised, starting at 7 am. Workshop Managers' offices and Europeans operating at mining sites in the area were all in two-way radio contact. Cars and pick-up trucks were all fitted with two-way radio operation from a Central Radio Control Room. Between 7 am and 9 am was a busy standby period when the Chief Mining Engineer would contact production locations requesting information regarding that day's activities and enquiring if any delays or problems were envisaged and likely to hinder production, and if so he would liaise with the necessary department heads and assist in solving any setbacks. Similarly, the Chief Mechanical Engineer would contact his staff for the latest updates and probably learn from his field service engineer that a certain D8 tractor required major work that could only be done in the main workshop and a low-loader vehicle would duly be despatched to the site to transport the machine to the workshop for a major overhaul. Not everything proceeded according to plan every day and occasionally tempers were frayed and harsh words were spoken in the heat of battle; unfortunately these occasions were not enacted privately by people behind closed office doors but heard by all and sundry who were issued with radios.

At 9 am everyone within striking distance of home was allowed an hour's respite to partake of breakfast; those in distant locations enjoyed the same privilege but taken from a lunch-box instead of a frying-pan. Unfortunately it became a time of husband and wife gossip and the early morning misfortunes, forgetfulness and follies of some were freely recounted and analysed. Words quickly spread.

The Personnel Officer appeared to view the Radio Control Room as a favourite location and had a penchant for moving expatriates around from one bungalow to another quite frequently. There appeared to be no logic in these moves and you would complain in vain; reason was there none. Many occupiers were keen gardeners and it was amazing to see the results they had achieved in such a hostile environment. Many people ventured the opinion that the Personnel Officer waited until a plot was neat and tidy before moving the gardener on to a more demanding site, thus eventually creating a kind of ATMN Garden City.

November to March was the dry season period and April to August the wet season. September and October heralded shorter rains that mostly started shortly after finishing work at 5 pm when we would start our vehicles and waste no time on the homeward journey, especially those of us residing off the beaten track, as the dirt roads could quickly become waterlogged and hazardous unless you possessed a 4x4 vehicle. Over a long period of time the very heaviest rainfall had usually been recorded during the months of June, July and August, and many machine production hours were lost due to unworkable, saturated ground conditions. It had therefore become company policy to close the mining operation down during this period and bring all heavy earthmoving equipment into the workshop yard for complete overhaul where necessary and major maintenance and repair to the remaining plant. This three-month period of work was meticulously planned throughout the remaining nine-month operating period and we worked closely with the Stores Manager to ensure the spare parts required would be readily available during this crucial time.

During this three-month period of heavy rain and major maintenance, it was amusing to see 20 Euclid dumpers meticulously lined up across the yard in a regimental row starting with the number 1, printed large and white on the sides of the machine, and continuing down the line to 2, 3, 4 and 5 and eventually reaching 10, 11, 12, 12A, 14, 15 and on to 20. Our Chief Engineer was highly superstitious and refused to acknowledge the unlucky number 13. The row of caterpillar tractors also bore witness to this. All maintenance of individual machines was devoid of the number 13, which was replaced by a bold 12A.

The expatriates' contracts were drawn-up for a stipulated 18-month working period followed by three months' paid leave in country of origin; flights to and from Nigeria were paid by the company. Workshop staff had all leave suspended during these critical three months but the remaining employees (administration, etc.) were encouraged to take their leave during this time.

The Transport Department had many American vehicles in the fleet - Chevrolet saloons and pick-up trucks and Chrysler saloons, together with British Bedford trucks and Land Rovers for the more demanding terrain. Expatriates could hire out cars for the weekend at reasonable rates if sightseeing further afield was on the agenda.

Apart from the repair and maintenance of heavy earthmoving equipment and the planning this entailed, expatriate supervisors were faced with other daily problems. However 'politically incorrect' it may be to broach the subject in these modern times, the facts must be stated: the African workman is financially poor and needs everything he can get to support his family, usually his parents and maybe brothers and sisters. Everything is of some value to him and whatever he can obtain by fair means or foul can be sold to someone who requires the item. We therefore had to construct a separate tool room with an attendant storeman inside the workshop to house the tools and equipment required daily to get the work completed. Each tool or spanner, hammer, gauge, etc was booked out to the individual workman and had to be returned before the end of work that day when the register was checked for missing items. This was an imposition we could have done without, but unfortunately if the situation had been left unattended few tools would have remained after a short time.

I often used to say to the African workshop staff, often quite openly, "If there were league tables for theft, Nigerian workmen would come top of Division One every year." They would always fall about laughing and never took offence no matter how many times they had heard it; often they would perform quite a passable impersonation of me saying it.

The other main problem was the cultural diversity thrown together in the workshop, where Yoruba, Hausa, Igbo and Fulani worked and underlying tension was always to the fore, especially between the Hausa and Yoruba personnel. Religion, not ethnicity, divides the nation and whenever possible we segregated them into tribal groups when selecting their working tasks to avoid possible confrontation.

Dragline and excavator operators were the only people to work a night shift, and their 24 hours operation left them ideally suited to the task of voluntary barmen at the clubs in the southern and northern regions of the mine; this rotation of barmen meant that drinks were readily available after the usual closing times if customers were interested.

The General Manager had fully-staffed accommodation in both areas to facilitate his frequent travelling between both areas at any given time. Cocktail evenings that he and his wife arranged and attended were frequent in both areas, as a quota was required for these occasions due to the large expatriate community, and everyone regularly received an invitation.

A young expatriate couple had purchased a new dark blue Austin A30 saloon car in Jos for use around the area, but they almost immediately regretted the decision as it was quite small and unsuitable for the rainy season's dirt roads. I had made many friends in the southern camp and hiring transport, I often travelled there at weekends and stayed over Friday and Saturday night, returning on Sunday. The Austin A30 had little mileage on the speedometer. I offered a ridiculously low price for the car; my offer was accepted and I could be observed from that moment on travelling between camps at weekends in my highly polished vehicle.

The demand for tin was declining and production was falling rapidly; as a result many employees were gradually being made redundant, and this also applied to the expatriate community. I too was informed that on completion of my contract my employment would be terminated. I was very disappointed as I had thoroughly enjoyed my work and made many friends. Several people made good offers for my Austin A30, but I declined them all, having already decided and planned our future. The Austin and I were going to travel to Lagos, board a passenger/cargo ship and enjoy a leisurely journey to England, where the car would be used during my paid leave and the search for another job overseas. "You're mad!" was the general opinion.

The wet season had just ended as my contract came to its conclusion. I fervently hoped the public works road graders had been busy concentrating on the dirt roads I would encounter on my journey to Lagos. During the wet weather vehicles that can negotiate these roads leave ruts where their wheels have travelled an also push a build-up of mud along the centre. The A30 has a ground clearance of six inches, so I envisaged a shiny engine oil sump casing if roads had not been maintained. I placed a spade in the car boot alongside the toolbox.

I allowed myself three days to travel to Lagos at a comfortable pace, and if everything proceeded as planned I would enjoy a good night's sleep at my stop-over hotels and avoid travelling after dark on the 600-mile journey. My route took me from Bukuru via Lafia, Makurdi, Enugu, Onitsha, Benin and Lagos.

Thoroughly rested, I emerged from my Lagos hotel. My journey had been accomplished according to plan with recourse to spade or toolbox not being necessary—very tiring but there was always something of interest to witness along the way. The Nigerian driving standards, roadworthiness of vehicles and overloading of buses and trucks with both people and goods had come as no surprise, since I had lived alongside a main highway for many months. The Austin A30 was covered completely in thick dust, the dark blue colour of the bodywork hardly discernible. There was enough time to visit the nearest garage and after a thorough wash and polish we presented ourselves at the dockside ready for loading and boarding the *Calabar*.

The ship was a cargo/passenger vessel capable of carrying 13 passengers, and the journey home would take seven days. The passenger accommodation was excellent, as was the copious amount of food and drink. Entertainment of various kinds, deck games, etc, were available and equivalent to the larger luxury liners. We had a full complement of passengers; many were no strangers to this type of travel by sea and preferred the experience rather than flying home, and if you have time to spare and are proceeding on paid leave I can understand their reasoning. I suppose much depended on the small band of passengers integrating and being ready to join in with shipboard activities.

The passengers and senior crew members had meals together and the tables were allocated according to any shared interests they might have. I joined the Chief Engineer's table for obvious reasons, but other matches were made where possible. I had many interesting conversations with the Chief Engineer during the voyage and he invited me to witness operations in the engine room on several occasions.

On arrival in England I waited until my car was unloaded and then proceeded on a pleasant journey home to Narborough.

During my service engineer years travelling around the country, and later on my rail journeys to and from London attending interviews for various contracts during my leave periods, it was noticeable that signage of all descriptions was spreading rapidly. This was becoming a blight on the countryside. It was mostly comments and information regarding the twinning of towns with remote places in far-flung countries overseas. Large signs appeared on the platforms at Leicester Railway Station welcoming the visitor or immigrant to the City of Leicester. These signs in foreign languages greeted everyone, including the local populace, who emerged from the carriages of overcrowded mainline trains after standing for two hours or sitting on their luggage. Welcome to Leicester. "There is no restaurant car or buffet on this train", the station manager would announce as the boarding passengers surged forward from platform to train.

At the height of the Cold War the main roads into the City of Leicester had signs which announced boldly, 'LEICESTER IS A NUCLEAR-FREE ZONE'. I fervently hoped the relevant Russian authorities had been notified so that aircrafts with their bombs could be diverted.

Before the motorway and bypass days, Stamford in Lincolnshire on the A1 Great North Road requested: "STAY AWHILE AMIDST OUR ANCIENT CHARM'. Unfortunately there was no alternative, as you waited in your transport for the traffic jam to move once again.

CHAPTER 11

THE BACHELOR YEARS IN WEST AFRICA (3)

GHANA, 1958-59

The wrought-iron gates to 65 Abbey Road were open as I turned the car into the long concrete driveway, passing the brick gate pillars with their Masaboin nameplates boldly bearing the house name. I slowly moved along the concrete driveway flanked by the low brick wall with its panels of wrought-ironwork and stopped outside the garage. It felt good to be home again.

It was good to be home again, but apparently the home itself was not as good as it should be. I was to listen in dismay as my parents and sister Pauline recounted various tales of the unexpected they had experienced during my time away, and these grim accounts could all be laid at the door of our builder, Wimpey, one of the country's largest house builders at that time and also engaged in many construction projects such as road-building, open-cast coal mining, etc, plus contracts abroad.

At this point I must introduce Joe the Site Foreman, who will figure prominently in past and current events. Joe had been contacted for advice when my mother wished to purchase a new gas cooker to install in the Wimpey-built kitchen. A space had been left for this appliance and she required assurance that whatever model was purchased it would slide comfortably between existing kitchen units. Joe's foreman's hut was on a plot overlooking our house and he only needed to cross the road to deliver his judgment. "Any gas cooker on the market today will fit—it's been researched," he said, returning to his car parked alongside the hut, his head disappearing under the raised bonnet.

The latest gas cookers of that period had a flint-operated gun attached to the side which when removed from its holder automatically lit a flame with which to ignite your cooker hobs (the same principle as a cigarette lighter). On arrival my mother's new gas cooker refused to enter the allotted space due to the side-mounted gun, and modifications to the adjoining kitchen units were required.

My parents were annoyed when one of the tiles surrounding the fireplace in the dining-room crashed onto the hearth without warning - amazingly, the tile did not break. Foreman Joe was called in to survey the damage. "That's a faulty fireplace, we need a new one," said Dad. Joe departed and returned with a workman carrying a tin of glue which they used to fix the offending tile. "That will not last five minutes, it's a faulty fireplace so why don't you replace it?" said Dad once again. The workman and his tin of glue departed. Joe also departed, returning to his car parked alongside the hut, his head disappearing under the raised bonnet. The same thing happened once again shortly afterwards, I was told, and in exactly the same way with the same tile and the same remarks. It may have been a different workman with a new pot of glue (that I cannot verify). Dad tapped the fireplace tiles sharply with his knuckles to demonstrate to me the hollow sound signifying that many loose tiles were ready to fall.

I did not witness these incidents, as I was abroad in Nigeria at the time. The following also occurred during my absence: winter was approaching and the coal fires in the living and dining rooms would be fully utilized (the houses of the 50s were predominantly heated by coal fires; central heating became a standard feature later) and so it was in our house. My parents were horrified as frequent puffs of acrid smoke entered the room instead of being transported up the chimney. Joe was called to witness this phenomenon and give his opinion: "It's downdraught from the tall trees at the bottom of your garden," he said, unfazed.

"Your tree theory is nonsense, plus they are too far away from the house to have any effect," Dad said. "You must think we're idiots, can't you see the chimney's blocked?"

He argued, but to little avail. Joe departed, returning to his car parked alongside the hut, his head disappearing under the raised bonnet.

Dad pointed out a few more minor examples of shoddy workmanship and that evening I witnessed first-hand the smoke problem emanating from the fireplace and with a knife carefully and with the utmost ease I removed the offending tile and laid it on the hearth, where it would probably have fallen in due course. It was rapidly drawing to the end of the site working day as I walked over to Joe's hut and informed him of the problem. It was our first meeting and he was anxious to get home. "We'll deal with it tomorrow," said Joe. Fuming and finding it difficult to control my rising anger, I returned home assuring myself that tomorrow could not come soon enough. Tomorrow would herald the showdown.

The following morning I strolled across the road as Joe arrived in his car. I followed him inside the hut and reminded him of our previous meeting and its cause. "I'll be across as soon as I get things organised." Several hours later I visited the hut to give him a reminder. "I'm on my way," he remarked as my anger mounted. Hours later, around midday, he arrived with a workman who carried a pot of glue and stuck on the tile.

"So you're not going to change the fireplace?"

"No need" was the reply. He repeated his tall-tree tall story and brushed aside any assumptions of a blocked chimney. I had no desire to cause a scene in front of my mother, and waited until they had departed with their glue before following them shortly afterwards.

Joe was seated as I entered the hut, obviously sharing a joke with several workmen. I enquired what he intended to do about my problems, and with an air of bravado and arrogance obviously with a desire aimed at impressing his workmen he shrugged off my enquiry. Battle lines had been drawn. I stood over Joe and heatedly demanded that chimney-sweeping brushes be pushed up the chimney, where I was certain a blockage had occurred. Joe's arguments and excuses continued and finally I played my trump card. "You see that car standing in my driveway? If you do not push some sweeping-brushes up that chimney today, you will see that car depart early tomorrow morning bound for your Head Office in Nottingham. I've got plenty of time during my leave to get things completed to my satisfaction."

Joe became subdued, but the excuses kept coming: "I can't do it today, the brushes are at our site on the other side of Leicester.

"That's your problem," I said as I departed the hut.

One hour later Joe arrived with a bevy of workmen, who fed

the sweeping brush up the sitting-room chimney. Its progress was soon halted, and despite all efforts it refused to proceed further. Everyone was engaged as they toiled; voices became whispers as bricklayers appeared at the side of the house and started removing chimney bricks. I stood nearby amazed as a few bricks turned into many and eventually a large solid mass of concrete was exposed which took several men to remove and negotiate down the ladder rungs to ground level, where I had noticed Joe appear and address the bricklayers with furtive hushed asides, hand gestures and pointed finger directions.

As soon as the lump reached the ground, several workmen were ready to spirit it quickly away. I enquired where they were taking the lump.

"To the tip," they said.

"That's my property," I said, "just put it in my garage."

I followed them closely until the operation was completed and the lump was deposited in the garage. The bricklayers were now busy repairing a large hole in the chimney.

"Now we sweep the dining room," I demanded as Joe appeared. The excuses continued as he assured me it was clear. "Prove it," I remarked. A chastened Foreman satisfied my demands—the brush was passed up the chimney without any further unfavourable incident. That will suffice for today, I thought as they left the house. I closed the door and was oblivious to any adverse comments that might have ensued between the Foreman and his gang, probably directed at me. Bricklayers could be heard outside busily filling the void with new bricks as hastily as possible before prying eyes and curious neighbours asked embarrassing questions. A wry smile formed as I gazed out of the window towards a locked garage door.

Through the following weeks I hounded Joe mercilessly,

especially when I could observe him alongside the hut, head under the raised bonnet of his car. Gradually with my sheer persistence the faults were being remedied, although whenever Dad and I mentioned the fireplace the subject fell on deaf ears and we would remind him that we were both tradesmen, not idiots to be taken in by his nonsensical reasoning. He informed us that he was a carpenter and their work was more skilled and arduous than either a turner or fitter's. We countered by stating that a faultily-worked piece of wood was easily disposable and inexpensive to renew, whilst a turner could scrap a piece of steel worth hundreds of pounds during the machining process and a fitter could ruin an engine, gearbox, transmission, etc by faulty workmanship. On several occasions Joe would dart quickly into an unfinished house to avoid contact as I walked along the road, obviously thinking I was approaching once again to harass him. "It's okay Joe, I know where you're hiding!" I would shout as I passed by.

"I'm just going to the newsagents." Loud laughter followed from the workmen inside.

'Workshop Manager required for a small diamond-mining company in the Gold Coast' was being advertised in the national newspapers. I applied for the vacancy and received a letter inviting me to attend their London office for interview. The interview date arrived and I made early preparations in order to catch my Leicester to St Pancras train in good time. Dad had left for work, but my mother and sister Pauline appeared to be in a state of disarray and on investigation I found them surveying the end wall flanking the stairs, which had watermarks staining a large area of the wall and its wallpaper from ceiling to stair-carpet. I was working to a strict time schedule, so I hurriedly confronted

Joe in his hut, informing him that the tank in the airing cupboard must have a faulty seam that was no longer watertight and therefore required replacement without delay.

Joe appeared with his plumber and they inspected the tank from their position at the top of the stairs. I stood at the foot of the stairs, knowing that I must depart immediately. "I hope you'll have that replacement tank fitted before my return tonight, Joe?"

"There is nothing wrong with this tank, it was tested before installation," he said. "I think your sister has spilt or thrown water over the surface of the wall."

My blood boiled. Never had I been goaded into retaliating like this before. I was insulted and amazed at his temerity. My sister was fifteen at this time.

"A new tank, Joe!" I fumed.

"This tank's okay," replied Joe.

"Personally I couldn't care less," interjected the plumber. I was flabbergasted by his remark.

"You heard that Joe, I have witnesses. You and your plumber may live to regret that statement." I glanced towards my mother and sister and left hurriedly.

It was difficult to relax as I journeyed to London. The morning's events were preying on my mind. I now knew my course of action, and I was anxious to return home and make progress.

The interview held many surprises; the biggest was being introduced by the Head Office Manager to two sisters who owned the mine. I would guess one was in her mid-thirties and the elder sister probably fortyish. They informed me that they each visited the mine separately as often as possible and the visits were usually of six weeks duration, but everything was flexible. The mining operation was overseen by European staff, each

Outside the front gate of 17 Shanklin Drive with friend, aged 6 (1936).

Aunty Nelly (right) and Uncle Jack Pearson with Aunt Annie,
Mother with me and cousin Ruth.

Mary the Second with Mother

Sitting on our front gate
(17 Shanklin Drive). Note the brick
shelter in the background.

The Fair Isle clan - friend Joe and me with cousin Liam and Dad.

Uncle John Meredith (left) with friend at Army camp, pre-war.

John with his sister after the war, early 1950s.

The Lincolnshire Poachers – the allotments with Gordon Drake's pigeon loft, leading to the poaching fields beyond.

Mr and Mrs Chalker with their grandson, me with Spot.

Mother and Tony guard the letterbox.

National Railway Museum, 2013: Spectacular smoke effects combined with lighting raised the profile of post-war steam record holder Sir Nigel Gresley.

Mother, Dad and Pauline

Mother, her sister Emily and Pauline

Liam, Mother, myself, Pauline and friend   Pauline

Dad and Mother on the steps of St Paul's, 1952

Pauline

With Mother and Dad   Dad

Mother (right) with sister Emily   Mother (right) with friend

The author

Paul and Mark, 1966

Another shot of Paul and Mark, 1966.

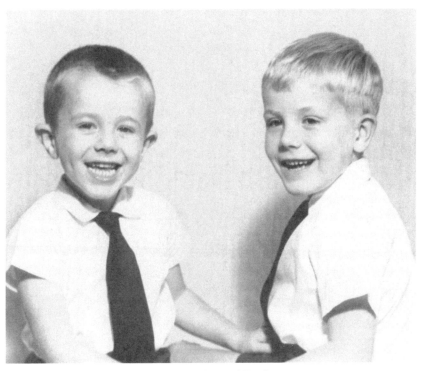

Mark (left) and Paul

Pauline and Jean, 1963

Grandparents Polly and Joe with Paul and Mark, 1976.

Paul and Mark, 1970

The Bradley family, 1970

With Paul and Mark, Sierra Leone early 1970s.

Farewell the dashing up and down to Bo, Senehun and Taiama town,
Farewell to tracks and touring wheels, farewell those uninspiring meals
My case is packed, it's time to go, so farewell road, Taiama–Bo.

Mother had died from cancer, 1969.

Jean with Sherry, mid 70s, Narborough.

Visit by Polly and Joe, 1978. More preparation and detailed planning preceded their visits than were required for the wartime evacuation of Dunkirk.

Scott and Jean, 1999

Scott and me, 1999

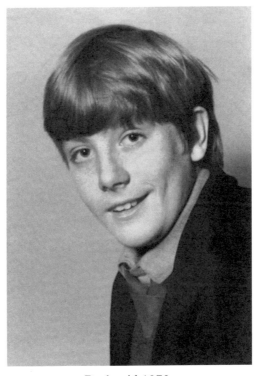

Paul, mid 1970s

Mark, mid 1970s

Recently retired, July 1987

Jean

Jade

Scott

Approaching Grantham on September 4 2013, Mallard passes the
landmark of St Wulfram's Church for the first time since 1962.

responsible for his own department. Other details were discussed and accommodation was good, I was assured, with each European having his own bungalow. Off-duty entertainment on the site was nil, but situated approximately five miles away was the country's largest diamond mine, and we automatically became club members able to enjoy all their entertainment facilities. Apparently I had been pre-selected as number one candidate for the position if the interview progressed according to plan.

They issued me with the contract and hoped that I would read it carefully at my leisure and sign on the dotted line, after which a travel date to the mine would be arranged.

The train journey home from St. Pancras to Leicester passed quickly, as my thoughts were dominated by the early morning events and I knew that I would not relax until my strategy had been implemented. My arrival home was greeted with the news that the offending tank had been removed and a replacement installed. Unfortunately Dad was not around during the removal, otherwise he would have demanded the faulty tank be placed in the garage next to the lump before it had been spirited away. Not to worry. I informed the family that for me it would be a late night/early morning affair, as an important letter needed to be written and posted without delay.

My Wimpey house purchase file was at hand as the letter listed the faults encountered in the short life of the property, the unhelpful attitude and remarks of people who should know better plus some detailed emphasis on the fireplace, the concrete lump and the leaking tank. My employment overseas was mentioned and I informed the reader that if my employers heard that I had uttered the words "I couldn't care less" I would be on the next aeroplane home, employment terminated. On my Wimpey-headed correspondence I sought out the most suitable director to receive my missive at the area headquarters in Nottingham, and it was posted early the following morning at Leicester Main Post Office. Within 24 hours I received a telephone call from Wimpey asking if I could receive a visit from the Area Manager responsible for the site, and I replied that I would welcome a visit. "He is on his way," I was informed.

When the Area Manager arrived he brandished a copy of my letter, saying, "Never write a letter like this to a director again, you can contact me on the phone."

I replied, "I've been in the construction business a long time and know the score. If I had contacted you by phone, would you be standing here now? I don't think so. You've had an uncomfortable meeting with the director and been told to get over here immediately and find out what's going on at *your* site."

Introductions over, Dad and I showed him the offending fireplace. He ripped out not one tile but many and smashed them on the hearth; I am sure he felt better. It had probably been a terrible morning for him so far. We proceeded to the garaged slab and returned to the stairs to view the damp wall. A knock on the door heralded the arrival of Joe and the plumber, who accompanied us on another tour of the devastation.

"Are you the person who said, 'I couldn't care less'?" the Manager enquired as he confronted the hapless plumber.

"It was just a figure of speech," replied the plumber.

"A very dangerous figure of speech!" said our Manager, who also queried the whereabouts of the faulty tank, expressing his desire to inspect the vessel. The Manager returned shortly afterwards to inform us that the fireplace would be replaced, plus any other work we required that was outstanding. My mother was to supervise a complete house redecoration with wallpaper and paints of her choice; transport and driver would be at her disposal at any time she wished to select these items. The costs would be paid by the company. The Area Manager departed knowing that a tedious report lay ahead concerning Masaboin, errant site staff and faulty supplies.

I never encountered Joe, his car or the plumber on site after this occasion and made no enquiries as to their whereabouts, having no interest in their fate. I shed no tears for Foreman Joe, Prof. VD (Professor of Verbal Diarrhoea).

My leave was coming to an end and a date had been arranged for my flight to Accra. The Austin A30 was no longer required and a fair sale price had been offered by a Leicester garage. The house had been decorated and all faults rectified. It was time for the next adventure.

Arriving at Accra Airport I was greeted by a company driver, and we immediately departed for the mine, which was near Tarkwa, 90km or an hour's drive away on a good surfaced road. Near Tarkwa we left the main road and proceeded along a dirt road through a densely-forested area for approximately five miles before entering the mining area.

My workshop was well equipped with tools and everything necessary for the repair and maintenance of the plant and transport on site. Apart from the General Manager there was a European Supervisor at the Diamond Separation Plant, two in the Earthworks and Mining Department, and one who supervised the diamond sorting and grading.

Cayco was an efficient company; the whole operation was run on a smaller scale than the large, vast complexes of the usual international organisations. There were fewer and smaller tractors

(Caterpillar D6s instead of D8s), a smaller transport fleet of cars, dumpers and lorries, etc. There was a railway running around the site from earthworks to separation plant transporting everything in wagons, but this system was of smaller gauge (engine, tracks and wagons).

It was not long after my arrival that we were notified that the eldest sister (and co-owner of the mine) would be paying a visit. This was partly due to the fact that our Diamond Sorting Supervisor was due some leave in the United Kingdom and she usually took over this diamond-grading operation while he was away. There was a Citroen saloon car permanently stored in our garage for her use on these occasions and this was checked and made ready. The bungalow accommodation she used was given the same treatment.

I soon discovered the lady had no pretensions of grandeur and mixed freely with the staff when the working day came to an end, and then on most evenings we would be invited to her bungalow for a meal and drinks. She appeared to enjoy her visits immensely - and why not if you are daily witnessing newly-unearthed diamonds and assessing their worth, especially if you are a co-owner. Being a high-flying businesswoman in the country, she was anxious to curry favour with politicians and administrators (and vice versa) especially in the current climate.

The Gold Coast gained independence from Britain on the 6th March, 1957 and became the Republic of Ghana. Many prominent people on the Accra scene were invited to visit the mine whenever she was in residence and the staff were never excluded from these social gatherings. I enjoyed these relaxed occasions and had the pleasure of meeting some of Ghana's affluent society, with whom the conversation was always interesting. Mr Moxon, the Government's public relations chief, had recently organised a

Louis Armstrong tour and a capacity audience had attended this jazz legend's concert in Accra. Being a jazz fanatic I eagerly listened to his encounters with this great trumpeter.

Our lady enjoyed the Accra social scene and together with another member of the staff, I accompanied her on one occasion. I had originally declined her invitation because my heavy maintenance schedule was centred around the weekends, when I had easier access to plant and transport. The lady discussed the situation with our General Manager, who then told me to delegate for the weekend in question, although I got the impression he was not wholeheartedly in support and did not share in my sense of good fortune. This lack of support was compounded when he discovered that I was to receive a large sum of money for the trip and would submit all expense receipts on return (the lady's instructions).

In Accra we stayed at a luxury hotel and made many new friends. It was strange being the custodian of our finances, but as the lady said, it looked so much better when the gentleman was paying the bills.

On our return journey we had left the main road and were proceeding along the dirt road through the forest to the mine when we encountered a fallen tree, the trunk blocking the road completely. These very tall trees would often fall due to the heavy rains saturating the roots and base. Great attention was always paid to this mine access road, as we depended on the route, which was in constant use.

Our problems were at their height during the March to June rainy season, and it was now raining heavily. There were three of us in the car; it was around midnight and I had no intention of sitting there through the night, so I clambered over the offending tree trunk and made my way to camp approximately three miles away. On reaching the workshop I collected a four-wheel drive vehicle and returned to the tree trunk with the Citroen on the opposite side. I helped the two occupants to clamber over the trunk and enter the four-wheel drive Land Rover. We arrived back at the mine; the rains still came and would probably persist throughout the night. Saturated, our sodden attire clinging to our bodies, we bade each other goodnight and made haste to our bungalows and a hot shower.

Being soaked was a constant occurrence during the rainy season and I had become accustomed to the discomfort, which was part of the job. Anxiously I checked the one thing I was perturbed about—ah yes, the expense receipts were quite dry!

The weekend maintenance had been completed without incident and workmen with mechanical saws had cleared the road of timber, while the grader levelled the dirt road of any ruts or obstruction. The Earthworks Supervisor and I had been discussing some problems we had encountered on site when we saw the General Manager walking along the road leading to my workshop. We both removed two ball-bearings from our pockets and proceeded to rub them together between our fingers, producing a clicking sound. This scenario had been taken from the book and film *The Caine Mutiny* where the sea captain (Humphrey Bogart) is affected by severe stress and imaginary situations are blown out of all proportion; he then reverts to this clicking action with ball-bearings. This was a cruel joke in which all the staff appeared to participate at various times. Our General Manager was well past the usual retirement age of fifty-five common throughout Africa and was probably nearer sixty-five. He was becoming an ever-increasing irritant to me as each month passed due to his daily interference in workshop staff, all due to his obsession with culverts and drainage in general.

At his insistence we were digging drainage trenches and culverts all around the mine, most of them unnecessary. He regaled us with stories of impending doom when the rains started, which proved wrong as the wet season ended without disaster. I can only imagine that in his dark, distant past serving abroad he had witnessed flash floods or similar weather occurrences. Relations became strained.

Very close to our mining site a large international diamond mining company was situated. Relations between both companies were good and our staff visited and enjoyed their hospitality whenever possible. We made many friends there, attending their cinema showings and club functions. I had a particular friend who worked in the heavy equipment workshop; he showed me around and informed me that their problem was securing experienced expatriate staff and if ever I thought of... I secretly envied their whole environment and yearned to get back among the big machines.

We were often accompanied by our lady owner and as stated previously relations were excellent between the two company mining neighbours. Rumours abounded regarding the previous history of the companies. Allegedly our co-owner's father was a prospector employed by the large mine and after retirement he bought the land where our small mine now operated. A very rich seam of diamonds was discovered and the rest was history. Apparently there was a well-reported court case that ensued as a result. Fact or fiction? I suppose with research the whole story could be verified. Fact: The father was a surveyor at that mine. Fact: It was a very rich seam.

One of our bachelor friends at the large mine would invite us to his bungalow for late-night drinks and while we were there he would exhibit a large pet snake which he would feed with various rodents. He was a colourful character who we regarded as slightly mad. A few days after one of our visits we were informed that he had been discovered dead in his bungalow from septicaemia (blood poisoning from bacteria) caused by the aforementioned process. Whether it was the rodent or the snake bite that caused his death I do not know.

Our large contingent of Cayco private security guards were kept busy, especially during the hours of darkness, when illicit miners would be discovered digging and washing the soil with their primitive equipment consisting of pans and spades, and the torch lights would be seen flashing around, denoting diamond smugglers at work.

A letter had been forwarded from home in Narborough. It was from ATMN in Nigeria with the mine informing me that the tin-market had made a recovery and they were offering me my old job back. The terms of the contract were favourable with increased salary and uninterrupted company pension terms. I was delighted to accept and notified them immediately. This news was received at the right time, and I was able to resign and give the necessary notice before completing my contract.

The General Manager was contrite on receiving this information and asked if our differences had any bearing on my resignation. I was able to reassure him that it had nothing to do with his actions, but the question was asked again on several occasions during my remaining time on the site. Our lady co-owners requested that I visit the London Office on my return to the United Kingdom where a discussion could probably iron out any differences.

On returning home my parents informed me that Cayco London Office would like me to telephone them. It was not something I wanted to do, so I delayed any action for several days until I received a call from the co-owning sisters requesting a meeting in London. I declined, stating that it would achieve nothing: I would not be changing my decision. Future prospects at the mine would be unchanged and there were not enough challenges in the work.

I replaced the phone with a sigh of relief. That chapter of my life was over and it was time to move on to another challenge. I thought I knew where I could find one.

CHAPTER 12

THE BACHELOR YEARS IN WEST AFRICA (4)

NORTHERN NIGERIA 1959-60

Arriving at Rayfield and later visiting the Heavy Equipment Workshop I discovered that there had been no drastic changes. A few expatriates had departed but otherwise it was 'as you were'. Even our favourite pastime of 'musical bungalows' was fully operational and I was destined to join the game immediately.

On my last tour I was located about two miles from the workshop just off the main road under a high rocky outcrop around 100ft at their highest point where a dusty track led off the road to three bungalows set some distance apart. My old bungalow was farthest from the main road; now my accommodation was the bungalow nearest the road. I was delighted to be back working on the big machinery and slotted into my duties seamlessly as though I had never been away.

Many expatriates acquire pets, usually a dog. Lloyd Bishop was no exception to the rule. Lloyd was an accountant in the

Rayfield Office and the family's field spaniel had recently produced a litter. Having once owned this breed of spaniel in my schooldays I paid him a visit, and the outcome was inevitable - a puppy and I returned home to begin a firm partnership. What to name this small, black bundle of mischief? Nothing popular, nothing common, so he was named Lloyd after Lloyd Bishop. Neither Lloyd had any objections.

On rare occasions an expatriate arrived who had slipped through the net of the Personnel Officer at the initial interview and hoodwinked his way into a job he was not suitable or qualified to hold. We had a supervisor arrive in the workshop who fitted this description, and doubts were soon raised regarding his previous experience of working with and repairing heavy earthmoving equipment. I was allotted the task of surreptitiously observing his progress, and although I objected, stating that being considerably older than me he would probably have greater experience than a person aged 28, my reasoning was to no avail.

The new addition to our workshop staff regaled us with adventures in the Arctic wastes working on Snowcats (a caterpillar tractor adapted for Arctic conditions). The Allis-Chalmers tractor I had been overhauling with my African mechanics had recently been completed and was ready for initial testing in our spacious workshop yard, which was to be my next task. I suggested that our friend test the machine on my behalf, a sort of 'be my guest' gesture which he readily accepted. Loath to give too many instructions to our Arctic explorer, I tentatively enquired as to his familiarity with the controls, ie clutch and footbrake operation, steering (usually standard on tractors of this type). He cut short my interrogations, brought the tractor engine up to full throttle and hurtled through the open workshop doors, proceeding without deviation through the yard towards the high wire meshed fence surrounding this industrial area. Travelling at full speed and going straight ahead, hands and feet firmly affixed on the controls, but offering no movement, his rigid figure seated on this runaway tractor, he advanced towards the fence and main road beyond. I followed his progress transfixed with horror. Was he showing off, trying to impress and intending to veer away at the last second? No. Crashing through the fence and over the busy main road, his straight-ahead course was finally halted by a ditch!

Amazingly, no one had been injured. The route through the workshop had been clear of personnel and the yard had no standing machinery blocking the path of this unleashed tracked monster. I was later informed by one of my African staff near to the accident scene that seconds before impact there had been an uncoordinated flurry of hands and feet which did nothing to alter the course of the tractor. Our chancer (a term used for this type of individual) came away with minor cuts and bruises and was immediately dispatched back to the UK, where he could apply to companies willing to further his experience in Antarctica or probably employ him in Iceland (the supermarket).

The mine operated on Saturday morning with various departments closing at midday for the weekend break until Monday morning. 11 am saw a general wind-down when workers collected their weekly wages from their staff offices, during which time the expatriates would congregate for a chat and cup of tea before dispersing for the weekend. My cook/houseboy would provide lunch before he had his afternoon off duty. Lloyd and I would then climb to the top of the rocky outcrop alongside the bungalow, where I would sit reading with Lloyd sitting in attendance, ever watchful and making sure nobody turned off the road and entered our compound. We would both survey the terrain below, the traffic passing by on the main road and the

Hausa village beyond. It is a vivid memory that has stayed with me throughout the passing years. Not for me the European Club with the afternoon filled with noisy, idle chatter from alcohol-consuming members. That could come later; this I much preferred.

The Site Service Engineer responsible for the maintenance of our Euclid fleet of 20 bottom dumpers and belt-loaders was due his three months' leave in the UK, and I was able to take over these duties during his absence.

An event which caused much local excitement was the opening night of the first cinema in Bukuru. All the expatriates on the mine had received an invitation to attend the wide-screen showing of *The Robe* starring Victor Mature, which had only recently been released and boded well for the future success of the establishment. The Europeans were reluctant to attend the opening performances, fearing a large African presence outside demanding entry without invitations, which could result in a possible stampede.

A group of five bachelors, myself included, joined the throng collecting outside the cinema, which had a heavy police presence, and as we made our way through the jostling crowd we encountered no hostility. The police manned the doors and opened them intermittently and long enough to allow the European ticket-holders access, around six entering each time. Looking around this lavish addition to our amenities we could see no other white faces, only the gleaming white teeth and smiles of a happy African community.

Bob, one of our workshop staff, was an avid reader of crime and detective stories and when visiting Jos he would purchase any magazines and books relating to this subject. One particular magazine printed in the USA was a favourite; it featured true crimes and the articles were written by crime reporters. The features had lurid headlines, 'That's not coal—that's Daddy' being one I remember, describing how a young boy discovered his murdered dad buried under a heap of coal in the coal-shed. Bob was so impressed with their macabre and gruesome articles that he wrote a letter to the Editor stating that his magazine afforded much pleasure to a lonely expatriate in Nigeria and I believe he overplayed his situation with words such as *solitary*, *inhospitable*, *dangerous*, etc.

The letter was duly published in the magazine, with dramatic results. A postal worker contacted Bob and requested that he collected his mail, possibly with a pick-up truck, as he was not talking about a handful of letters. Parcels and letters had arrived from all parts of America, written by all kinds of people, some offering hospitality if ever he visited the States, ladies wishing to be pen pals, etc. The parcels usually contained vast amounts of chewing-gum, which was distributed far and wide. Many back copies of the magazine and other periodicals were received and could be collected from our workshop office (or library). This influx continued weekly for several months and we were all amazed at the generosity of our American friends.

The inevitable happened once again and several expatriates engaged in a further round of our Personnel Officer's pastime of 'swap the bungalow'. Fortunately furniture did not have to be moved in the bungalow exchanges as it was all of a standard design, so personal possessions were the only items involved.

Lloyd and I were easily adaptable and settled quickly in our new quarters close to the workshop and directly by the main roadside. My cook/houseboy, Isiako Wassi, moved with his wife to accommodation at the far end of the compound, which Lloyd also welcomed as they prayed together at various times of the day with Isiako kneeling on his mat praying and Lloyd alongside howling in unison.

As I stated previously, I had many friends in our southern area mining site and the wives would often travel together by car to enjoy a day of serious shopping in Jos. To do this they had to pass through our northern area with my bungalow being situated mid-journey. I had issued an open invitation to anyone travelling this route to regard my bungalow as a toilet stop, and Isiako would be available to serve tea and biscuits, etc if I was at work and not available. This was greatly appreciated and I would often hear from Isiako that two, three or four 'madams' had visited in the morning on their way to Jos and again in the afternoon on their return journey. He would then give me a 'thank you' note signed by all the visitors, adding, "Can I please have some money to buy more biscuits, the tin is empty?"

Isiako and his wife were always cheerful and had a great sense of humour. They would visit the local market whenever they found an opportunity, usually by informing me that I required potatoes, tomatoes etc. I would give them a few shillings to replenish our stock, the emphasis being 'our stock' because a certain quantity of vegetables would be siphoned off for their own use. This was common practice, recognised throughout the expatriate community; it was accepted and never begrudged. The heaps of produce laid out by the market traders were plentiful in quantity and sold under the 'penny penny' system designed to be suitable for the African customer and what they could comfortably afford. A European would fill their shopping basket for a few shillings and we regarded the produce we purchased as a bargain. Gossip was also traded freely with other cook/houseboys at the market and titbits regarding Europeans and their families were highly sought after and eagerly received, later to be passed onto credulous members of their own European household.

Sometimes when I returned from work around 5 pm Isiako would appear with his wife. "My wife has made these cakes for you," he would say as his wife placed a large plate of heaped delicacies on the table before me. "Thank you very much," I would reply, knowing that they had a similar plate of cakes on their table made from the ingredients in my pantry. They were among the best cakes I have ever tasted.

Fitting a new set of tracks on a tractor was an operation that was carried out frequently in our workshops. A worn track would be removed and completely overhauled - new track shoes, track pins and track links would be assembled on our track machine. The tractor would be jacked up clear of the ground and the reconditioned track laid alongside. This heavy track required at least ten men armed with long crowbars stationed at intervals along the length of the track. Working in unison, each man would slide his crowbar under the track and lift/slide the track under the tractor until it reached the desired position, whereupon the tractor would be lowered onto the track.

Watching these ten Africans during this operation would fill me with frustration and despair, as only around four of them applied their full strength to the task, with the others shirking. Grabbing a crowbar I joined the team, shouting words of encouragement as I endeavoured to get them working as one powerful body all together. The lift/slide operation was stalling badly when I felt a searing pain from my right foot. I looked down and realised I had momentarily taken the weight of the track on my big toe, which was now swelling up rapidly.

Dr Branch was the mine doctor, and on arrival at his surgery I was taken into his office where on inspecting my ballooning toe he proceeded to completely clear the top of his desk and afterwards brought in a plentiful supply of towels. Sitting on a chair I was told to rest my lower right leg on top of the desk and he then surrounded the leg and desk top with towelling. Working from the other side of the desk he proceeded to lance the offending bulbous toe. Blood spurted in all directions.

"As a result of this you may get gout in later years—fiftyish," he said. "I will fill in a form for c company records; you may be able to claim should the need arise." I left the surgery wearing open-toed sandals. The right toe still appears larger than the left due to the squashing, and the nail grows thicker and is harder to cut. I never did get gout, but I never did assist the track gang again.

There were always lizards clinging to the outside walls of my bungalow and frequently chasing around the whole four sides without falling to the ground; this annoyed Lloyd immensely as they moved speedily and often beyond his reach as he dashed around the compound trying to catch them. Knowing he would be outpaced from a standing start he would commence his run from inside the bungalow; gathering speed as he passed through the open door, he would turn left or right following the outside wall and hopefully surprising a resting lizard. Plan B was to race around the outside walls, hoping that as he turned a corner he would achieve a similar result. This often worked, the only problem being that as I sat reading a newspaper a dead lizard would be deposited in my lap. I would look up to discover Lloyd standing in front of me, wagging his tail.

During this last tour I had been writing to Jean Denton, who lived in Sheffield. Jean had requested a pen-pal in some magazine I discovered somewhere. I cannot remember the name or subject matter of the magazine, but we began corresponding and exchanged photographs. Sheffield was only 62 miles from

Leicester and I had a longer period of leave to come (nearly four months) having completed a longer tour than usual. We both agreed it would be nice to spend some time together.

I hired a Ford Zephyr car for the duration of my leave; it would be waiting for me to collect at Heathrow Airport.

THE MARRIED EXPATRIATE YEARS

1960 – 1987

CHAPTER 13

THE MARRIED EXPATRIATE YEARS

NORTHERN NIGERIA 1960-63

Collecting my hired Ford Zephyr at Heathrow, I travelled along our first recently-opened motorway to Leicester, a novel experience in those days. Everyone and everything at home was in good shape and the following morning Jean and I had arranged to meet at 10 am on Sheffield Town Hall steps. The 63 miles from Leicester to Sheffield was pre-motorway and being unfamiliar with UK traffic conditions, I failed badly on the timing and arrived around thirty minutes late. Jean was nowhere to be seen. I paced around for another thirty minutes before travelling to Park Hill Flats, which were easily found as the two high-rise buildings had become a landmark locally.

Arriving at Jean's residence, I nervously prepared myself for whoever would answer the doorbell. The door opened and Jean stood before me. Greetings were exchanged, and I followed her into the flat. The other members of the family had all departed to commence their Saturday activities. Many people say there is no truth in the remark, 'love at first sight; do not believe these doubters, as I can verify it does happen! It happened to me, and at that moment I knew the girl for me was right here and the situation called for a rapid response. There was no time to waste.

Apparently Jean had arrived at the Town Hall on time but decided to return home when I failed to arrive. The flat was large enough to accommodate her parents, two brothers and two sisters whose ages ranged from 11 to 19, so as the flat was occupied by only the two of us at that moment, I was apprehensive of meeting other members of the family whenever they arrived home. Introductions were completed at regular intervals as they appeared on the scene; however, Jean and I decided to visit the cinema in the evening for a little privacy and further conversation. The film? *Elephant Walk* (an African colonial adventure).

I returned home to Leicester late that night and returned to Sheffield the following day (Sunday), where we spent the day together before I returned home once again. This hectic kind of schedule continued the following weekend when Jean enjoyed time away from her work as a GPO Telephonist until on the second weekend after first meeting I invited her to stay at my house in Narborough; she accepted and was duly able to meet my family. The following weekend saw Jean spending the long Christmas holiday period (1960) with me and my family.

The travelling to and fro increased in pace. Often I would travel to Sheffield during the week to pick up Jean after her work and we would travel to Narborough for some special event or concert at the De Montfort Hall in Leicester; we would then return to Sheffield ready for her work the next morning and I would return home once again. That's when everyone finally realised matters were becoming serious between us. I remember the incident when Jean visited their family doctor and explained our situation regarding limited time together before I departed for Africa once again. He signed her a sick note for one week's duration.

Weekends alternated between me staying at Sheffield and Jean staying at Narborough. Time was quickly passing and my leave was drawing to a close. I chose my time carefully. Jean was spending the weekend at my house - it was quieter and more private than the Sheffield flat. I proposed and was accepted. Arrangements were in overdrive, and I bought an engagement ring the following day.

Our General Manager at the mine had stipulated that any expatriate bachelor who married in Jos could have two weeks' paid leave with his bungalow, staff and transport in the Southern Area included as part of the deal. I mentioned this to Jean, who would have been delighted to take up the offer but unfortunately times were very different in those days and both sets of parents would have been dismayed at the suggestion. The deed had to have been seen to be done, even for 30 and 27-year-olds. We both agreed on a low-key, nothing lavish, registry office wedding.

I was due back at the mine two weeks after the wedding and the evening before my departure Jean and I travelled from Narborough to Sheffield in the Ford Zephyr; how many times we had travelled this road in the last 3½ months I do not know. Arriving at Jean's flat, we were shown the bedroom that her parents had prepared for us on this last night before separation. My flight from Heathrow departed early the following morning and the Ford Zephyr required handing back to the dealers at the airport. My luggage, passport, tickets, etc were all packed and ready to go but, alas, in Narborough. The overnight stay in our

Sheffield suite was impossible with my tight time schedule. Jean and I said goodbye for a few weeks until we would be reunited in Jos. Despondent, I headed for home.

Bob was waiting for me on arrival at Jos Airport, and after placing my luggage in the boot of the car we headed for Rayfield office.

"Anything exciting happen during your leave?" Bob enquired.

"I got married," I replied.

The car swerved violently as Bob almost left the road, heading for the ditch nearby. He was incredulous, as I was probably accepted as a confirmed bachelor by this time. As we entered Rayfield office my target was the Personnel Officer, with Bob following close behind and imparting to everyone within earshot the vital information he had recently been given.

On hearing my news, the Personnel Officer assured me that everything would be arranged immediately regarding passport, visa, jabs, ticket, etc, and my wife would arrive in approximately four weeks from now. "If you had informed us, you could have taken a few extra days' leave," he said. I was stunned and, thinking about that bedroom in Sheffield, I left the office.

I moved back into my bungalow by the roadside. Lloyd had been well looked after by Isiako and his wife during my absence. We began to prepare the bungalow ready for the 'new madam's' arrival. A second-hand Standard Vanguard saloon was purchased at a bargain price and came complete with a specially-made and fitted protective tray on the underside of the car which would be useful and effective during the rainy season on our dirt roads. Independence regarding transport requirements was a big plus. Isiako was keen to spread his news to all his friends at the market in Bukuru.

After four weeks Jean arrived at Jos airport and we headed in our car to the bungalow. Over the next few weeks the women of the expatriate community were quick to welcome her into their activities, and coffee mornings were enjoyed at various bungalows. She was adapting to her new life seamlessly.

About seven weeks after Jean arrived, we discovered she was pregnant. We had naturally discussed children and were eager to have them, so no precautions were taken. Jean was twenty-seven years old at that time; thirty and below was regarded as the critical age for successful childbearing in those days, so we prepared to let the situation take its own course. We were delighted and shocked that it had happened so quickly.

4th December,	1960	First Met	
2nd March,	1961	Wedding	
16th March,	1961	I return to Nigeria	14 days
16th April,	1961	Jean arrives in Nigeria	
26th May,	1961	Jean Conceives	40 days

If getting pregnant proved to be so straightforward, we decided we would have to take precautions in the future.

The inevitable happened and we were moved to another bungalow away from the main road and situated along a dirt road. It was larger and well planned, so we did not complain. Visits to our mine cinema on Sunday evenings were a popular event, and Dr Branch would sit next to Jean on these occasions, a sort of moral support in her pregnancy. We had many friends in the Southern Area and would often visit their club and attend their various Saturday evening functions.

Towards the end of Jean's pregnancy, I returned home after work to receive the news that Lloyd had been missing since lunchtime, and despite a widespread search by Isiako there had been no sight of him. I continued the search on foot and off the beaten track until dark without success. Frequent trips with torch around the bungalow area during the night proved fruitless and daybreak brought no sign of Lloyd. I spread the word around as I started work that morning but was dismayed when he was still missing at lunchtime, twenty-four hours from the last sighting. I spent my lunch hour searching the local area, and just before returning to work I searched our outside garage once again. Our Standard Vanguard was inside. I looked underneath and found Lloyd - dead. Isiako and I removed him carefully and wrapped him in a blanket. I was heartbroken but also very worried. Luckily the Veterinary College was only a few miles away.

At the College I handed Lloyd over to the staff and informed them of the circumstances and mysterious death. They assured me that a full examination would follow and requested that I return after I finished work that day. The afternoon seemed endless as I fretted over the outcome. Arriving at the College I was dreading the news I was likely to receive. "Your dog was attacked by a poisonous snake and the venom entered the neck, which swelled-up and choked him," they told me. It may appear callous, but I was greatly relieved and a huge weight was lifted from me. The staff sympathised but could imagine my relief from this burden, especially when I informed them that my wife was pregnant.

The word I dreaded hearing was 'rabies'. The disease can be carried by African dogs and can be transmitted by a scratch, lick or open wound. Effective treatment with vaccines needs to be taken for twenty-one days. All persons known to have been in contact with the affected dog must also receive the treatment. Lloyd had received his anti-rabies vaccination and wore a disc on his collar to signify this. Unfortunately this law is often ignored by Africans.

I was allotted company transport during working hours, so our own car remained in the open-doored garage for long periods. Lloyd had obviously returned there after being attacked. In the latter stages of Jean's pregnancy I became anxious and would creep out to the garage and satisfy myself that the car battery was fully charged and we were ready to jump into action when the time came; hence the car would be started and checked at least once every day. I had convinced myself that action stations would occur in the middle of the night.

The special date duly arrived and nothing seemed to be stirring. A further week passed and Jean and I visited Dr Branch.

"The baby's a week late," we cried.

"Well, you've got the solution," replied the doctor, looking at me. He suggested I take Jean for a ride in my Land Rover and visit some of my machinery on site, with the accent on 'bumpy terrain'. "Bounce Jean up and down a bit," he concluded as we left.

It was Saturday afternoon when we commenced our grand circuit and bumps tour; it was midnight on Sunday when I started the car and we departed for Jos Hospital with minimum delay. My forecast had been correct! The European Matron greeted us on arrival: "Your wife is in good hands now, Mr Bradley, see you in visiting hours tomorrow." My summary dismissal complete, I returned home.

On my way to work the next morning I informed Jean's friend, who was our nearest neighbour, of the previous night's events. All the mine transport was equipped with radio contact to the main Radio Communications Room in Rayfield, and as I travelled around on site at approximately 8 am my thoughts were with Jean, and I looked forward to seeing her after work, around 6 pm. A call came through to me on my radio: "Your wife has delivered a baby boy weighing 8lbs 7oz. Everything is okay."

Jean's friend had visited her after my news and requested the message be relayed to me on her way home. The news spread quickly, and further discussion would ensue as the staff passed on the news over breakfast with their wives.

It should be remembered that in the 1960s there were entirely different views held regarding childbirth. In those days it was regarded as 'women's business' and women supervised the whole operation. If the woman was having the birth at home, the expectant father was encouraged to leave the premises and ideally visit the local pub until called for. Maternity hospitals operated a similar system and the father being in attendance at childbirth was unheard of. Similarly the father would not be expected to down tools and immediately rush to his wife's bedside during or after the birth. He would visit after his day's work had ended.

Jean returned home and embarked on the chores of motherhood. Nappies required washing; these were pre-disposable times, and baby food was purchased in bulk. There were no after-birth health visitors—just her women friends who were mothers themselves, and she appreciated the advice and assistance they offered.

Paul was a 'lazy baby' apparently, a term used by the medical profession for babies who are difficult to feed. His baby food would be pushed back out of his mouth. The mixtures contained in these jars looked revolting enough, but when it was ejected from the corners of the mouth it became a disgusting sight. Breast feeding for Jean became a painful experience as he refused this milk and as a result she spent long periods bent over the bathroom sink disposing of it; hence her breasts became very sore, she was heavily bandaged and reverted to bottle-feeding, which did not solve the problem as he refused the bottle. I have spent much time with Paul's bottle; he needed the milk, and the obvious solution was to slightly enlarge the hole in the teat, which I did with a sterilized needle—unsuccessful. This operation continued with a succession of larger needles, all sterilized, all unsuccessful. Eventually, in frustration and with patience wearing thin, I used the point of the scissors and rotated them until a sizeable hole was created. The bottle teat entered Paul's mouth, his eyes bulged open widely, and he looked amazed - success at last! I think I forgot to sterilize the scissor-point.

Paul rarely slept through the night and I usually spent many hours transporting him around the bungalow, with one of my arms folded across my chest; he would stand on that arm facing to the rear over my shoulder as we moved around from one room to another in perpetual motion. His other request (demand) was that I sing or hum a particular tune that he liked while he bounced up and down in time to the song, and whenever I stopped his head would swivel around from his rear view and he would stare at me until my song was resumed. I counted kitchen and bathroom tiles as we travelled through the night. Floor tiles would then be included as we passed through the kitchen once again before a further attempt was made to transfer him from numb, aching arm to bed.

The Hausa women from their village nearby would pass our bungalow, but before proceeding on their way they would show much interest in viewing and discussing our clothes line in the garden, and their conversation would become animated due to Jean's underwear being displayed. The Hausas wear very little of anything and some villages and their inhabitants are still very primitive. One lunchtime I arrived home and Jean told me that Isiako had met the village chief, who had expressed a wish to visit 'the new master', meaning our baby Paul. Jean, of course, had conveyed the message that he would be most welcome, whereupon shortly afterwards Isiako announced that the Chief was outside. Jean was astonished when the Chief standing before her was completely naked. Embarrassed and averting her eyes whenever possible, she handed Paul over to the Chief, who was highly delighted, and holding Paul he transferred his greetings and congratulations to Jean through his interpreter, Isiako. A delicate situation handled superbly.

Paul could be soothed when fretful by playing Dave Brubeck jazz records, and I thought this boded well for the future and we would share musical tastes; this was sadly never to happen. His christening was held in Jos. Many attended, and it proved to be a great and memorable social occasion.

The situation at the mine with regard to tin production was unsettling, with rumours of redundancies rife. We were nearing the completion of our tour and I asked Jean if she fancied a change. Whatever I decided was okay as far as she was concerned, so I applied for a vacancy being advertised in the UK national newspapers. In due course I received a reply informing me to make contact when I returned home. Although I had a wife and a seven-month-old baby to support, I never had any qualms about resigning my job and was confident I would secure a further overseas appointment within weeks of arriving home.

Jean and I departed from Jos Airport with rather more than we arrived with, a baby complete with carrycot, not to mention the various accessories required when travelling with this addition to the family. Arriving at Kano, we had an hour or two to relax before boarding our flight to Heathrow. There was always a good atmosphere in Kano Airport, with Europeans happy to be going on leave and African waiters eager to take your drinks order, knowing that they would be suitably rewarded with a sizeable tip.

Shortly before joining our flight, Jean handed Paul over to me while she attended the ladies' room, and I sat with him in my arms. Several people, both European and African, stopped to admire him. Jean was returning and as she walked towards me I realised how fortunate I was to be married to this wonderful person. I was so proud of them both. Finishing my drink, I passed Paul to his mother who carefully placed him in his carrycot. Life is good, I thought, as we walked towards the embarkation desk.

On board the aircraft we discovered we had been allocated the front seats facing the bulkhead; these afforded more space and leg-room, with a shelf fixed to the bulkhead which could be lowered to accommodate a carrycot, which could then be strapped to the shelf. We sat gazing at our contented baby as cabin crew peered into the cot and enquired of his well-being.

Jean and I stretched out our legs in the ample space before us and enjoyed our drinks. Life was good. It can't get much better than this, I thought once again.

CHAPTER 14

THE MARRIED EXPATRIATE YEARS (2)

MALAWI: 1963-1966

Before leaving Nigeria with our baby Paul, Jean and I discussed the problem of grandparents and how to solve the visiting problem when one set of grandparents lived in Sheffield and the other grandparents lived in Leicester, both eagerly awaiting the arrival of their grandson. Announcements had been placed in the birth columns of both local newspapers, and whoever was honoured with our arrival, the words 'favouritism' and 'disappointment' could be levelled against us by the losing party.

Mainline express trains run from St Pancras Station to Leicester and Sheffield, usually the same train, with Leicester the first stop. It all appeared straightforward during the planning stages in Nigeria; I would accompany Jean and Paul to Leicester Station, where I would leave. They would then travel on to Sheffield. Jean was happy with this arrangement and assured me she could manage Paul, carrycot and suitcase. "It's England and

I am sure people will be ready and willing to assist a mother and baby in any way possible," she remarked. Our plan would pacify the losing grandparents (to some extent). Jean hoped to introduce Paul to interested parties (relatives, etc) for a couple of days and she asked me to then hire a car and pick them up, solving more problems, before we all returned home. We would visit Sheffield again in due course during our leave. It all sounded excellent - what could go wrong?

We arrived at St Pancras Station and immediately heard the station announcer informing passengers of a train leaving for Leicester (no Sheffield destination). Almost immediately another train on another platform was leaving for Sheffield (no Leicester stop) in 15 minutes' time. This was not in the plan, but Jean suggested I take the imminent Leicester departure as she would manage okay. I saw Jean and Paul onto their platform and hurried away to catch my Leicester train. It should now be noted that this was the early sixties, before mobile phones were available.

My parents had been previously informed of the plan and readily accepted that this was the best way to deal with the situation. I had arrived home as planned and we were busy exchanging our latest news when the telephone rang; it was Jean with news that they had arrived home in Sheffield safely - but minus the luggage. The railway authorities (British Rail) at Sheffield had been informed. Apparently when she boarded the train the carriage luggage rack was full, so she placed her luggage in the corridor (passengers were able to pass without difficulty), where she was in a position to see it at all times. Shortly afterwards she encountered a 'jobsworth' in the shape of a British Rail carriage attendant who informed Jean that her suitcase could not remain in the corridor. Jean pointed to the luggage rack, baby in carrycot, and stated that as the train would only stop for three minutes at Sheffield Station she would not have time to waste and needed everything to hand. He insisted she remove the offending luggage, escorted her onto the platform, with baby and carrycot, and placed the luggage in the adjoining guard's van, showing her the exact position near the door where he had placed it, adding that she could easily nip from her carriage to the guard's van and retrieve her luggage without difficulty. Luckily she was allowed to travel with baby and carrycot and not leave them in the guards van! Welcome to England, land of the jobsworths.

I arrived at Leicester Station early the following morning and joined the queue at the British Rail Lost Property Office, which was obviously doing good business as the line contained many unhappy travellers. I had come to vent my anger at anyone in officialdom who bore the roaring lion emblazoned on his British rail uniform. I realised the incident required handling at Sheffield and I would serve little purpose here - but let's have a rant anyway. Eventually I was facing authority and proceeded to lambast British Rail with my story of tramping through darkest Africa with porters bearing our luggage on their heads (lies), travelling on Nigerian trains and unable to see our luggage through crowded, sweating bodies (lies), by Land Rover through the jungle with luggage strapped to the roof (lies), our luggage passing through busy airports and onto British Airways flights (true), travelling with luggage from Heathrow to St Pancras by London Underground (true), luggage arriving safely at St Pancras Station (true), only to be lost by British Rail on a mainline express somewhere between St Pancras and Sheffield.

Behind me in the queue people were listening intently and voicing their support with each passing stage of my journey. At the conclusion we were all agreed as one and am sure were ready to vault the counter and take retribution on the hapless official at a given order. Soon after returning home Jean telephoned to say that her luggage had been returned; apparently it had been taken from the guard's van and left on the platform. No comment—discuss.

I collected Jean and Paul from Sheffield after a couple of days and we returned home to Leicester. This pattern of visiting continued throughout our leave. My interview with Crown Agents in London was successful and I accepted a position of Workshop Manager with the Ministry of Works, Plant and Transport, which was engaged on road development in Malawi, Central Africa.

Dad was very proud and excited with the arrival of Paul and it appeared that the first part of his dream was taking shape, as he always said that his one ambition was to be retired from work and surrounded by grandchildren. Liam, my cousin, had been visiting us for the weekend and was returning home on Monday morning. Dad was excited and anxious to visit his brother in Grantham and show him the photographs of Paul he and my mother had accumulated over the months since his birth.

Dad had taken the day off work as maintenance man at the residential home for the elderly which was situated nearby on the main Narborough road. In recent years he had been diagnosed with coronary thrombosis and could not follow his trade as turner and machinist as he might at any time suffer dizziness, or worse, and fall into the machinery. He was unable to follow medical advice and find light work for several years, but he had secured this position, which had been approved, and he had thoroughly enjoyed his work among the elderly for several years.

Dad intended to catch a bus from our local bus stop into Leicester, where he would take another bus from Leicester Bus

Station to Grantham, a journey of 32 miles. Liam was also going to Leicester and arranged to accompany Dad into the city. They were both at the bus stop when Dad collapsed. A passing motorist stopped to assist and they took him to Leicester Royal Infirmary. He was dead on arrival.

Liam returned with the dreadful news and I made my way to the hospital. Dad's pockets and wallet were crammed tight with photographs of his first grandson.

The funeral day arrived and we were travelling to church. We left our estate and entered the main road. Covering the short distance to the residential home, we saw that all the residents were lining the pavement smartly dressed, the men with their hats and caps removed. Those that were unable to stand attended in their wheelchairs. It was a very emotional moment and a tribute all the family appreciated.

Around this time Jean announced that she was pregnant again. We both knew exactly when it had happened, as we had been extra careful up until this night when I had left our bedroom to check on murmurings from Paul. I returned, it was winter and it was chilly. Need I say more?

Dad's death coming so close to our impending tour in Malawi left me in a quandary. Not wanting to leave my mother alone at this difficult time, I contacted Crown Agents to enquire if it would be possible for my mother to accompany us if I paid all expenses. This was not a problem, but a passport and other documentation would take one month to finalise. Jean would accompany her to Malawi and I would go on ahead. We duly arranged to let the house during our absence.

My flight was to Salisbury, Southern Rhodesia (now Zimbabwe), where I enjoyed an overnight stay until leaving for Blantyre, Nyasaland (now Malawi) the following day. Reporting to the Ministry of Works in Blantyre, I was given a full insight regarding my future for the next three years. Apparently the accent was on tourism and Lake Nyasa would feature prominently towards this end. Running along the Great Rift Valley for 585km, it was 100km wide in certain areas and covered over 15% of Malawi's surface area. A road was to be constructed from Blantyre in the south of the country up to Karonga in the north and linking up with Tanzania's network at the border. Three Road Construction Units had been formed (RCUi-2&3) for this purpose and based in various locations along the route. The road was to pass as close to the lake as possible along the entire route.

The contract was for thirty-six months and your own private transport was necessary. Any model of car could be purchased and a loan would be granted - repayable in thirty-six equal monthly instalments from salary. There was a mileage allowance for travel on dirt roads and a slightly less amount for surfaced roads. This generous travel allowance was more than adequate to pay off my monthly car loan. Company transport was provided for work duties. This three-year contract was to be served in Malawi with no UK leave, although local leave was generous. On completion of the contract there was six months' paid leave in the UK.

Having wandered around the car dealerships in Blantyre, I decided to purchase a new Morris Oxford saloon. Two-tone cars were very popular at that time and mine was dark green along the bottom and white on top—price £750. I was now ready to report to Unit RDU3 near Ntcheu, which was approximately 100 miles from Blantyre and reached by travelling mostly on a dirt road. Arriving at the unit I lifted the car bonnet to discover that one of the brackets holding the horn had snapped due to the rough terrain, leaving the horn hanging loose. My first job was to make two new horn brackets from a heavier grade material and replace the original items.

There were six Europeans on site, all bachelors living in caravan accommodation except for the married Resident Engineer. Before leaving Blantyre I had been instructed to contact the District Commissioner in Ntcheu, who would supply me with a government bungalow for a limited period until he required it for one of his own staff. The brick-built bungalow was very spacious and stood in a one-acre plot of land; it was wired up ready for connection to a generator (which I did not have). I purchased six modern paraffin lamps, which worked effectively and looked excellent in their various locations around the bungalow. A cook/houseboy was easily acquired, as they appeared readily on the scene with references as soon as a new European arrived. The grass and vegetation on the plot had grown high and dense and had become a fire hazard, so I employed a gardener who started work immediately.

On completing a check of plant and transport, I discovered many things that annoyed me. Although the Resident Engineer was in overall charge of the unit, his jurisdiction did not override the functions of the workshop. As a government department I was responsible for my own plant and transport budget, which had to be strictly adhered to and all purchases made kept in a register of accounts. The workshop stores therefore were a vital key in my budgetary control and I was amazed when at the close of the working day the Resident Engineer appeared and asked for the workshop and stores keys, as apparently he did every day. I refused, whereupon he informed me that he would have to contact my Chief Engineer in Blantyre as it was standard procedure. Calling his bluff, I told him to go ahead and I would give the Chief Engineer the same reply.

The District Commissioner ruled over the usual set of government officials in his area, the doctor, Agricultural Officer, Veterinary Officer, Police Commissioner, etc, and after further detective work I learnt that our RE was very friendly with this clique and was able on many occasions to supply them with parts for their private cars: spark plugs, fan belts, brake fluid, etc (and not forgetting his own Mercedes Benz) from my stores. I did not expect to stay in my bungalow for any great length of time.

Some of the plant on site had been continually operated when it should have been brought to the workshop for overhaul. Track shoes and track rollers on some tractors required changing and we were extremely busy for some time; this again was due to overriding interference in maintenance affairs. Resident Engineers are civil engineers whose interests lie in production, and they usually show little interest and have scant regard for maintenance, so the two can be drawn into a constant battle.

Jean, Paul and my mother arrived after one month and settled quickly into their new surroundings. We returned to Blantyre after a few days, mainly to sort out my mother's UK pension, which was easily arranged so that she could collect it at any post office in Malawi. Thereafter I used to supply her with a driver and transport; she would then collect her pension from a post office in Balaka, about twenty miles from camp. Paul had his pushchair and she would walk with him around the local village each day, enjoying her conversations with the locals along the way. I was amazed how quickly she adapted to her new life in Africa.

We would travel to Blantyre once a month to stock up on necessities. It was a three-hour trip and we would make an early start and arrive for the shops, which opened at 9 am. I took my Morris Oxford into the dealership to show them my new horn brackets designed to withstand speeds on bumpy dirt roads and asked them to pass the information to the manufacturers in the UK to enable them to modify future cars destined for third-world countries. I showed them my rubber sealing strips around the doors and boot of my car and how the red laterite dust from the dirt road was starting to penetrate to the inside of the car after only a few miles and said that on my return to Ntcheu I would discover a dust layer on my provisions when opening the boot. I informed them that I had made comparisons with Peugeot and other makes after the same journey, and they were dust free. They did not show a great interest in my concerns.

Jean had been in Malawi for six months when Mark was born on 31st August, 1963. The doctor at Ntcheu had been following her progress regularly during her pregnancy. We had become close friends with him and his wife; we were also tennis partners. Jean was sure she was approaching the birth time and after checking with the doctor he told us to leave for Blantyre Hospital without delay.

I breathed a sigh of relief when we arrived after our 100-mile dash. It was the usual procedure on arrival; I was dismissed abruptly and told to return when notified. My Chief Engineer in Blantyre would keep me informed by radio, so I was not unduly concerned. The following day I received the news of Mark's birth. Mother and I travelled to Blantyre to collect them both.

My mother was obviously a great help to us all and Jean greatly appreciated her advice and day-to-day assistance. They were a good team and enjoyed their life together; it was also a good time for me, as I had the two most important women to me figuring prominently in my life. It therefore came as a shock to us both when my mother declared that the time had arrived for her to return home. Jean and I asked her to stay with us until the end of the tour and we could all return home together, but we could not change her mind.

Our local leave was due and we all spent a marvellous two weeks at Monkey Bay and Fort Johnson. Mother departed for home in February 1964, after spending twelve months with us in Malawi.

Jean had followed Mother's advice and the cod liver oil and malt ritual had been passed on and was now firmly established. A spoon or dummy, liberally coated, was supplied whenever the boys were fractious and it always solved the immediate problem for a few minutes, as the lips appeared firmly glued around whatever method was used to insert the substance into the mouth.

Shortly after Mother's departure we were notified by the District Commissioner that he required our bungalow for one of his own staff and we would have to find alternate accommodation. A low-loader transporter arrived almost immediately carrying a Terrapin prefabricated bungalow. Terrapin is the manufacturer's trade name and the bungalows are made in South Africa in a one-piece design for easy transportation and quick installation on site. Imagine the inside of this bungalow: you have entered a front door and stand in a wide corridor which runs the length of the building to the rear bathroom and toilet area. The width and height of this corridor is all you see before work begins; walls and roof have been folded and compacted around it. The outer walls fold out from this corridor and the roof (already hinged) is pushed up into position in two sections. It is then all bolted together. The bathroom and toilet fittings are then plumbed in, and kitchen units are supplied ready for installation and plumbing in; all that is then required is a spot of inside painting and decorating.

Our generator arrived with the Terrapin, as did the furniture and utensils. The whole operation could be completed in a few hours with five or six assistants; the main pre-preparation is a concrete foundation slab for the bungalow. Living/dining room, two bedrooms, bathroom/toilet and kitchen were then ready for use. Electricity was supplied by a generator—but you are probably wondering about the water supply. This water supply was delivered by what we used to call the 'Rhodesian Boiler', but names of countries gaining independence in Africa all appear to have changed; maybe it is now known as the 'Zimbabwean Boiler'. It consists of 45-gallon oil drums mounted on a brick structure raised from the ground, with pipework from the drums connecting to bathroom and kitchen fitments, and all gravity fed. Hot water is supplied by lighting a fire under the drum (or drums) feeding the hot water taps. The water was supplied to the drums on a daily basis by one of the workshop's water bowsers, which collected the supply from the nearest river (or Lake Nyasa). Everyone had their own water filters in the kitchen which processed the water before use.

The whole family, Mother, Jean, the boys and I, enjoyed many Sundays picnicking, when the Resident Engineer and I would form part of a cricket team consisting of the District Commissioner, doctor, Agricultural Officer and other local government officials, plus many of the local shopkeepers. They were relaxing, enjoyable days and conversation flowed freely, but perhaps I should exclude our Resident Engineer from that as he was unable to relax completely because of his concern for his beloved Mercedes saloon, which was always parked some distance away from the remaining transport and beyond the reach of any six-run cricket ball which was likely to damage its bodywork. He watched marauding children carefully, as their sticky hands and fingers were anathema to the carefully and frequently-polished bodywork.

I would remark that if he showed as much concern for my earthmoving equipment as he did for his Mercedes, the Road Unit would have had little to worry about. It fell on deaf ears. After completing his tour of duty he returned to the UK with his car and his wife.

Around halfway through our contract the Road Unit had made excellent progress and our allotted section of road was completed. We were designated a further section at Karonga in the far north of Malawi near the Tanzanian border; in fact, that section would eventually connect with a Tanzanian main road at the border. Whenever Karonga was mentioned in conversation with fellow expatriates, a deathly silence would follow. Nobody appeared to have been there, but harrowing stories would be told and shaking heads would advise against the move. "Terrible for a bachelor, but with a wife and two young children..." they would remark. Our Resident Engineer had no desire to move to Karonga; his contract was completed and he departed for the United Kingdom.

Jean and I discussed the situation and she had no objection to the move, deeming it quite an adventure. The Chief Engineer asked me how I felt about the move and I replied that my only concern was medical care, and getting immediate treatment for my wife and children in an emergency if the situation should arise. He assured me that there would be a charter plane dispatched to Karonga and ready to return to Blantyre for any medical treatment required for me and my family.

My schedule was to move everyone from Ntcheu to Karonga in the right sequence and be ready as required to commence work at the new campsite. A European trailblazer with his caravan,

African staff and equipment ready for site development would be the first priority. The twelve Foden trucks were split into two convoys travelling backwards and forwards with equipment from the workshops, spare parts boxed and labelled from the stores, etc. The ideal was for the two convoys to meet midway, one coming and the other going. The journey of 600 kilometres would take approximately 20 hrs.

Gradually one by one I released the six Europeans from our Ntcheu site and watched them depart for Karonga. Our site was beginning to look bare and desolate until finally we were the only people left and it was now our turn to make the move. I booked Jean, Paul and Mark into a hotel in Lilongwe and returned to site to help dismantle our Terrapin and see it loaded onto the low-loader. Our boxed possessions and furniture were loaded on the last convoy of trucks. Morris Oxford, convoy and Terrapin on the low-loader travelled together as far as Lilongwe, where I joined Jean and the boys for an overnight stay at the hotel. I sent the convoy on its way; they would be in Karonga before we arrived (with luck). Our bungalow on the low-loader also travelled ahead; we would no doubt catch up with them the following day on their long arduous journey.

Karonga is the oldest town in the far north of Malawi and in 1963 it was an isolated outpost. We caught-up with the low-loader and travelled behind for the rest of the journey. Arriving at our new campsite, we discovered that a concrete base had been laid ready for our bungalow. It was late in the evening and we retired to the camp guest house, which had been newly built for any visitors that may arrive in the future. The camp was built on the lakeshore and all personnel enjoyed views of a sandy beach stretching to the lake. Our bungalow was soon erected, decorated and ready to inhabit, and after work each day we enjoyed strolling along the beach, which virtually came up to our door, and where the boys would make sandcastles in our garden. The bungalow had been raised up off the ground on bricks approximately 12" from the ground to allow for ventilation; the air could circulate under the floor and cool the building, a form of 'underfloor cooling' as opposed to 'underfloor heating'.

Occasionally we would hear shuffling during the hours of darkness caused by iguanas under the bungalow. Sometimes an iguana would run past the boys as they played outside, but they were harmless and the boys carried on regardless.

There was a local landing strip where a small Beaver aircraft would arrive on Tuesday morning on its scheduled stop before flying on to Mbeya in Tanzania; it would then appear again on Thursday morning on the return trip to Blantyre. Karonga had only the dirt runway, no out-buildings or other airport facilities. We were the only family on the camp, with six other Europeans who were bachelor caravan-dwellers. There was very little available locally with regard to provisions and we all possessed a large standard wooden-box (which we called the 'chop' or food box); Jean would go around in a Land Rover with her African assistants every Tuesday morning collecting these boxes together with their order books. She would then meet the incoming aircraft, load the boxes and hand the order books to the pilot, who would later drop the boxes and books off at Mbeya Airport, where local supermarket staff would collect and supply our needs before returning the packed boxes to us on Thursday when Jean would be waiting to collect and deliver to our staff.

Beer and spirits were also in short supply locally and whenever deliveries were made they disappeared rapidly. The *MV Ilala* toured around the lake weekly, its itinerary being most unreliable, so whenever the bush telegraph warned of its impending arrival all Europeans would dash to the lake shore together with the local shopkeepers, and transactions would be completed as the cargo was being unloaded.

The local market was always an interesting place to visit every Saturday with the stallholders displaying their wares on the ground. All the various types of fruit and vegetables were arranged in their standard heaps, all priced at 'penny-penny', and you came away with a full shopping basket at a bargain price. The abattoir was another hub of activity and not recommended for the squeamish or vegetarians. Animals were slaughtered and joints of meat selected by the customer and virtually removed before your eyes, wrapped and handed over. Jean would leave the market carrying meat that was still warm, so there was no doubt at all that it was fresh.

This much-enjoyed Saturday ritual was rudely interrupted by President Banda's Malawi Youth, an undisciplined, disorganised rabble of young men eager to enjoy some form of authority, however incapable they were, in their new republic. A road block had been set up on our route to market and we were informed that we (Jean, the two boys and myself) could not pass until we had been searched. The annoying part of this encounter was the fact that the members of this rabble knew who we were and what we were doing there. I did not enter into any argument but returned to camp and contacted our Chief Engineer in Blantyre from our radio room. I explained that I was not prepared to have my family subjected to these impositions and if this treatment was to continue I would return with my family to Blantyre, where we could enjoy the high-life of other European families. I also reminded him that we were the only European family in the area enjoying our life here, but we were unwilling to suffer restrictions of any kind as we assisted in fulfilling Dr Banda's dream of a lakeshore road.

A few hours later I was called to the radio room, where the Chief Engineer informed me that he had travelled to Zomba (Administrative Headquarters) regarding my complaints and all Europeans on our Road Development Unit were to meet in the Karonga Community Hall on the following Monday morning, when President Dr Hastings Banda would address the meeting.

Monday arrived and we assembled together with local African dignitaries and the Malawi Youth delegation. Dr Banda addressed his comments mainly to the Malawi Youth, stating that for many years ahead Europeans would be needed to help develop the country and we must work with them and not against them, also stressing that he did not want to drive them away to South Africa and other countries who could reward them more financially. Let the Europeans go about their work in peace and cause them no problems. He required the Malawi Youth to tear down their barriers and disband, as he desired the lakeshore road completed as soon as possible. After this visit we were able to continue without further hindrance.

The 'Engineer in Charge' of the three Road Development Units would visit every two or three months, when Jean and I always made it an excuse for a camp get-together with meals and drinks served at our bungalow. The boys enjoyed the attention they received and the party spirit of these occasions until it was their time for bed, and it always amazed me how quickly they fell asleep despite the chatter and noise from the room next door. The Beaver aircraft on the internal flight to Karonga had pilots who were always eager to converse and discover the work their passengers were engaged on. When our engineer visited and they learnt of his interest in the new lakeshore road the pilot would diversify slightly and fly very low down the length of the road under construction affording our visitor an early bird's-eye view of the progress being made.

Jean, the boys and I continued to have wonderful local lakeshore holidays at Fort Johnson, Monkey Bay etc, although we had our own piece of lakeshore just outside the door where we enjoyed spectacular sunsets and breakfast looking out over the lake. The area around the campsite was a type of black cotton soil, and one of the bachelors and I created an allotment which supplied us with tomatoes, carrots and many other salad ingredients in abundance which we supplied to the European and African staff. Tomatoes grew easily on open ground from seeds scattered around, and were so plentiful that we begged any visitors to take as many as possible when departing.

Our three-year contract was coming to an end and we now had to consider the boys' education. Nothing would have been available to us in the area if we had embarked on a further three-year tour. Sadly we had to plan ahead, and this would mean saying goodbye to friends and our beautiful lakeshore home.

My replacement arrived and immediately offered me an excellent price for the Morris Oxford, which had served the family well after its initial horn-bracket malfunction and still looked as good as new. I must mention that all our vehicles were fitted with seat belts; the legislation came in Malawi long before it arrived in the United Kingdom.

Paul and Mark had been surrounded by Africans for all of their lives and were quite relaxed whenever they were around, whether they were friends or strangers; however, Europeans had always been thin on the ground and it was these white people they were wary of. We did not relish the thought of arriving home on leave and having the boys shying away from their grandparents, and as we had six months' leave ahead of us we decided to embark on a month-long voyage on the luxury-liner *Uganda* to slowly integrate them into their white community. The *Uganda* was carrying cargo and due to stop at many ports for at least one day on the voyage from Lourenço Marques in Mozambique to the UK, including Dar es Salaam, Tanga, Mombasa, Malindi, Cadiz, Barcelona and Marseilles.

CHAPTER 15

THE MARRIED EXPATRIATE YEARS (3)

TANZANIA: 1966-1969

Paul, Mark, Jean and I arrived home after our four-week voyage on the *MV Uganda*. Mother had settled into her usual routine after her Malawi adventure and my sister Pauline visited frequently with her children. The usual routine of travelling between Sheffield and Leicester resumed as before. My next step was to secure another overseas position, but this time with an important proviso - there must be schooling for the boys available.

Construction News was always a reliable source of information, and I was soon replying to one of their job advertisements with my up-to-date CV. There was a quick response from the Chief Engineer, who happened to be on leave at his home in Manchester, and he asked if he could come over to Leicester, where we could discuss the situation. This suited me fine - I had never been interviewed in my home before, a unique experience.

The appointment was for a Workshop Manager, Plant and Transport at Williamson Diamonds Limited in Tanzania, East Africa. The Chief Engineer interviewed me at my house and was also able to meet my family. He assured us that the educational facilities were excellent, with teachers recruited from the UK. Apparently we would find life at Williamson Diamonds much more enjoyable than our primitive existence in Malawi. I was offered the job and informed that I would receive the detailed contract as soon as he could make the necessary arrangements.

The new contract was received and signed. The company were using Rapier draglines and Aveling-Barford 9½ yard dumpers among the equipment at the mine, and it was arranged that I would spend one week at the London Brick Company near Bedford, where some draglines were operating, and a further week at Aveling-Barford, Grantham, where the dumpers were manufactured.

It was interesting to spend time at Aveling-Barford after leaving the company ten years previously. Many of the old faces were still there doing the same job they did a decade ago. I was in conversation with Cyril Bennett, an old service engineer friend, when the 5 pm end-of-working-day whistle blew. All service engineers grabbed their coats and disappeared. When I enquired where they were going Cyril replied, "Home, to join their families and watch television. They work a normal day. If a machine's broken down it stands until tomorrow, no unsociable hours; times have changed since our day." That's the understatement of the year, I thought.

Our leave period ended and the family packed their bags once again for pastures new. We arrived at Dar es Salaam Airport, where we were met and escorted to our company aircraft, which had 'Williamson Diamonds Limited' emblazoned along the side.

It was a twin-engined Dakota, so I felt quite at home already. As it was nearing Christmas, many of the seats had been removed to make room for Christmas trees and decorations. A first night in the clubhouse was a familiar way of meeting people on first arrival.

Mr Williamson, a surveyor, had discovered diamonds in the Shinyanga Region of Tanzania and then concentrated his attention on developing a township, Mwadui, near the site, boasting top-class facilities with the necessary expertise brought in to fulfil this ambitious programme. The residential area had bungalows with well-kept gardens spaced out along tarmac tree-lined avenues and roads. Facilities included a 19-hole golf-course, four tennis courts, swimming-baths, supermarket, fire station, police station and a hospital housing the latest surgical equipment and staffed by two doctors and five nurses. A fleet of company buses operated throughout the township on a daily schedule. The Williamson Airport was operated solely for the benefit of the mine and its staff, with three aircraft, three pilots and three flight mechanics. The aircrafts' regular routes were to Dar es Salaam and Nairobi, transporting spare parts, provisions, etc. The wives and children of the expatriates employed on the mine could fly free of charge to Dar es Salaam or Nairobi whenever they wished for shopping or other appointments. Take-off was around 7 am, returning the same day around 5 pm.

All employees were encouraged to own their vehicles for easy access around the township, and second-hand cars were freely available to purchase whenever the Transport Workshop brought their fleet up-to-date. All staff residing in the township carried a Class C (township only) pass. Employees who required access to the industrial area and administrative offices were issued with a Class B (township and industrial area) security pass, and the few staff working in the Diamond Sorting Area carried a Class A security pass. Accompanied tours were available at certain times to enable Class C pass holders to visit the more secure areas and places of interest which otherwise they would never see.

The industrial area comprised three large workshops: The Plant and Transport Workshop, my responsibility, with two European foremen, thirteen European supervisors and 200 mechanics, electricians, paint-shop staff and clerks. The second building was the Welding Shop with a European Manager, European foreman, welders and platers and the third was the Machine Shop with European manager and foreman plus African turners, millers, drillers, etc. I also managed a separate Body Repair Shop and Re-spraying Shop. There was also a large Stores Department with European manager and staff. The Administrative Offices housed the Chief Engineer, surveyors, secretaries, etc.

Each year I would write off approximately 20 of our older vehicles and replace them with new models, not necessarily of the same make or manufacturer. Over my years abroad I had been consistently disappointed with British firms' after-sales service and the procuring of spare parts required for urgent repairs. The Peugeot, Toyota, Nissan, Daihatsu, etc dealerships would usually have spares readily available, whereas with Land Rover, Leyland etc there could be lengthy downtimes when spares were not available and this common occurrence could see the vehicle standing for six months if the part was delivered by sea, which meant that a costly air-freight order was inevitable.

This annual ordering of new vehicles created great interest among the salesmen, who descended on my workshop, in force and many of the UK representatives were disappointed to hear that in most cases I thought their product superior but I was choosing the foreign dealers who I could rely on to supply me with the spare parts without extra delays and costs.

One of the perks of the job was permission to bring into the workshop employees' private transport for any repairs required, provided it did not interfere with any mine procedures or schedules. I was also told to 'lose' most of the costs incurred and keep them as low as possible. Three private vehicles at any one time was the figure I had decided we could comfortably work with. Among the vehicles I was writing off the fleet was a Peugeot 304, still in good condition, so I purchased it for our own family runabout. My allotted work transport was a Land Rover and this was also the case for most senior personnel. The Chief Engineer and I decided these were a costly waste in most cases unless you were working out on site, and most of us only used them on tarmac roads to and from the industrial area to our homes in the township. Accordingly we ordered twenty Morris Mini saloons and pick-up vehicles, which proved to be a great success.

Wherever possible the wives of the employees were found work with the company, and Jean became the Chief Engineer's secretary, working in the Administration Offices. Other ladies would work in the supermarket. Jean passed her driving test in a Land Rover and afterwards ferried the office staff to and from work. I was playing tennis regularly again at the weekends and winning one or two trophies, playing one tournament in Dar es Salaam.

There was one occasion during our stay in Malawi when Jean, Paul and I has been engaged in a long conversation in the kitchen. We entered the living room but could see no sign of Mark, so a hurried search ensued indoors and out, until we noticed his hands grasping the top of the sofa. He was hanging down the back with his feet off the floor. I lifted him from this position, whereupon he scampered away unperturbed. There had been no cries of distress, or any other sound, during this episode.

Afterwards we discovered that climbing onto the back of the sofa was a favourite pastime, but sometimes he lost his balance and fell the wrong way, landing on the floor at the back of the sofas instead on the cushions.

The family visit to the Williamson Supermarket was a regular occurrence, and after the boys had led Jean and me around the aisles, ensuring that their favourite products had been loaded into the trolley, they usually disappeared to join friends outside who also found the regular shopping expedition rather boring. During one of these visits several of these young people came up to me to say, "Mr Bradley, Mark's climbed up one of the poles outside and he's stuck!"

The offending pole was one of many supports for the overhanging covered walkway outside. Mark had reached the top, where the pole joined the canopy, and this appeared to be the only thing stopping him from ascending even greater heights. With legs and arms firmly wrapped around the support, he nonchalantly surveyed the concern of the gathering onlookers standing below.

"You'll have to climb up and get him down," said one of his associates. This was beyond my capabilities without a ladder, as, unlike my son, I could not climb like a monkey. Relying on a firm command, I ordered him to descend immediately, which he did, as expertly as a fireman sliding down a greasy pole - or the aforementioned monkey.

Apparently he had been watching challenges and attempts to climb the pole by friends and acquaintances much older than himself, and all had failed miserably, until silently he had passed through the throng and demonstrated the art of shinning up a pole. The strength in his arms amazed me.

Paul and Mark were progressing well at the mine school,

which employed teachers on contract from the UK. At one point they both required some dental attention, so we boarded our aircraft, flying to Nairobi for a couple of days' leave. We had booked rooms at the Norfolk Hotel, which dates back to the old colonial days. The boys had an afternoon appointment with the dentist, where both were given chloroform before the treatment. They were still asleep when I carried Paul from the taxi and placed him on a sofa in the Norfolk lounge. Residents enjoying their tea and biscuits looked on in shock until I explained the situation. I then hurried out to the taxi and carried in Mark, placing him on another sofa, which required a further detailed explanation to the astonished residents. Both boys came round shortly afterwards.

Our 18-month contract at Williamson Diamonds was drawing to a close and we were offered a further tour which we were happy to accept, but first came our three months' UK leave.

My sister Pauline had been visiting mother regularly during our time overseas, and she now shocked us with the devastating news that Mother had breast cancer. I immediately contacted her doctor, who was a family friend, and expressed my difficulty in not knowing what to do next regarding my work - what action do I take now? Do I now get work here in Leicester to be near Mother? Is it incurable?

He informed me that it was incurable, that he was unable to say how long she would survive and that I could not be expected to put my life on hold for a situation that might happen in months or maybe years. As a family friend he promised he would be keeping a close and regular watch on future developments. My sister had given me the same advice, and said she and her husband would be there for her during my absence. If her condition deteriorated seriously, they would take her into their home.

Jean had been stating for some time that the boys had never experienced the holiday camp atmosphere and we really should not deprive them a moment longer. I had resisted, insisting that I was not the holiday camp type. The pressure continued, and eventually Jean presented me with a brochure opened at pages showing top grade accommodation complete with television, etc.

"You can always stay in and watch the cricket," she said.

I relented grudgingly. As we advanced towards Cleethorpes the boys began jumping and cheering in the rear of the car: the holiday camp loomed ahead and as the comedian Stanley Holloway used to recite, "Blackpool, land of gaiety and fun!" For Blackpool read Cleethorpes.

It was midday Saturday when we moved into our accommodation, and by 6 pm Jean was complaining of stomach pains. We retired to bed with her still complaining of the pains. The morning dawned, still with stomach pains. I insisted that Jean should go across the road to the doctor's surgery whilst I prepared breakfast for the boys. She duly departed.

Then I heard the wail of a siren, but thoughts were concentrated on the Cornflakes. There was a knock on the door and on answering I was informed, "Mr Bradley, your wife's been taken to Grimsby Hospital."

A frantic time ensued as the boys were hastily prepared for our rush to the hospital, where on arrival I was told she had been rushed into surgery with appendicitis and it had just been caught in time. We returned to the holiday camp until we could visit Jean in the evening, and the following days were spent trying to keep the boys happy by feeding coins into various machines and watching them passing relentlessly on numerous roundabouts and donkey rides on the beach followed by our evening visits to Jean in hospital.

On Friday evening I enquired if there was any chance of Jean being discharged the next day (Saturday midday we had to vacate our accommodation). "We will have to wait and see what the doctor says," was the reply. On Saturday on our way home I visited the hospital for their verdict. "We will have to wait and see what the doctor says," was the reply once again.

"When is that likely to happen?" I enquired.

"I don't know," came the answer.

We set off for Leicester and home. Soon after arriving home, the telephone rang. "Your wife has been discharged and is ready for collection." Cleethorpes - land of gaiety and fun!

On arriving home Jean told me of her conversations with other women on the ward who were in no doubt that she must be pleased that her operation had occurred while she was here and not in Africa. Jean thought it would have been churlish to mention that if this had happened at Williamson Diamonds Hospital she would almost certainly have been the only in-patient and would have received the undivided attention of two doctors and three nurses.

We returned to Williamson Diamonds and resumed where we had left off on the previous tour.

The Chief Engineer and I were often on different wavelengths. He was an electrical engineer and i was mechanical, so it was inevitable that differences occurred along the way. It was during one of these awkward periods that his private Volkswagen was laid low and required attention, and as mentioned previously, I had sole discretion over whose vehicle warranted precedence over others. Jean, in her position as Chief Engineer's Secretary, rang me to ask if the said Volkswagen could have some attention, to which I replied that I had my full allocation of private vehicles, we were terribly busy and I would be in contact when a suitable slot could be found. These telephone calls continued for several days, all with the same outcome. I received a call from the Chief Engineer's wife: "Ron, I know you're terribly busy but could you give me some idea of when the Volkswagen could be repaired - any chance next week?"

"I'll come and collect it right away," I replied.

We sat with our tea and biscuits. "I don't know how you work with him, he is such an obstinate, awkward man at times," she said, referring to her husband.

"I've worked with worse," I replied smiling, adding, "I don't think the car requires much work, nothing serious, I'll bring it back when it's repaired."

I delivered it the following day. On hearing that I had collected the Volkswagen the Chief Engineer came out of his office and said to Jean, "What made you marry a man like that?"

"He's all right when you get to know him," she replied.

Several weeks later the Chief Engineer said he wished to discuss with me a letter he had just received. This was an official Government document stating that the pace of Africanisation was to be stepped up and in 12 months' time there would be only two Europeans in the workshop, myself and a senior foreman. This meant that thirteen Europeans would be made redundant.

Many of my supervisors were Italian and had been here with their families since the end of World War Two in 1946. "I don't envy you your job of breaking the news to these men," I said to the Chief Engineer.

"It's not my job, it's your workshop and your job," he replied. "I leave it to you how you tackle it."

I walked through the large sliding doors of the workshop into the noisy interior of revving engines and over 200 industrious men, African and European, first-class men and first-class tradesmen who I had grown to respect. I climbed the stairs to my office dejected and hoping I could reach that sanctuary before being confronted with the latest problems. I looked down on the scene below. Where to start? What to say?

Over the following year I was forced to make twelve Europeans redundant, one every month, followed by the inevitable leaving party at the club, which included my speech (twelve variations on the same theme), all rather depressing. Coupled with these events was the death of our Welding Shop Manager from a heart attack and shortly afterwards the death of our Machine Shop Manager, both wonderful men who gave me great assistance and advice in numerous ways whilst making my workshop life so much easier. I was feeling jaded; there was little joy around any longer.

The usual routine was to call at the post office to check if we had any air-mail; this was done on my way home from work. There was a telegram from Pauline. My mother was dead.

I arrived home and silently handed Jean the telegram before hurriedly disappearing into our bedroom, where I sat on the plain wooden chair in the corner and held my head in my hands. I cried silently. The boys were playing in the garden outside the window. Over time the bare, tiled floor became wet from tears. Jean had silently placed a cup of tea beside me on the floor where I could see it. Night fell and she had closed the curtains.

I sat on my hard wooden chair in the corner, in darkness, and the dampness spread on the tiles below. It was 10 pm. Jean had seen the boys to bed and came to persuade me to leave my corner and come into the living room, where a hot drink was waiting. I sat on the sofa and lifted the *Daily Telegraph* up in front of my face; it was a large newspaper, ideal for sheltering behind. I did not read, just stared ahead through tear-stained glasses that constantly slipped down the wet bridge of my nose.

We climbed into bed and I held Jean tightly in my arms. There had been two women in my life, and now I had lost one. What would I do without Jean? I relied on her so much. I drifted off to sleep.

Five days later on my way home from work, I called at the post office and there was another telegram. It was from Pauline, to inform me that mother was now seriously ill with cancer. It was the telegram that should have preceded the previous one. I was upset, because if this had been received sooner I would have gone home to the UK immediately. I know I could not have changed anything, but at least I would have been there with her.

This tour had been the opposite of the first one; so many sad events had happened and for us Williamson Diamonds would never recapture its old glory. We could not return and would be seeking pastures new. Jean decided to go home with the boys a month early in order to get the house organised.

CHAPTER 16

THE MARRIED EXPATRIATE YEARS (4)

SIERRA LEONE: 1969-1970

Jean had dealt with all outstanding items since returning home, and there remained little for me to do = except find another job, of course. The house was furnished by my parents and reflected their ideas. It now appeared that the 'day of reckoning' had come for Jean and me. Since our marriage nine years before we had never had to worry about housing or furnishings as we were always supplied with these items (Government Issue, we used to call them) on our contracts abroad, so were always free from this expenditure. The time had now arrived to put our own house in order.

We were now ready to encounter the 'six-week syndrome', an affliction common to British salesmen and highly contagious. Two bedrooms were to be completely revamped and we had decided that Limelight furniture (beds, dressing-tables, chairs, ottomans, wardrobes and overhead storage cupboards) would be suitable in both rooms.

Waring and Gillow were our Leicester stockists and we entered the store joyfully like a newly-married couple ready to feather their nest. The salesman perused our brochure with its carefully-ringed items, checked our carefully calculated price-list and with a broad smile formed by the thought of a sizeable commission remarked, "Yes, that's fine. Delivery in six weeks." I explained that I required the items immediately, as I would probably be overseas in six weeks and I also needed to fit the overhead storage units. If he could not deliver we were not interested, we added. The Manager was called and after a telephone call to the London Office we were promised a quick delivery. The items were delivered two days later.

Within a few days of arriving home I attended the optician's for my regular eye test and selected some new spectacle frames. "Yes, that's fine. They will be ready in six-weeks," said the assistant. Protesting and using the same reasons as before, I asked the Manager to append a special note to this effect with the order: "If not delivered within six weeks, cancel order."

If you are being measured for a new suit I guarantee that when you depart the outfitter's premises the tailor will have informed you, "your suit will be ready in six weeks." When attending any sales course I am sure that the instructors insist that the 'code of practice' must be adhered to and six weeks quoted as the 'salesman's safety net'.

I made enquiries regarding my spectacles after five weeks had elapsed and was assured they would arrive before I departed overseas. I telephoned the day before leaving but they failed to arrive. "It's too late, cancel," I had to inform them.

A company mining rutile (titanium dioxide mineral) in Sierra Leone required a Workshop Manager. I forwarded their application form and was successful at the interview. "When would you like to take up your position in Sierra Leone?" enquired the Personnel Manager. "Oh, in about six weeks," I replied.

Sherbro Minerals were an American organisation. The mining of rutile takes place near Nitti Port in the Southern Province and the area contains the largest deposits of the mineral in the world; in fact, the area around Gbangbatok and Mattru is known as 'Rutile' and its titanium-rich black soil contains the elements required when manufacturing paint, artificial knees and has heat-resistant qualities suitable for parts used in aircraft jet engines, to mention just a few of its many uses.

Mogbwema is the site of the mine and there a 400-ton dredge works day and night, its buckets scooping out the earth containing the titanium ore and loading it into waiting barges. The camp accommodation was built on top of a hill and the bungalows looked down into the heavily-wooded valley below, where monkeys could be seen scampering about, and sometimes children playing on their verandas were joined by inquisitive monkeys that quickly departed when the excited squeals of the children were heard. The bungalows were prefabricated and equipped to a very high standard. Every bungalow was identical, with exactly the same soft furnishings, table lamps, tables and chairs, kitchen units and kitchen utensils - everything identical in each bungalow, from the General Manager down to more lowly staff positions. I could never get used to the American electrical system of pushing and pulling plugs in and out of walls that had no electrical cut-off switch.

The earthmoving side of the operation was typical American 'biggest and best' and in my opinion was badly planned from the onset, consisting of three Blackwood Hodge twin-powered scrapers (one engine in front and one behind powering each), the largest and most modern scrapers of their day, and with a workshop staff that had received no training in dealing with their complex requirements, they were difficult to maintain. This was exacerbated by a failure by the Blackwood Hodge dealership in Freetown to supply anything like the spare parts required to keep these machines operating; hence it was a rare occasion when all three machines were serviceable. I also believed that these three lumbering giants would have been easily outmanoeuvred by six smaller basic machines achieving the same or better results. Alas, I was never able to prove it.

The scarcity of spares for these machines led to 'cannibalization', taking parts from one unserviceable machine to keep another in operation - a step which once taken is difficult to reverse.

This American company employed predominantly American senior staff with approximately ten further staff recruited from Europe. The Quaker influence seemed to permeate the entire operation, and as Europeans we always had the feeling we were being closely scrutinised, which was alien to any mining community who were noted for working hard and playing hard. The social club was a modest building where most of the Europeans congregated in the evenings for a few drinks, but the Americans were little in evidence, and when they were, they departed at a reasonable time. Just before 10 pm the Personnel Manager would often be seen walking slowly past the windows gazing in and making a mental note of personnel still intent on merry-making. Provisions were ordered in your own personal book which passed through the Personnel Office before the goods were supplied and costed. Any beer and spirits required were also ordered in this way.

It was at this time that my personal war with Blackwood

Hodge and its Freetown, Sierra Leone dealership started. Frequent trips to visit the Caterpillar and Blackwood Hodge dealerships to query the reasons for long-awaited spare parts became a necessity, and afterwards I would regain my composure after our heated arguments by retiring to the Paramount Hotel for a beer and sandwiches before continuing my quest around Freetown for other required items. Freetown traffic was always hectic, but luckily I had my driver.

Rumours were spreading that the company was on the verge of ceasing operations and pulling out of Sierra Leone. The despondency grew with each passing week, and as my tour was nearing completion I gave Sherbro Minerals my three months' notice of termination as required. Immediately afterwards I saw an advertisement in a UK newspaper that Crown Agents were looking for a Plant and Transport Workshop Manager for a road construction project in Sierra Leone. I forwarded my application.

Soon afterwards I received a letter from Crown Agents asking me to contact the Resident Engineer for the project, who was now visiting Sierra Leone. We duly met in the Crown Agent offices which had just been opened in Freetown in readiness for the forthcoming action, and he outlined the details, offered me the job on the spot and asked me to meet him again in London, where the contract could be signed and I could meet other people responsible for planning and securing the project. This news quickly spread around the Sherbro site, not from me but from my driver who had waited in the Crown Agent's Office until my business was completed. It came as quite a shock to others, who were wondering what steps to take next as dark forebodings continued to escalate.

A few days after this I received a letter from a consultancy I had dealt with previously who asked if I was interested in a workshop manager's job in Kuwait; if so, the interview would be in Kuwait. Jean intended to return home a few weeks early with the boys, so I thought, "Why not? Let's have a couple of days in Kuwait and see what happens."

I arrived in our Personnel Office and requested that my flight home be via Rome to Kuwait and then on to England. I was asked the reason for this diversion and was delighted to inform them that it was for a job interview. The Americans and Europeans quickly spread the news, discussing my plans and looking on as the storm clouds gathered over Sherbro Minerals and impending doom was forecast.

Leaving Freetown on the flight to Rome, it was soon evident that it consisted mainly of Italians who stood in the aisle and conversed as soon as the 'Unfasten Seat Belts' message appeared. This reminded me of my days at Williamson Diamonds in Tanzania, where a large Italian community worked, and they always congregated in groups (usually men) outside the supermarket, post office, street corners, etc. They appeared to spend more time standing than seated.

At Kuwait Airport I was met by a chauffeur-driven car and deposited at a five-star hotel. The following morning I was taken to an office and issued with examination papers relating to engines, gearboxes, transmissions, etc. There were some "what would I do if..." questions and quite a number of "yes or no" boxes to tick. I found the whole experience quite probing with regard to engineering knowledge and efficient in determining strengths and weaknesses—perhaps a method that could be adapted in the UK instead of being subjected to inane questioning by wet-behind-the-ears personnel managers.

Almost immediately I was told my marks were over 90%, and I was offered the job. A visit to a newly-built large workshop was next on the agenda, and I was informed that my first task (if I accepted the position) would be to travel to Pakistan and recruit skilled labour for the workshop. A visit to a large house which would be our accommodation was our next stop, and we would be required to furnish it to our taste (a loan would be available). A car would be a requirement and should be a prestige model (a loan was available). I received details of my salary per annum and was told they awaited my reply in due course.

CHAPTER 17

THE MARRIED EXPATRIATE YEARS (5)

SIERRA LEONE: 1970-1973

Arriving back home with two firm offers of employment was a very desirable situation, and I had now to choose between a contract in Africa or something new in Kuwait. It was a decision which I had no difficulty making. There were too many imponderables with the Kuwait offer; it appeared to be a lucrative package but the outlays were plentiful and unknown (car, furniture, rent, etc). There was also the big culture difference with the Kuwaiti people and their vast wealth employing Europeans, Asians, Indians and Pakistanis to do the work they had rejected. I was conversant with the African situation and knew exactly how far my salary would go and if I would have any surplus in the Bank at the end of the month. It was back to Sierra Leone, West Africa.

The Resident Engineer I had met previously in Freetown, and he now chaired this meeting in the London Office of Crown Agents together with other interested parties who had planned the operation. The project was to construct a completely new stretch of highway between Taiama and Bo in the Southern Province approximately 50 miles in length, complete with culverts and a major bridge spanning the river at Taiama. All equipment used had to be manufactured in Britain. The main earthmoving fleet would consist of six Blackwood Hodge scrapers and three Blackwood Hodge tractors. I expressed my forebodings, stating that there was nothing wrong with the equipment but I had reservations about their ability to supply spare parts and I had had personal battles in the past with the same dealership in Freetown that I would be dealing with now. I was assured by the Resident Engineer that their full co-operation had been guaranteed. The work was to be completed in three years and the Resident Engineer stated that he was now returning to Sierra Leone permanently and looked forward to me joining the team when I had completed my leave.

our road construction camp was still being set up, so Jean decided to stay at home with the boys until she heard from me that everything was organised and we had accommodation. A few more weeks also fitted in well with the boys' school term. The camp site was adjacent to Njala University and the vacant land we intended to use for our workshops and housing belonged to the university. After three years, when the highway was completed, the intention was to hand the housing and generators over for the use of their senior staff, while handing the workshops and equipment plus all the plant and transport (in working order) over to the Public Works Department. Njala is approximately five miles from Taiama. The contract was due to be completed in three years and the expatriates, of which there were eight, were due UK leave every six months.

When I arrived on site I was surprised to see most of my old

African workshop personnel from Sherbro Minerals, who informed me that soon after I had left, the rutile mine had closed until further notice. My old driver was among the many seeking employment and I gave him his old job back, driving me around, plus quite a number of reliable tradesmen were hired. Not every one of my old acquaintances was successful; one of my old foremen was rejected due to his unreliability and being absent frequently. He messed me about terribly at that time and I'm sure he knew the odds were against him when I appeared on site. It was a great advantage to be able to recommend good machine operators to the Europeans in charge.

Now knowing that Sherbro Minerals was not operating, I was keen to hire my old African foreman (the reliable one) who I rated as one of the best I had encountered. Apparently he was being paid by Sherbro to act as watchman over all the plant that had been mothballed until further notice. I arranged a meeting with him through my driver, who took me to his village. We talked for several hours, but I was unable to persuade him to move; his allegiance was still with Sherbro Minerals.

The large wooden crates were arriving daily and we were kept busy unpacking our prefabricated bungalows and erecting them. The furniture and fittings came with them, and soon we were a working campsite with new generators supplying all our power requirements. Njala University had been supplying us with meals and accommodation until our bungalows arrived. They also had a good primary school with European teachers and I was able to enrol Paul and Mark prior to their arrival.

The bungalows were all in position and work had commenced on the roadworks. There was a very tortuous roundabout route from Taiama to Bo, but our road was going to be a direct straight line between the two, through the forest and rocky outcrops, cutting many miles and much time from the journey.

Jean arrived with the boys, who enjoyed life on site tearing around on their bicycles. They also adapted quickly at their new school on the university campus. In the wet season it would usually rain conveniently around 7 pm, when Paul and Mark would take advantage of the rain splashing down from the edge of our bungalow roof on to the sloping veranda roof from where it cascaded to the ground. They would discard their clothes and armed with bars of soap take a shower - much more fun than the indoor version.

My worst fears soon materialized, and we had to park a Blackwood Hodge scraper after a few weeks due to lack of spare parts. This machine never worked again throughout the three-year construction of the road because of cannibalisation; we used parts from this machine to keep the other five working. We could never catch up with the spares required for this scraper until after the project was completed. Luckily we managed to keep the three Blackwood Hodge tractors operating throughout. The Manager of the Blackwood Hodge dealership and I were old sparring partners and had many heated arguments in his Freetown office, and his regular visits to Njala became less frequent because of my growing hostility, not to him (he was a decent man) but to his company's lack of after-sales service. Every time I visited his office I would come away with a car boot laden with baseball caps, T-shirts, pencils, pens, key rings, etc, with the BH logo emblazoned on them. The boys were grateful to receive models of their tractors and other equipment. I am sure he presented me with all these gifts in an effort to pacify me after I started complaining. It became a camp joke as more and more of these peace offerings appeared around the site being worn by various individuals.

Our Resident Engineer rented a company flat in Freetown with resident cook and houseboy, where the expatriate staff could enjoy a break from work. I allotted a Volkswagen Kombi for these expeditions but no driver; the expat would have to drive himself. This break spanned four days (travel to and from included), and when one party returned to camp the vehicle was handed over to the next family on the rota, a continuous process that gave all expatriates a four-day break approximately once a month.

Jean and the boys, with me driving, were returning from one of our breaks in the Volkswagen Kombi and it was raining heavily. We were about midway through our journey when a passing lorry threw up a stone which shattered the windscreen. The boys and Jean took refuge on the floor behind the rear seats and protected themselves from the rain the best way they could. I smashed out the rest of the windscreen and we continued on our journey, arriving back at camp in a very soggy condition. A trip not easily forgotten.

We were friendly with a young sports master who was one of the teaching staff at the university. He had formed a very useful football team who had enjoyed some success in the area and I asked our African staff if they were interested in forming a team. They were very enthusiastic, but could not see any way of raising enough money to buy football kit, footballs and other necessary items, so whenever Jean and I visited Freetown we would buy some useful items for raffles which we organised to raise money for the football team. The Europeans on site could see we were keen to succeed and supported us in every way by buying raffle tickets, and as I said earlier they were enticed by some worthwhile prizes.

We made rapid strides and practised regularly. I was

appointed player/manager and we became a well kitted-out team. The university sports master was on leave, so we were temporarily spared his boastful comments regarding his university outfit. He had never seen us play, but threw down a challenge, stating that they were ready to teach us a footballing lesson at any time.

The Njala University Football Club were anxious to play Crown Agents and although I suggested we wait a couple of weeks until their mentor/manager arrived back from leave this was regarded as a sign of weakness, that we were fearful, and so a local derby was arranged. I was the only white man in our team. I also had the dubious distinction of being the only player in the team with footwear - I had discovered long ago that all my team members could kick a football further and harder with their bare feet than I could with boots! I had always played on the left wing and I had now passed the forty-year mark and knew my limitations, so I substituted myself after the first twenty minutes.

Crown Agents won a hard-fought game. The Sports Master returned from leave and sought me out, saying, "This is supposed to be my job, training our football team, and you appear with your Crown Agents and beat us!" He took it well; we went for a beer and I gave him solace. "I demand a return match, I need to see these Crown Agents play," he said. We won again.

Paul was approaching eleven years of age and educational facilities in underdeveloped countries would now become a problem. Jean returned home in the later stages of the contract to attend to Paul and Mark's schooling.

Leave periods in the UK were now becoming more attractive, and the old three years and 18 month continuous contracts were being replaced by six-month periods abroad followed by UK leave. This contract was leave after six months.

ODE TO A ROAD

TAIAMA TO BO ROAD CONSTRUCTION PROJECT, SIERRA LEONE, WEST AFRICA. 1970-1973

Up they come from far and near
converging on a central sphere.
Britain's sons their finest hour
march through corridors of power
in that hallowed, supreme think-tank
known as Number Four the Millbank.

"You will be part of Y Division,
Go, uphold a fine tradition.
Build a road complete with bridges,
lay the culverts, dig the ditches,
Sierra Leone shall be your prize...
And don't forget to stabilize."

The locals stared with puzzled frown
to see these Agents of the Crown
arrive with baggage and machines
to fulfil their wildest dreams.
Three years in all they would remain
through scorching heat, relentless rain.

Spares you've waited for impatient
are arriving from the Agent.
Boxes long and crates so tall,
They are not bad blokes after all.
Parts to make you burst with song...
Bloody hell - they've sent them wrong!

Stupid buggers, silly sods,
how do they get their bloody jobs?
Consignment notes and inquisitions.
"Will you sign these requisitions?"
Signing, signing through the day, -
take the f........ things away.

Charts and graphs adorn the wall
of the RE's sacred hall.
Lines that stagnate, rise, descend,
will this torment never end?
Linear records like a dart
thrusting at a fitter's heart.

Charts are plotted, plant confusion.
Is it just a grand illusion?
It is fiction, is it facts?

Does it cover up the cracks
on the RE's office walls?
Is it true or just plain balls?

Analysis, planning and time-factors,
deadlines, downtime on the tractors
Ten days lost in late December,
that's a time I well remember.
Peace, goodwill to all plant men,
will ye no come back again?

Matted hair and sweaty palms,
sticking shorts and aching arms
probing with the long-nosed pliers
while balancing on ribs of tyres.
Engine seized, the pump had failed,
pull out bits of hot entrails.

Civil bastards all around
standing firm on sacred ground.
Some technicians, some are chartered,
what they learnt has long departed.
"How long will you be with that?"
Shout abuse and get some back.

Engineers, uncivil all.
Come to see you rise or fall,
They come enquiring or to scoff,
Or just to watch you strip parts off.
The RE comes but doesn't laugh.
You're blocking up his critical path.

At last it's time to ease the load,
machines stand idle on the road.
All staff are here on this occasion
to cut the tape, there's celebration.
"Three cheers!" the RE loudly cries.
The tumult and the shouting dies.

Farewell the dashing up and down
to Bo, Senehun and Taiama town.
Farewell to tracks and turning wheels.
Farewell those uninspiring meals.
My case is packed, it's time to go,
so farewell road, Taiama - Bo.

CHAPTER 18

THE MARRIED EXPATRIATE YEARS (6)

NIGERIA: 1973-1976

Returning from my tour in Sierra Leone, I arrived home around 3 pm. Jean had returned some weeks previously to arrange Paul and Mark's schooling, as it is virtually impossible to receive suitable education after primary school in third-world countries. Paul had reached 11 and Mark was 18 months younger. Jean greeted me with the news that Paul had been taken to the hospital by the school headmaster as he had suffered a cut just above the eye; apparently it did not look too serious but it was a precautionary measure. I immediately said it was due to stone-throwing, an act I had repeatedly warned and lectured the boys against committing.

The headmaster duly arrived back with Paul. It was not a serious cut and had only required dressing. Paul said he had been walking across the playground intent on other activities when he was caught by a stone; he was not and never would be engaged in stone-throwing. The headmaster agreed with this account and apparently knew the culprit's identity and said he would be 'spoken to'. I enquired of the headmaster if throwing stones was part of the school curriculum, as many of his pupils resided on our estate and all seemed adept in the activity of stone-throwing; in fact, one of the glass panes in our storm-porch had been broken by one of his pupils - a girl. I suggested that it could be stamped out overnight by a clip round the ear of any offender (as in my schooldays). The headmaster agreed, but said he was frightened to lay a finger on any child for fear of retribution by a parent.

Monk Construction Company in Warrington were advertising for a workshop manager on a highway construction project in Lagos. Nigeria. I applied and later at their request travelled to Warrington for an interview with the Chief Engineer, who explained that the company was keen to secure contracts in underdeveloped countries and this was to be their first, a highway from Lagos Airport to the centre of Lagos and continuing as the Lagos to Ibadan Expressway. Monk's was family orientated, with many employees long-serving and UK-based. They now required someone with overseas experience, I was informed. I offered my opinion that this contract in this place was probably the worst location to 'dip your toe in the water' and something smaller and remote might have been more beneficial. The job was mine if I accepted. It was a challenge - let's give it a try!

Lagos Murtala Mohammed International Airport, a name to strike fear into the most seasoned traveller, was a hive of bribery and corruption, pickpockets, bogus taxi-drivers and confidence tricksters. We were due home leave every six months, and although it should have been a pleasurable experience passing through the airport it became a time of dread, knowing you had to face corrupt officials who were capable of putting obstacles in your path, even delaying your departure if bribes were not received. In due course we employed a Nigerian public relations officer to oversee all arriving and departing Europeans safely through the airport with minimum hassle.

Before departing from the subject of Lagos Murtala Mohammed International Airport, I should mention that one of our European employees from Warrington had a fear of flying and was in a state of constant agitation whilst in the air and visited the toilet frequently, a situation he apparently was anxious to share with the cabin crew, while at the same time he hoped they would not regard him as a nuisance. We were both due UK leave around the same time, so he changed his flight and travelled with me. I took his window seat so that he was unable to look out of the aircraft. He duly informed the cabin crew of his predicament and they promised to assist wherever possible (by keeping a clear flight-path to the toilet, I assumed).

A steady stream of conversation ensued between us throughout the six-hour flight; he did not overly use the toilet and on reaching our destination proclaimed it was the most trouble-free, relaxing flight he had ever undertaken. We met again at the airport after completing our leave and boarded the aircraft for our night flight to Lagos. The flight had been uneventful and I looked out of the window to see that we were only a few feet from touching down on the runway. My companion was thanking me for my assistance in making the flight as comfortable for him as possible when suddenly and without warning the aircraft's nose was pointed sharply skywards at an acute angle and the pilot quickly announced, "Everything's okay - a Land Rover appeared on the runway so I thought I had better do another circuit!" All my good work was ruined.

Jean came to Lagos for a two-week holiday. Her return journey to the UK had been booked on a Nigerian Airways flight with Nigerian cabin crew. On arriving home she had to visit the doctor's surgery; food poisoning was the verdict.

The base for our road construction project was at Ikorodu, near the airport. Plant and transport workshops and the administration offices were located here. European staff were housed in accommodation rented by the company in Ikeja, the most upmarket suburb on the mainland. Power cuts were frequent and our generators were installed at the properties and required on most evenings when widespread blackouts occurred. Lagos was chaotic, with terrible overcrowding; the haphazard development had led to a drain on energy, and sewage facilities, water access, housing and transportation have all been adversely affected as it has grown too big too fast and the infrastructure has stretched to breaking point with inadequate sewage facilities leading to much of the human waste being carried along rainwater ditches which culminate on the city's tidal flats. Piles of garbage lie everywhere.

The Company and its employees suffered much abuse from the general public during the first year of this three-year project, because very little progress could be seen above ground and their expectations of an overnight solution to their transport problems did not materialise (and probably never would). We would be returning to our accommodation in Ikeja in company transport bearing the Monk Construction logo when inevitably a traffic jam would halt our progress. There would follow thumping and banging on the roof and side panels of our car, plus jeering faces at the windows chanting "monkeys,

monkeys!" and other unflattering remarks. Being our country's 'ambassadors on the ground' we ignored it through clenched teeth. Incidentally, this twenty-minute journey could never be achieved in less than an hour.

My work meant that I would be called out to difficulties or breakdowns to machinery on the road, and a contract requirement stated that we did not drive ourselves in company time but employed African drivers for this duty. Call-outs and inspections were a daily occurrence, and with traffic conditions so chaotic and highway codes non-existent I would often think back in the evening after my working day of the many accident near-misses we had encountered that day. Luckily your vehicle was unable to accelerate to any great speed due to the chaos enveloping you from every angle. During that first year, our lack of progress, in the general public's eyes, was due to our attention being focused on areas where vast flooding had occurred in the past after heavy rain causing traffic delays, as these areas became insanitary swamps. Our concentration had been focused on drainage and culverts with much concrete work being laid below ground level, often covered over and unseen. During our second year relations with the public changed beyond recognition as their shanty towns, markets and nearby roads remained free of constant flooding due to our efforts and progress could be seen on the actual highway.

One of the road construction staff called me out to the latest emergency. Their progress had been halted by a man's dead body lying directly in their path; it had been there for twenty-four hours as far as they knew and during this period they had been hoping someone would appear and claim him. This had not materialised, and milling crowds jostled by, schoolchildren, policemen, traders, all going about their daily business with scant regard for the dead man they were stepping around. Life is cheap in Nigeria, especially in Lagos. In Lagos, if you transport a body to the hospital or mortuary you have automatically accepted responsibility for it and you must pay any expenses incurred for treatment or burial.

I contacted our Resident Engineer and informed him of our predicament, whereupon he sanctioned our removal of the body via pick-up truck to the mortuary with the necessary paperwork, signature and cash required for burial or cremation as we had accepted responsibility. On our arrival at the mortuary it was their first question - means of payment.

Monk's operated a quarry just a few miles outside Lagos, and I visited the site frequently to check the earthmoving equipment. The road leading to the quarry was busy day and night with traffic, mostly heavy goods vehicles. On my return to Lagos on one occasion a man had been knocked down in the road, and was obviously dead. Several lorries had stopped at the side of the road adjacent to the fatal accident. I returned to the quarry the following day; the body had not been removed and so many vehicles had passed over it that it now formed part of the road surface.

A visit to one of our sites near the airport was a daily occurrence, and my driver was familiar with the long traffic delays at the busy road junction, where a policeman would be standing directing the traffic (no traffic lights). We had slowly worked our way forward until we were at the head of our line awaiting the go-ahead signal from our policeman. The policeman casually walked from his central point of the intersection, came over to my front passenger side window and said, "I notice you come this way often, I could make your journey quicker and easier by passing you through every time I see your Monk Construction car" (referring to our logo on the side).

"I will take my chances," I replied.

He slowly returned to his duties and the Lagos traffic moved once again. This is not an isolated example of bribery and corruption; I could list many examples. Our white-skin was an automatic attraction and a sign of wealth to the average African.

My driving licence was ready for renewal. I attended the necessary office at 3.30 pm and at 4.45 pm was told they were closing, it was too late, come back tomorrow. I reluctantly passed over a banknote which slid surreptitiously from my hand to his and into his open desk-drawer. "We have got a minute or two, maybe we have time for a new licence," he remarked.

Military rule operated in Nigeria from 1966 and was highly visible around the Lagos area. The unit in our locality bore the flashes of a black scorpion on a red background and were a brutal bunch who were quick to dole out punishment with their batons at every given opportunity. The people do not understand our idea of queuing or waiting your turn, and if a bus arrives at a stop it is a case of every man, woman and child for themselves. When the bus is full many will still endeavour to clamber aboard. The 'scorpion' brigade would gladly intervene, wielding their batons and striking men and women (some with babies strapped to their backs) around the shoulders until they were forced from the bus steps back on to the road. Understandably they were hated by the public.

Many times my driver and I would be out on site as the end of the working day approached, picking up workshop staff who I had earlier in the day assigned various tasks on the earthmoving equipment. If there was a large number who required a lift back to base, we would take a pick-up truck. Unfortunately the five or six mechanics in the open-backed pick-up would play a game of 'He who dares wins' with our 'scorpion' acquaintances roaming the vicinity, calling and shouting various uncomplimentary remarks (aided and abetted by my driver). Sometimes the 'scorpions' had transport and gave chase, with my mechanics now reverting to hand signs and laughing which added to the tension as my driver sped towards the safety of our large workshop gates manned by our security staff. In one instance the 'scorpions' were in hot pursuit as we neared the open gates. "Shut the gates, shut the gates!" the mechanics shouted as we sped through.

The gates were shut, but as several 'scorpions' drew their batons and threatened consequences unless the gates were opened, they obliged and the army moved in. My mechanics did not like to arrive back home to their 'villages' in dirty overalls and grimy boiler suits, so we had large shower and changing rooms in the workshop complex where they could all get spruced up and change into their everyday clothing before returning home, where other 'villagers' probably were lured into the assumption that they had VIP jobs in Lagos.

The 'scorpions' searched the workshop area high and low but could find no trace of the offending mechanics. I had rapidly taken up position at my office desk with head down perusing some paperwork as they passed my window. During this time the end-of-day whistle blew, and the cleaned-up mechanics/civilians nonchalantly walked through the gates unrecognised on their way home.

Brutality was the order of the day, and robbery was the order of the night. I shared a bungalow with Bill, another member of our European staff. We were great friends and were moved from our previous accommodation in Ikeja which now housed four younger members of staff to new accommodation suitable for senior members who desired a quieter and more relaxed existence; this bungalow was semi-detached and the adjoining bungalow was of the same plan, but the opposite way around to ours. The bungalows were in a large compound with a company security guard stationed at the entrance at all times. Our driver also had his accommodation in this same compound. I should mention that all windows had vertical steel bars embedded in the brickwork surround approximately six inches apart; this was in order to deter robbers. There were inner security steel lockable doors made up from steel bars on each door leading to the outside compound, so in the evening your house became akin to a prison cell. This emphasis on security was common practice. Welcome to Lagos.

The adjoining bungalow was empty when we moved in but was soon occupied by another member of staff who was married; this young couple we knew very well and were always a part of our social gatherings. My bedroom was at the end of our bungalow and was separated from one of their bedrooms by a brick wall (being semi-detached). On their moving-in day I was in my bedroom and was amazed how clearly I could hear the couple's conversation coming from the bedroom next door. I immediately informed them of my discovery and suggested they might consider using the second bedroom at the far end of the house. I talked in a natural way from my bedroom to prove my point and they were grateful for this information.

I have my reasons for explaining this incident, as several weeks later I was in my bedroom around 8 pm when I heard the terrified cries of the lady next door shouting from her bedroom: "Ron, the robbers are here, the robbers are here!"

Dashing from my bedroom to the front door, I found Bill standing in my way.

"Where are you going?" he asked.

"Can't you hear the cries for help?"

He then gave me a sobering lecture, asking me what my actions would be after confronting at least two or three robbers almost certainly armed with machetes, knives or other weapons - I would be of no assistance whatsoever. He was right of course. We turned off all the lights and hid in the kitchen. Frantic activity could be heard in the compound next door, but there were only spasmodic attempts to gain entry to our bungalow. We furtively rang the police and warned as many of our friends as we could in whispered tones down the telephone. The plaintive cries of "Ron, the robbers are here" could still be plainly heard between consistent attempts to break into their bungalow (or so we thought from our hiding position).

We heard activity outside our kitchen window, and thinking it was the robbers, we kept silent until a voice from underneath the window whispered, "Give me the Land Rover keys." It was our driver; we slowly and quietly opened the window and dropped the ignition keys into his hand. A few seconds later we heard the Land Rover engine start and our driver 'ran the gauntlet' through the compound and through several robbers who tried to stop him. He sped to the police station to summon help.

The robbers then knew they had to make a quick getaway. Bill and I had gone to the bungalow next door and informed our couple that everything was back to normal and we were all recounting the evening's adventure when our driver and the police arrived. Our driver was suitably rewarded.

We were constructing a bridge over the railway line near the airport; the supports had been completed and now we were ready to lift some long, heavy steel girders onto these supports with the aid of a large mobile crane. I was always amazed each time a train came around the bend with its overcrowded carriages and human bodies sitting, squatting and lying on the carriage roofs, some dangling precariously from the carriage roofs and a myriad faces peering out of open windows and bodies clinging to the carriage sides by various means. It was obvious that the railway authorities should be contacted and asked to co-operate in this operation by ensuring that no train passed through and underneath whilst these steel girders were swinging about above ground and being positioned. Monk Construction and the Railway Authority agreed on a time that would be trouble-free for both parties.

The day and time arrived and we commenced our work free of railway worries. There was a loud piercing 'whooeeee!' from the train as it appeared round the bend with its overcrowded carriages and human bodies on the carriage roofs, some dangling precariously down, and a myriad faces peering out of the windows and bodies clinging to the carriage sides. The steel girder swung around in the air just above the carriage roofs. We all held our breath.

"You can open your eyes now," I heard someone say.

Our Quarry Manager suddenly resigned and departed the scene, which left us in a quandary until a replacement could be found. I was asked to oversee the operation for a short period and was allotted a European member of staff to assist. The bungalow at the quarry comfortably housed two people with Brian and me settling into our temporary jobs without difficulty. Lorries from other companies arrived at all times and were supplied with their stone requirements; it was a highly successful business operation and outside sources paid for the materials supplied. One of the rooms in our bungalow had previously been transformed into an office space where two African accountants worked during the normal daytime shift, and they kept records of these transactions with the money received being kept in their office safe.

The Chief Engineer, based in Warrington, England, was on

one of his tours of inspection and came to visit Brian and me one Friday after his recent arrival in Nigeria. We toured the quarry and discussed various operations; knowing that I had many years' experience in quarry maintenance, he was keen to hear my observations on certain aspects of the operation, especially what I had learned of the financial aspects in my short tenure. He informed both accountants that he required their presence in the Lagos office early on the following Monday morning, with all records and paperwork appertaining to sales up to date and balanced. Apparently the financial side was under close scrutiny - the books were not balancing.

On leaving our quarry bungalow he gave us favourable comments, and before departing asked if we had any outstanding problems.

"Only one," I replied, "We've got some large rats in the vicinity of the bungalow and we have noticed them roaming around at night, hence the poison laid around the outside of the bungalow." He appeared very concerned and as he entered his car he said, "You can do without rats. Let me know how you get on with their extermination."

It was midday Saturday and some quarry staff were leaving for their weekend break, including the two accountants. Brian and I entered the bungalow and could smell smoke; we immediately noticed it was coming from the accountants' office. We fought the fire for as long as possible, but the bungalow was completely gutted in less than thirty minutes and we were left with the clothes we were wearing (shorts, short-sleeved shirt, etc). The fire brigade arrived, but the bungalow was an empty shell by this time.

Taylor Woodrow Construction Company had a site a few miles away, and as soon as they heard the news they came to our rescue, arriving at the quarry and transporting us to their camp. We knew many of the expatriates there, and they supplied us with food, accommodation and clothing until we could make a start reorganising clothing, missing passports and visas etc the following Monday in Lagos. I will not take this experience any further; it caused us much hassle at the British Embassy in Lagos arranging new documentation, with much hassle filling in insurance claims and a certain amount of money being forfeited in bribes in order to get things moving. It will not require any great detective work to realise who the guilty party or parties were in this case, and they were later brought to account.

Early on the Monday morning I arrived in Lagos. Entering the Chief Engineer's office I said, "Wally, we've got rid of those rats."

"Excellent, how did you manage that?" he replied.

"I've burnt the bloody bungalow down."

My work meant that I frequently needed to attend unserviceable machinery on site, and this meant leaving the workshop for long periods. When not directly supervised, the African employees would stop their work, down tools and gather together in groups to engage in the latest gossip or just have a rest. During my tours I always found the most difficult job was finding a good African foreman who would supervise and push the work along while I was away from the workshop.

I advertised this position in the local press and thought I had discovered the ideal candidate in this instance; he was well educated with good qualifications and I called him in for an interview. I explained what I required and he was pleased to accept the position of Workshop Foreman. Unfortunately he proved to be a disappointment, joining forces with the rest of the workshop employees and joining their groups for conversations instead of pushing them to keep working. The reason for this, I believe, is that the African foreman probably lives in the same village as most of his workmates and therefore needs to be a popular member of the village community, whereas a European foreman, who is probably ambitious, can get completely away from his workmates after working hours, usually living many miles away in another town, and so is not so concerned with who he upsets during working hours.

The three-year Highway Project was completed and the opening day was approaching. Our Resident Engineer voiced concerns, stating that the African drivers were not conversant with the modern motorway systems; indeed they had scant regard for any road codes. He contacted the local Army commander and wondered if he could assist with personnel to patrol the route and inform motorists of the correct procedures to be observed on the highway, how to enter the system and how to leave, etc. Delighted to assist, he placed many men at our disposal, but stated that they would need to be told exactly what action was required at these various intersections along the route.

Operational Day arrived, and our Resident Engineer told us to take transport and operate in pairs, standing aside and leaving the Army to proceed with instructing whilst we stayed nearby watching the developing situation and acting only where necessary; in other words, "do not get involved." We each carried two of the Army personnel to a given site, informed them whether the vehicles should be entering or leaving the slip-road where they were stationed and then removed ourselves from the immediate scene ready to observe from a distance.

A Mercedes approached and started to enter the motorway down the exit slip road. The Army man stopped the car and ordered the suited, smartly-dressed African businessman out of his vehicle, whereupon he drew his baton and beat the man about the head and shoulders until he sank to his knees begging for mercy. The second Army man, who had been some distance away now approached, and placed a large army boot in the Mercedes man's midriff. We heard afterwards that instances similar to this were occurring at several points along the route. The following day's newspapers announced that the opening had been a great success. Monks Construction secured other contracts in Nigeria, notably in Jebba, where I was able to spend some time during our Lagos wind-down after completing our highway contract ahead of schedule. They also secured work in Aba.

Jean had spent a few weeks with me during the contract but was unable to join me full-time owing to the boys' educational requirements back home. The leave period in the UK after six months' service in Nigeria made life more bearable. The company also offered me a valuable extra perk by suggesting that on returning home on leave, if I cared to fly on from London to Manchester Airport (Monks' headquarters at Warrington were only a few miles away) at the company's expense, there would be a car waiting for me to use during my leave period. When my leave was complete, I could drive the car to Warrington and they would drop me off at Manchester Airport. This occurred every six months and was much appreciated.

My expatriate friends said how fortunate I was to have survived three years of daily travel on Lagos roads without being involved in an accident.

238

CHAPTER 19

THE MARRIED EXPATRIATE YEARS (7)

SAUDI ARABIA: 1976-1978

Jean's parents enjoyed regular visits to their favourite caravan park at Cleethorpes, travelling to and from Sheffield by bus. Jean would often join them there for a short holiday break, which I encouraged. During my leave we had invited them once again to spend some time with us in Leicester and their visit was drawing closer, so a plan of action needed to be scheduled without delay.

Jean's dad had suffered with emphysema for many years, a condition in which excessive air is present in the body tissue, especially in the lungs, causing breathlessness, and before they visited we would draw up a list of suitable places we could take them to visit that did not entail too much walking, especially places devoid of hills, steps or other obstacles likely to cause shortage of breath. This was more easily said than done, and we frequently spent days before their visits on reconnaissance in various areas to ascertain suitability for various sightseeing tours we had in mind. Historic Castles and stately homes were definitely off the agenda, as were museums and art galleries. All would have been dismissed and the entrance fees would probably have led to one of their favourite expressions, "not worth the money", their idea of an interesting day out being a visit to a shopping centre where the local branches of Boots, Marks and Spencer, Debenhams etc could be compared for size and quality with the same stores they were conversant with in Sheffield. We always said that more preparation and detailed planning preceded their visits than were required for the wartime invasion of Dunkirk.

They were not easy guests, and after we had collected them from Sheffield and brought them to our house in Narborough they would sit down with their cups of tea and look you straight in the eyes with an unspoken, "Well, we are here - how do you propose to entertain us?"

At home in Sheffield virtually every day, weather permitting, Joe and Polly enjoyed nothing more than walking around the shops and having a snack or meal before returning home. A day spent indoors reading or watching TV was not comparable, and not to be considered against their daily routine.

During one visit, as a result of her mother's restlessness while housebound, Jean travelled with her from Narborough to Leicester by bus and from Leicester to Birmingham by train, where they enjoyed their day visiting the large stores before returning home later in the day. The following day a similar trip was made to Nottingham and the next day saw them in Coventry. The fourth day was spent on a local trip to the Leicester shops. I asked her mother what differences there were between Boots, Marks and Spencer, Debenhams etc in their various locations, but I never did receive a suitable answer, only "It's nice to look round the shops."

Joe stayed home with me during these visits, so I recorded a few programmes and films on the VCR (video cassette recorder—remember this was pre-DVD and the like) which I thought might be of interest to him. I think we failed to pass the ten-minute mark on each occasion before he fell into a deep sleep.

Jean and I had visited Sleaford prior to their arrival and inspected its suitability for a visit from Joe and Polly. The car parking was only a short walk from a suitable bench which would afford a rest before they went to a nearby café for refreshments before entering the town and visiting the shops. This visit later took place; we parked the car and headed for the aforementioned bench, where a local resident sat calmly stealing a few quiet minutes with his favourite newspaper. We approached, and by this time Joe was suffering one of his breathless, heavy-breathing, wheezing attacks. Our local resident shot to his feet, with hurried steps crossed the road and without glancing back disappeared round the corner back to the sanctuary of wife and home, and he never stopped to fold his *Daily Mirror*. Joe produced his trusty inhaler and we proceeded to the café for refreshments.

I was outside, busy at the front of the house when my neighbour appeared saying, "You'll soon be off, where are you going this time?"

Nothing had been said to anyone regarding my future activities and I replied, "How did you know I was going away?"

"Oh," he replied, "you always give your wrought ironwork a new coat of silver paint just before you depart overseas."

I had never given this any thought before, but he was correct.

The *Construction News* carried an advertisement for a Workshop Manager in Saudi Arabia; the tour was for two years' duration with an attractive leave period every three months. Jean was quite happy with the situation and told me to go ahead as she knew I would be happier as an expatriate rather than taking a job around the Leicester area and commuting daily. I had now reached my mid-forties and I was aware that whatever I had achieved abroad and whatever experience I had workwise counted for nothing in the UK, as at my age you did not fit into the scheme of things. I had always thought that around the age of thirty-five a decision was required - the expatriate life, or shelf-stacking in B&Q. We had discussed this situation over the years and I once again informed Jean I was willing to take work around the home area, but she was happy with our current lifestyle.

I decided it was now time to try a new culture, the Middle East. Once you get in the West Africa rut you tend to be typecast, the general opinion of personnel managers being that if you've survived there for a few years and have volunteered to return, why risk a newcomer? It's like the old expatriate joke about the prize draw: first prize -one week's all-expenses-paid holiday in Nigeria. Second prize - two weeks' all-expenses-paid holiday in Nigeria.

Plant and Transport Manager, Pre-Stressed Concrete Factory, Jeddah, Saudi Arabia. My flight to Jeddah was uneventful, except that about an hour before landing the cabin crew announced that no further beer or spirits would be served and then proceeded to clear up, removing all evidence that alcohol had been consumed aboard the aircraft. On arrival at King Abdul Aziz Airport there were no 'Nothing to Declare' exits and you were well advised to unlock all your cases ready for a meticulous search of every piece of baggage. Customs were on the lookout for DVDs which might contain images of a sexual nature, and magazines and newspapers featuring sexual themes.

Our industrial site was approximately 30 miles from Jeddah along the desert road leading to Mecca, the Muslim Holy City.

Europeans are not allowed within a 30-mile radius of Mecca and signposts along the route inform you when to leave the road. Our site was in the desert along this road and about as close to Mecca as we non-Muslims could go. The factory specialised in pre-stressed concrete slabs of various lengths and thickness, which were used as load-bearing walls in the building industry.

'Pre-stressed' referred to the manufacturing process where long strands of wire rope approximately ½" thick were placed along a heated bed running the length of the factory. These wire strands were attached to a machine at each end of the bed, which then hydraulically tensioned the wires to a given pressure or stress level before cement was poured over them and dried on the heated bed. When this operation was completed, the dried slabs of concrete were cut by mechanical saw into the lengths required. Three of these beds were in operation, forming different widths of slabs in a 24-hour operation. Alongside this operation there was a fibreglass moulding factory, producing mouldings to order. Two miles into the desert we also operated a quarry. Two large road tractor/trailer units were operated by Europeans who transported our products throughout Saudi Arabia and were licensed to operate internationally. Large generators powered the whole site.

The company employed six Europeans on site, but the labour force were mainly expatriates from India. We always had construction machinery and projects in operation at Mecca, and the Asian workers could enter and maintain them, but unfortunately when they had a particular problem to solve I could only discuss it with them and offer my assistance in other ways. I was often frustrated and it would have been much simpler if I could have seen the problem.

Our accommodation was a two-storey building on site with

senior staff on the top level. Each person had his own private bed-sitting room with television, radio and cassette player (pre-CDs). There was a communal dining-room, with a television, and kitchen. Saudi television featured very few items of interest to Europeans and was dominated by religious programmes and constant views of the Grand Mosque at Mecca with prayers and rituals happening throughout every day. There were a few 'wholesome' programmes shown that were deemed suitable for all viewers; these included the 'Doris Day Show' (the singer, film actress and regular girl-next-door type) and 'The Waltons' (three generations in one house who all retired for the night at the same time, switched off their bedroom lights at the same time and said goodnight to each other so loudly it could be heard well beyond the confines of their house). The Saudi TV censors had nothing to worry about.

The Saudis enjoyed their football, and whenever their national team played at home or abroad those matches would be televised. They were playing a friendly fixture in Spain on one occasion and we all sat around the TV ready to watch the game. Both teams formed a line in the centre of the pitch, national anthems were played and we made ready for the presentation. Suddenly from the tunnel out onto the field ran 22 scantily clad cheerleaders, each carrying a bunch of flowers. Our mouths dropped open - what was happening? Where were the censors? After a few seconds the screen was blanked out until the girls had departed from sight. We could imagine the panic among the Saudi censors, who were probably falling over themselves in a frantic effort to reach the switch.

Sometimes the censors would sanction a film they had obviously not viewed previously in its entirety. Passionate meetings of the sexes were frowned upon and the usual scenes of long-awaited reunions where lovers first see each other across the airport concourse and rush forward with outstretched arms are blacked out long before the four-minute mile ends in an embrace and kisses.

The month of Ramadan is dedicated to fasting, prayers and charity and work ceases during this period. The TV specialises in showing the Ramadan soaps across the region, and these are hugely popular. Pilgrims arrive and there is a Minister solely responsible for Hajj affairs, who allocates quotas to Muslim countries for the number of pilgrims they may send. I have attended King Abdul Aziz Airport in Jeddah during this period and the whole floor area has been strewn with visiting pilgrims; stepping gingerly over prone bodies was the order of the day. Our factory site was just off the Jeddah to Mecca road, which became very busy with pilgrims during this period, and caution was required when driving.

Friday is a day of rest, and the TV news on that evening is dominated by a list naming wrongdoers including rapists, thieves, etc, followed by a list of punishments allotted to each individual. Rape could result in death by hanging and theft often led to the amputation of a hand. These sentences had usually been administered that day in the main square of Riyadh or Jeddah and were open events free to witness by anyone interested in the macabre.

After work we would often take a trip into Jeddah and pay a visit to our Head Office, where we would drink endless small cups of tea with sugar and no milk. On finishing your tea it would automatically be replaced with another cup by an observant and attentive office boy; a firm 'no more' would be necessary to stop this constant flow of tea, a social custom. In Head Office I would be intrigued by the 'family tree' on the wall, which should have depicted the company structure but only mentioned the Saudi hierarchy.

We all had our Saudi equivalents. My Plant and Transport Manager I rarely saw on site; he was not concerned with or interested in happenings at the factory and did not really wish to get involved, content to leave the day-to-day operation in my hands. When he visited he sat in my office, and did not require a briefing or want to be shown around on a tour of inspection. Whether he was qualified for the job I do not know. He asked if I would employ his son (approximately twenty years old) and teach him the work. I agreed and he made a few appearances in his Cadillac car, showing how bored he was with the whole idea of work, so I suggested he return to Jeddah and his friends. The Saudi youth do not embrace the idea of work and expect to start at the top in management. Our European names and positions did not appear on the 'family tree' - we were replaced by our Saudi equivalents.

On our journeys to Jeddah I was always fascinated by the behaviour of the camels that were often transported around in the back of pick-up trucks and sat quite placidly, nonchalantly viewing the passing scene as they sped along the highway. "Camel train? Never heard of it," they seemed to be saying. Incidentally, I have often observed a camel train passing a few yards from noisy earthmoving equipment (tractors and scrapers) with not the slightest concern.

Our quarry was two miles from the factory, and I always walked through the desert between locations for exercise. Camels would often be busily grazing as I passed amongst them. They would carry on regardless until one would notice me out of the corner of his eye and carry out a marvellous 'double take' when it realised I was not an Arab but a European. Others would follow, and I always found it hilarious.

A visit to the souk in Jeddah was always fascinating, and the rows of shops selling gold items and jewellery were like Aladdin's caves. I have arrived at the entrance to these shops just as the bell summoned all Muslims to prayer and as I sat and waited for these shopkeepers to return and unlock their premises I would look around this quiet, deserted souk full of gold and think that if this was the UK there would be a robbery with getaway car at the ready. The shopkeepers would return from their prayers and from open display cabinets I would select my 22-carat gold object. Everything was priced on weight, not craftsmanship or intricate detail. I always purchased items for Jean whenever leave time came around.

Another favourite buy in the souk was cassette tapes - do I have to explain again? Although most of them were pirate tapes from Japan, they were very good quality. With local TV being mostly uninteresting we relied on our cassette-players as the main form of entertainment. When visiting the souk (or any other place) your car could be left unlocked and containing whatever you had purchased in full view on the seats without fear of anything being stolen.

Often on Friday evenings there would be activity adjacent to our factory site when groups of Saudi men would arrive in their cars and pick-up trucks. They would then erect a large marquee where food would be served and music played. Afterwards the men would dance together and enjoy a weekend of merrymaking. No women were ever present on these occasions.

CHAPTER 20

THE MARRIED EXPATRIATE YEARS (8)

SAUDI ARABIA: 1978-1981

Having completed my two-year contract in Saudi Arabia, I returned home and found everything running smoothly, thanks to Jean, who was organising absolutely everything during my absences abroad. I received my wages each month, withdrawing a certain amount for expenses to see me though until the following payday; the rest would be sent home to Jean, who was the family accountant and administered our financial affairs whilst at the same time administering the required amount of discipline to two teenage sons. Paul and Mark have never caused us any trouble. I suppose discipline is a strong word to be using in this case, but thanks to Jean, they are growing-up level-headed individuals.

Over the last few years they have both had their paper-rounds, operating from our local Narborough newsagent. They also seem quite adept at repairing bicycles with their mates, taking over the garage for this operation. They have now advanced to motorcycles, but not before Jean enrolled them for lessons with a qualified instructor. Paul and Mark have both commenced apprenticeships in fitting with machine-tool manufacturers in Leicester, although with different companies. Jean has started work as a receptionist at the local doctor's surgery in Narborough, which gets her out of the house and meeting people.

I was offered a position as Plant and Transport Manager in Saudi Arabia with Joannou and Paraskevaides, the largest construction company in Cyprus. They had been awarded several large contracts and were recruiting senior management from the United Kingdom, as there was a dearth of experience in the company, especially in working on overseas projects. There was no lack of engineering graduates and many would be working in an assistant capacity on these contracts and gaining practical on the job experience. They were yearly tours with UK leave every six months.

The main office and workshop compound was in Riyadh, the capital city, and our main work would be centred on road construction in Najran and Abba with modern banks and office blocks to be built around the Riyadh area. Western expatriates usually lived in walled compounds with good facilities; we had a canteen/restaurant with Cypriot cooks on site, so we were spared food shopping or cooking meals. Senior staff had hostel accommodation with your own furnished room complete with TV and radio-cassette player. The communal rooms were also equipped with television, snooker tables etc. Although we lived in walled compounds there was very little crime and I suppose we were just following the Saudi way of life, where the family is the central point and privacy is essential. Saudis shut themselves away behind walls, shutters and curtains, and social life takes place within the family. Amusement parks are usually forbidden to them or restricted to family sections, and there is little in the way of outside entertainment. Restaurants also have a family section, whose occupants are hidden away behind partitions or walls.

The Riyadh souk is a very interesting place, and you soon realise how few Saudi women there are about. Their lives appear even more restricted than their counterparts in Jeddah, and by law they must be fully veiled and accompanied by a male guardian. In the shops or supermarkets the wife will have in attendance a maid or two and will gesture towards the item required, whereupon the maid will pack the basket or trolley. No Saudi women are permitted to drive a vehicle. Their life appears to consist of supervising the home and entertaining women friends at home and visiting their homes, the art of doing nothing in a life of enforced idleness.

The young Saudi people grow up in a culture of entitlement, many owning cars they drive around in a state of perpetual boredom with no work and little to occupy their minds. Often they take their 4x4 vehicles into the desert, where they hold races in the dunes and perform various stunts. Jeddah and Riyadh are cities built for the car; there is an absence of people in the streets and no social space. After midnight the streets are deserted.

Saudis have a high opinion of Americans; their limousines are sought after, the Supermarkets are piled high with all brands of American food and electrical goods. Young Saudis dream of escaping from their stultifying, boring lives at home and travelling to America. The military acquires its equipment from America and trains them in its use. Despite all this, America and Israel are regarded as responsible for all the troubles in the Arab world. One-fifth of the population are foreigners, from America, Europe, India, Pakistan, Bangladesh, Philippines. It is a closed society with so many foreigners in its midst, the Asians being mostly engaged as drivers, waiters, etc and employed on tasks the Saudis do not wish to be associated with. The women work as nurses, maids, etc. The universities turn out religious scholars, mostly unemployable, and not enough engineers, computer programmers and accountants. Saudis would be lost without their American cars, Lebanese food, and the Indians and Filipinos who attend their daily needs. Prayers are attended five times daily, during which everything comes to a standstill and the restaurants and shops are shuttered.

My time was divided between the workshop in Riyadh, where we were engaged in many large-scale building developments, and Najran, where we had a road construction project. My visits to Najran entailed travelling internally by air on Saudi Arabian Airlines (Saudia) where usually I was the only European on the flight. When the Saudi women saw me boarding they would hastily adjust their veils, even to the point of covering their eyes. This reaction contrasted starkly with a flight home on leave to the UK, where I had a seat directly behind a Saudi man and his wife, both dressed in their national attire, the white ankle-length robe worn by the man, topped by a chequered ghutra, and the all-over black woman's aboya and hijab.

Soon after the flight was airborne and safety-belts could be released, they both left their seats and disappeared from my view. It was some time later that I realised that they had not returned, and I thought no more about it until two people in Western clothing came and occupied their seats. It was the returning Saudi couple, he in a smart suit, shirt and tie, and she in full fashionable Western outfit with lipstick and the full make-up package. They proceeded to order and consume alcoholic drinks obviously enjoying the Western way of life whenever possible.

My first task on arrival in Najran was to inspect a tunnelling machine and decide if it was worth purchasing to use on our road project, which was to run through several rocky outcrops. The machine had previously been used by a construction company building a dam just over the Saudi border in Yemen. Unfortunately Yemen had few friends, especially in the western world. I had all the necessary paperwork to enable me to enter Yemen and was always under the watchful eyes of heavily-armed guards throughout my short stay. The tunnelling machine received my approval and was a bargain buy at the price requested. It was to carry out sterling work for us in the months ahead.

Najran is a mountainous area that receives little rainfall, but when it does occur it is usually heavy and can result in flash floods due to the water cascading down the mountains. We were engaged on repairs to roads and bridges washed away by these floods. The Falklands War was occurring during my tour and we were able to follow the action on our TV coverage. I was interested to see that the luxury liner *Uganda* which in earlier years brought the family home from Malawi was now based in the Falklands and acting as a hospital ship.

One of the Indian surveyors was due for leave and was preparing to fly from Najran to Riyadh and onward to India. He had left the site and started his homeward journey when by pure chance the Surveyor's Department noticed that one of their theodolites was missing from their stores; a thorough search ensued, but it could not be found. A theodolite is an instrument used in surveying, with a rotating telescope used for measuring horizontal and vertical angles. After all avenues were exhausted on site the Chief Surveyor contacted Riyadh airport and asked that Customs Officers search our man in transit to ascertain if he was carrying the theodolite. If he was, the request was to let him proceed to India with the instrument and in due course his employment would be terminated. This course of action did not satisfy the Saudi authorities, and our transgressor was escorted back to Najran Prison to serve a suitable sentence for theft. The prison was a stark building where inmates relied on family or outside sources for their well-being. The company were supplying his meals for the six months he was incarcerated.

I was aboard the aircraft on my way home after completing my latest three-year contract in Saudi Arabia, and on take-off was eagerly awaiting my first lager for three months, my last having been consumed on the flight to Saudi three months before.

"Can I get you a drink?" said the stewardess.

"Just place two lagers there on the table side by side," I requested.

"It's all right, I'll be coming round again frequently," she replied.

"I've seen you before, you'll just disappear never to be seen again," I said.

She returned, placed three lagers side-by-side and grinning, quickly departed. She knew the score.

CHAPTER 21

THE MARRIED EXPATRIATE YEARS (9)

TANZANIA: 1981 - 1984

When I arrived home, Jean informed me that she had received a telephone call that morning from a company interested in interviewing me for a job in Tanzania, and would I contact them as soon as possible.

Paul was now twenty years old and serving his apprenticeship as a fitter with a machine-tool manufacturer in Leicester, while Mark was eighteen, and also an apprentice fitter with a different machine-tool company. There had been instances in the national press where apprentices had been made redundant when companies were facing a downturn in orders and their apprentices were first in the firing line. This is abhorrent to me and smacks of the bad old days when companies would terminate the employment of their apprentices on their twenty-first birthday when their wages jumped dramatically on reaching tradesman status. It was a form of cheap labour practised by many engineering companies (Ruston & Hornsby of Grantham being a prime example and my dad being one of their victims).

The parents of an apprentice virtually agree to subsidize him for the six or seven years of his apprenticeship; in return the employer will teach him a particular skill. That should be a binding agreement between the two parties, and nothing should be allowed to sever it. Tradesmen should be laid off before apprentices are affected. I forwarded a letter to the Institution of Plant Engineers (I am a member) on this subject with a copy to the Rt. Hon Nigel Lawson, our local MP for Blaby district. Norman Tebbit, Secretary of State for Employment replied.

Caxton House Tothill Street London SW1H 9NA

Telephone Direct Line 01-213 7789

Switchboard 01-213 3000

GTN Code 213

Our Ref   PO 2832/1981

The Rt Hon Nigel Lawson MP
House of Commons
LONDON   SW1A OAA

18 SEP 1981

D Nigel.

Thank you for your letter of 28 August enclosing a copy of a letter from your constituent, Mr R Bradley, to the Institution of Plant Engineers. Mr Bradley comments on apprenticeship arrangements generally and the financial rewards for obtaining engineering skills. These are, of course, essentially matters for agreement between both sides of industry.

As to redundancies, the engineering industry has been to their credit, until recently, reluctant to make apprentices redundant, though a significant factor in current engineering apprentice redundancies is the high proportion resulting from firm or plant closures. Mr Bradley may not be aware that in recent months, however, the Government has become concerned about both the increasing number of apprentice redundancies and the considerably reduced level of recruitment of new apprentices by industry, and has made available substantial funds to help relieve both of these difficulties.

In the case of the engineering industry, these funds have enabled us to increase the monies sufficiently to boost craft and technicians apprenticeships by an additional 4,000 this year, and to help protect some 2,000 apprentices who are expected to be made redundant during the year. In the case of the promotion of new apprenticeships, there are two forms of support, either by making substantial grants available to employers willing to recruit extra apprentices this year, or by sponsorship of the first year training of others.

In the case of redundant apprentices, there are again two forms of support which we offer; grants to firms willing to adopt a redundant apprentice, or sponsorship of continued training for those who cannot immediately be found new employers.

You asked for some information about the incidence of unemployment amongst engineering apprentices. Separate unemployment figures for apprentices are not kept nor are exact numbers of engineering apprentices made redundant known. However, you may be interested to know that, between 1 September 1980 and June 1981, 2,255 apprentice redundancies were reported to the Engineering Industry Training Board, of which 832 were found new employers and 1,107 were sponsored in continued training by the Board while efforts to place them were continued.

Please thank Mr Bradley for raising these most important issues. I hope what I have said will convince him that the Government is not complacent about the situation.

My interview with Wade Construction Company was successful, and I prepared for another visit to Tanzania, East Africa as the Plant and Transport Manager for a new township we would be building to accommodate the employees of a paper mill. This new mill was being constructed by the Americans near Iringa, and Wade Construction were building a large township nearby to house the employees when the mill was completed and operational. Our main offices were based in Dar es Salaam, and we had a small airstrip near the camp which connected us to the largest city and was useful for visiting personnel but not capable of receiving large aircraft and cargo, so the transportation of vast quantities of materials and spare parts necessary for the project came by road. This was achieved by three Leyland land-trains travelling constantly between the camp and the docks and airport in Dar es Salaam.

From: The Rt Hon Nigel Lawson MP

HOUSE OF COMMONS
LONDON SW1A 0AA

23rd September 1981

Dear Mr Bradley,

Thank you for your letter and enclosres of
the 28th August about the position of
indentured apprentices in the engineering
industry.

I took this matter up with the Secretary
of State for Employment and enclose his
reply with this letter.

I am glad you wrote to me about this and
I hope you will find Mr Tebbit's letter
helpful in explaining the present position.

Yours sincerely,

Ronald Bradley Esq.,
65 Abbey Road,
NARBOROUGH,
Nr Leicester   LE9   5DB

On my arrival there were only two of these land-trains operational; the third was parked near the workshops with a faulty engine fuel-pump. This was a complex repair and we did not have the necessary calibration equipment to rectify the fault. A complete new fuel-pump assembly had been ordered, but we had been awaiting delivery for many weeks. The land-train's performance was integral to the operation and meant that any downtime on the remaining two vehicles became critical. The faulty fuel-pump had been forwarded to the Dar es Salaam Leyland dealership for repair, and after many weeks in their possession it was returned. We fitted the pump, but it was unreliable and therefore returned to them, where it now remained.

Near my home in Narborough there was a large Leyland Service Depot and during my first leave in the UK I paid them a visit to enquire if they were able to repair one of their fuel pumps, as obviously Dar es Salaam were finding it difficult. They assured me it would present no problem if we could get it to them. I informed our Manager in Dar es Salaam, and after retrieving our faulty pump it was arranged that one of our workshop expatriates who was going to the UK on leave should personally travel with the pump and on arrival deliver it to our London Office, and they would forward it to Leylands at Narborough.

Our workshop expatriate duly escorted the fuel pump to Heathrow Airport, but he rapidly grew tired of its bulkiness and weight, and decided he would rather travel on to Scotland than across London to our offices, so he abandoned the pump in a left-luggage locker, then phoned the office and told them where it could be collected or retrieved. He then departed for the Highlands. One of the office girls was given the task of collecting the pump from Heathrow.

On my return to Tanzania and our office in Dar es Salaam, the Manager regaled me with the full story. I enquired if his contract had been terminated. "That would be too easy and not very satisfying," he remarked, refusing to elaborate.

I returned to site and was very soon reunited with our errant fuel-pump, which in turn was reunited with the land-train engine, and the three land-trains once again joined forces delivering our supplies and equipment from Dar es Salaam. Our workshop expatriate? He returned from leave, carried out the customary procedure of reporting to the General Manager at the Dar es Salaam Office, entered with a smile and was told, "You're fired!" He was transported with ticket to the airport and caught the next flight back to the Highlands of Scotland.

Two of our expatriates had travelled to Dar es Salaam by road and were on their return journey back to site. One was driving their Nissan Patrol and the other was in the front passenger seat; they had picked up one of our African foremen in Dar es Salaam and he was travelling back with them. The last few miles to site were along a dirt road which our Foden dumpers used on their frequent trips to our quarry. At one section of the road, a flat, straight section, the Nissan and a Foden met coming in opposite directions; the two vehicles did not touch each other, but the Nissan veered into the bush and rolled over several times before coming to a standstill. The African Foden driver had stopped to give assistance; the two expatriates in the Nissan had suffered cuts and bruising but no broken bones as far as could be ascertained at this stage. The African foreman passenger was dead.

I was one of the first on the scene, and I took a few photographs and cordoned off the area. We arranged for transport to site and medical attention for the expatriates and I accompanied the body to site. I contacted our Site Contract Manager and informed him that I had misgivings regarding the accident as everything pointed to a speeding Nissan Patrol, tyre marks in the road, etc. The Foden driver corroborated this, although the expatriates vehemently denied it. If the police confirmed my suspicions it could lead to a lengthy prison sentence for the expatriate driver, according to my previous experiences where a death had occurred. I suggested to our Contract Manager that we should get them out of the country without delay and before the police get involved, our reason being that both expatriates required urgent medical attention, preferably in the United Kingdom.

It was around 4 pm and darkness would fall around 6 pm. Radio contact was made between the site and General Manager in Dar es Salaam, the aforementioned plan of action was agreed upon and our General Manager organised a private flight to pick-up the injured expatriates. As the aircraft would be landing after dark and our bush runway had no lighting, I rapidly contacted everyone with vehicles and requested their presence along each side of the runway. Our lorries and earthmoving equipment were also lined up. When we received radio contact that the plane had taken off from Dar es Salaam and knew its estimated time of arrival, all vehicle lights were turned on and focused along the landing strip lighting up the surrounding area. A successful landing was made and the two expatriates were flown to Dar es Salaam and whisked away on the next flight to Heathrow. Better safe than sorry.

The township contract was completed well in advance of the estimated completion date, while several other smaller contracts were secured and completed.

CHAPTER 22

THE MARRIED EXPATRIATE YEARS (10)

LESOTHO: 1984-1987

I had always promised myself that I would retire from working in tropical climates by the age of fifty-five, as I had seen so many of my contemporaries rapidly decline in health and even die after attaining this benchmark; company retirement and pension plans were set at this figure. Unfortunately I had not quite reached my goals financially and was certain that one more year overseas coupled with some dedicated saving could solve the problem.

Jean and I agreed on the plan, and in the interim would use my leave period looking for our retirement home. Jean's favourite county was Lincolnshire, which she had always remembered from childhood days travelling on buses and trains from Sheffield to various holiday destinations in Lincolnshire, and I suppose that particular period for her was a time of great happiness and fond memories. Her ambition had always been to retire to Lincolnshire, and I had no quarrel with that as I was a native of that county.

At this time many Londoners and people from the southern counties were retiring and selling their expensive homes and moving into Lincolnshire, where property was much cheaper. At weekends the hotels and guest-houses were filled with these property hunters and I have been informed by many of these hunters and seekers, who were later to be our friends, that secrecy was in evidence as they discovered excellent property in various locations and were anxious to keep any information to themselves.

We travelled around Lincolnshire in our search. We intended to downsize, as both Paul and Mark had left home and a bungalow would be a natural choice. A small estate in Long Sutton village near Spalding was being built and we had requested the plans from the builder and selected our favourite site. On our site visit they had not started to build our bungalow, but we booked the plot. "The bungalow will not be ready for at least another year," said the agent. "Just right," I replied, "I've just signed a twelve-month contract in Lesotho."

On our return home my thoughts drifted back down the years. How many times had I been in this situation, ready to depart once again for a tour abroad which would see me absent from home for months, sometimes years, ahead? This was to be the final time. The milestone was within reach and departure number 13 was drawing ever closer.

Two events usually happened a few hours before departure. I could guarantee that switching on the television would herald the imminent showing of an aircraft disaster movie, usually on the evening before I travelled. This occurred regularly during my bachelor years and later when Jean and I would travel together. We watched and never gave the film another thought.

The second event was a ritual I observed down the years and I remember it happened before my expatriate days. The National Service absences from home, the four-week lodging periods in Sydenham before a home weekend was due, the service engineer times when weeks were spent in South Wales, all heralded the placing of a vinyl disc on the record player, and always the disc was Duke Ellington and his orchestra playing 'Take the A Train'. It always happened very close to my departure time and to me to signified that I would return safely and once again enjoy one of my favourite records:

> *Hurry, hurry, hurry, take the A Train*
> *To get to Silver Hill way up in Harlem*
> *If you should take the A Train*
> *You'll get to where you're going in a hurry*
> *Hurry, hurry, hurry now it's coming*
> *Can't you hear the tracks are humming*
> *If you should miss the A Train*
> *You'll miss the quickest way to get to Harlem.*

The lines did not rhyme, but you could not fault the rhythm. The vocalist usually departed into 'scat' singing after this initial statement, but some versions were minus a vocalist.

> *I ain't much to look at, I ain't nothing to see*
> *But I've got a train waiting for me*
> *I'm hoping to catch the A Train*

As for me - well, it was time to depart, hurry and take the express train, the quickest way to get to St Pancras, as the song might have said.

JP Sullivan (Consultants) required someone to be based in Lesotho, southern Africa and act as Consultant to the Ministry of Works and Transport. My flight to Lesotho was via Johannesburg in South Africa. The lowest altitude in Lesotho is 1000m, which is why it is known as 'The Kingdom in the Sky', and the lowlands around Maseru would be highlands anywhere else. I arrived in the late evening at Maseru Airport and was immediately surprised how cold it was; it is the capital and the only big town. I was booked into the Lancers Inn in the centre of town, which appeared to be pleasant and full of character.

Ponies appear to be the preferred means of travel around the country; there are no highways, but the tarred roads are kept in good condition. No sleek, modern luxury buses are to be seen, minibuses in various states of repair being the norm. May to July are the winter months; it often snows in the highlands and is extremely cold at night. August to October is spring. November to January are summer months and most of the rain can fall during this time. February to April is autumn. Lesotho gained Independence on the 4th October, 1966. Life expectancy is 35 years, largely due to HIV/AIDS, among the worst figures in the world.

The subject of accommodation was soon mentioned and they had several bungalows for me to view, apparently under the impression that I would be anxious to get organised as soon as possible, so there was an air of surprise when I announced that I was perfectly happy to stay at the Lancers Inn for the duration of my contract. The organisation of cook/houseboys, food, meals, etc which I had been part of over the years was wearing thin, and if I was able to leave all these duties to someone else at Lancers then that appeared quite attractive to me at this time.

The Lancers Inn was a sandstone building set in attractive

gardens just off Kingsway Avenue, the main thoroughfare through town. In a convenient central location it housed comfortable rondavels and chalets with en-suite bathrooms. A pool, beer garden and excellent restaurant made up the amenities. The owner and his wife became great friends during my stay; he, like me, was a jazz fanatic and after reading my monthly *Jazz Journal International* forwarded by Jean I would pass it over to him for his perusal, with the added 'to be returned' of course.

I was very fortunate to be able to accompany one of our engineers and travel to our various locations around Lesotho for approximately a week on a courtesy visit assessing their problems and requirements. Back at the workshops in Maseru I found the Transport Department running quite efficiently; it was the Plant Workshop that I was concerned about. Lesotho is completely surrounded by South Africa and many of the labour force find employment there, working in the mines during the week and travelling home at the weekends. This goes a long way towards easing Lesotho's unemployment problems. Our workshop plant breakdown problems appeared to be mostly solved by outside agencies in South Africa relying on Caterpillar service engineers etc to solve their difficulties. Bloemfontein in South Africa was only a short distance from Maseru and all the main dealerships had representation there and frequently visited our workshops, anxious to secure work and orders for spare parts.

The stores held spares received years previously and unlikely to be required in the future. Many were for obsolete machinery and plant we no longer used. I was able over my twelve-month period to sell back to the dealerships most of this unwanted stock; they still had a use for it.

Every month I produced a detailed chart showing for how many hours out of the weekly 44 each tradesman was fully occupied, and the results at first were shocking. Gradually I reduced this culture of relying on outside sources by introducing more work to be done in our workshop, at first the simpler tasks and then the more complex repairs. The African foreman and supervisors were reluctant to change, and many hurdles had to be overcome as we progressed from the easy to a more challenging and active environment, but the monthly charts were showing a marked improvement.

Shortly after arriving in Lesotho I bought myself a second-hand Daihatsu saloon from a local dealer. This proved a good investment and never let me down throughout the tour. The border with South Africa was only a mile down the Kingsway Road from the Lancers Inn and the Maseru Bridge linked both countries. South African police manned this border crossing and your passport would see you through without any difficulties. On Saturday I would often travel to Bloemfontein, which was only a few miles inland, and enjoy a day sightseeing.

As the tour was rapidly drawing to a close I started making enquiries in the UK regarding a car for use in our retirement. Jean and I had enjoyed a holiday in Cyprus during one of my leave periods and we hired an Austin Metro saloon during our visit which proved reliable and transported us all around the country. I have always been reluctant to pay more than £5,000 for a car and am quite satisfied with a basic model with no fancy trimmings and added extras. The brochures arrived and I asked Jean what colour she preferred. Her choice was a chocolate brown colour. I cannot remember the official colour name. All details and necessary paperwork were forwarded to the dealership and they arranged to have the car waiting for me at Heathrow Airport on arrival.

The local dealer was pleased to buy back my Daihatsu for the same price I paid for it originally, so I had enjoyed a good year of economical motoring. The situation in the workshop had improved dramatically, with the employees taking on most of the work with growing confidence and resisting the urge to call in the South African dealerships whenever any major breakdowns occurred; unfortunately my fear was that they would revert to their old ways as soon as I departed the scene.

The Range Rover dealership in Maseru was celebrating the launch of their latest model and I received an invitation, along with other local businessmen and dignitaries. Engaged in conversation with a group of their representatives, I joined in their enthusiasm for the new model and enquired if their spares department would be capable of backing up new sales, as I had experienced difficulty with securing parts for current models over the last year. The group quickly dispersed and moved away - obviously I was spoiling their party!

We received news from the wife of a previous expatriate employee that a few months after leaving Lesotho for retirement in the UK he had dropped dead on the golf course. I arrived after his departure and never met him. It made me think deeply about my own situation once again.

It was time to leave Lesotho and the Lancers Inn, where I had enjoyed interesting conversations over evening meals with fascinating guests who were passing through during my residency. The steaks were also the best in town! My overriding impression of Lesotho during working hours was of being cold and usually shivering more hours than I was comfortably warm, which meant I needed little encouragement to return to my office and take a position near my electric fire. The Lancers' rooms were centrally heated and very comfortable at all times.

Arriving at Heathrow, I was greeted by the representative

from the dealership, who handed over the keys to my new Metro. As we approached the car-parking area my eyes were busily searching for that chocolate brown colour, but it was nowhere to be seen.

"Sorry about the colour, but you've got your second-choice of Targa Red," said the representative with a smile.

"Thirty-two years and British car dealerships never change," I replied.

"I don't understand," said the bewildered representative.

"It doesn't matter," I said, turning the ignition key and driving smoothly into retirement in our new Targa Red Austin Metro saloon.

SUMMARY

1987 - 2008

1945 to 1955	Aveling-Barford Ltd.	Apprenticeship, Service Engineer
1955 to 1957	Sierra Leone, West Africa	Iron-Ore Mine
1957 to 1958	Nigeria, West Africa	Tin Mine
1958 to 1959	Ghana, West Africa	Diamond Mine
1959 to 1963	Nigeria, West Africa	Tin Mine
1963 to 1966	Malawi, Central Africa	Road Construction
1966 to 1969	Tanzania, East Africa	Diamond Mine
1969 to 1970	Sierra Leone, West Africa	Rutile Mine
1970 to 1973	Sierra Leone, West Africa	Road Construction
1973 to 1976	Nigeria, West Africa	Road Construction
1976 to 1978	Saudi Arabia, Middle East	Pre-Stressed Concrete Factory
1978 to 1981	Saudi Arabia, Middle East	Road Construction
1981 to 1984	Tanzania, East Africa	New Township Construction
1985 to 1987	Lesotho, Southern Africa	Public Works Department

Professional Qualifications gained as Plant
& Transport Manager.

Registered Technician Engineer - R.TECH.ENG.
Member Institution Of Plant Engineers - M.I.PLANT.E.
Member British Mistitute Of Management - M.B.I.M.
Associate Member Institute Of Road Transport Engineers
A.M.INST.R.T.E.

I consider myself one of the last of the breed of truly freelance expatriates able to carve a full-time career from working abroad in under-developed third-world countries.

Personnel Managers

xx

My 'Number One Hate' is Personnel Managers, and I state this without hesitation or reservation. I probably have had more dealings with this occupational hazard than most during my working career, having successfully gained employment with various Companies on fourteen occasions, not counting a few failures.

Present-day job-seekers, although limited in choice, have access to vacancies made easier through Job Centres, computer access and applications (i.e. curriculum vitae structure and presentation). I sympathize with their unenviable quest seeking employment in these difficult economic times and consider myself fortunate to have sought employment during times that were easier and employers fought hard to recruit staff and fill their job vacancies. Unfortunately they will eventually encounter the Personnel Manager who will be no better (and probably worse) than in my day.

Having sought job vacancies in the 1950's, 60's, 70's and 80's B.C. (Before Computers) I compiled and often updated my curriculum vitae which had to be very detailed regarding the types of Plant and Transport I was familiar with. These C.V's were then produced in quantity at the Printers (no home copiers available) after which I would forward a copy with covering letter to the company advertising the vacancy. From every ten letters dispatched during the job-seeking period I would consider myself fortunate to receive two replies. If fortunate enough to receive a reply it inevitably contained the dreaded 'Application Form' which was the ultimate in frustration and probably designed by the Personnel Manager in question. The detailed information submitted on your C.V would be ignored in favour of this standard issue Form which probably conformed with the size of his filing-cabinet. The Form would consist of various sized boxes, large boxes for your date of birth, Christian and surname and ridiculously small boxes for job experience (especially when you have worked for over ten different Companies) when you were inclined to write in the boxes 'Please refer to the damned C.V'. I attended one interview where, when entering his office, the Personnel Manager remarked, "You don't look like an earthmoving type!" I replied that he "didn't act like a Personnel Manager and we were obviously wasting each other's time"— upon which I turned to leave the office. I was eventually persuaded to continue with the interview. I cannot understand how I failed to secure that appointment.

The hour-plus time spent on completing these Forms would usually go unrewarded, in most cases not warranting a reply. In my opinion the headquarters and any other properties of the Institute of Personnel Managers should be closed and redeveloped as Job Centres, the Institute and its qualifications declared void and all members issued with 'Job Application Forms'.

Following my discourse on 'Number One Hate' I suppose 'Number One Regret' should be mentioned. I have been extremely fortunate throughout my life in having parents and a sister who I loved, a wife who I adored, two boys who are a credit to us, and five grandchildren who I worship. It has been a good life and I have always followed a goal which I have managed to achieve in most cases, therefore regrets are of the minor variety and very few. My one main regret is not being a Chartered Engineer (a Member of the Institute of Mechanical Engineers M.I.MECH.E) but this would have entailed three years full-time College which I, or my parents, could not afford and I regret not being able to prove to myself that I could achieve it. I am a Registered Technician Engineer (R.TECH.ENG) one rank below degree level. Many job vacancies have been denied me because they have stipulated they must be filled by a degree-holding applicant even though I have had the utmost confidence in being suitable to fill the position, therefore missing many opportunities to further my experiences with Personnel Managers.

During my working life in Africa and the Middle East I had encountered instances where European friends I knew had reached the usual retirement age of fifty-five and returned to their country of origin whereupon shortly afterwards we would be notified by a wife or member of the family that their death had occurred. In one instance during my employment with Williamson Diamonds in Tanzania two of the three Workshop Managers died suddenly, one being the Machine Shop Manager and the other the Welding Shop Manager. I was at that time the Plant and Transport Workshop Manager. I had always vowed to retire from my expatriate activities at the age of fifty-five. Several friends had continued working after this age but their rapid deterioration was noticeable and I intended and fervently hoped to enjoy many years of retirement after this milestone.

LIFE EXPECTANCY

LESOTHO - 35 YEARS

SIERRA LEONE - 41 YEARS

NIGERIA - 51 TO 56 YEARS

GHANA - 59 YEARS

TANZANIA - 50 TO 71 YEARS

Many things have changed since my time in Africa and this should be borne in mind when reading these accounts from 1955 to 1987.

SIERRA LEONE:
1955 TO 1957 & 1969 TO 1973

Devastated by Civil War lasting from 1991 until 2002. Much has been written concerning the atrocities committed during this period. Marampa Iron-Ore Mine at Lunsar was abandoned, its control cabins and conveyor-belts now lying idle where during my time there we supplied 40% of Britain's iron-ore.

NOTE: SIERRA LEONE 1955 TO 1957

The Rutile Mine at Mogbwema was rich in titanium used in the manufacture of toothpaste, artificial knees and suntan lotion. The Mine was the site of the largest deposits of Rutile in the world; during my time there a 400-tonne dredge was operational, its buckets digging out the titanium ore. In 1995 rebels invaded and ransacked everything in sight, taking Europeans and workers hostage; some escaped and fled into the bush spending many weeks in hiding .

In 2004 work commenced again; in 2007 a new dredge—the Solondo—was commissioned. This dredge collapsed sideways in July, 2008 with 50 workers on board of which two were never recovered.

NOTE: SIERRA LEONE 1969 TO 1970

The Taiama-Bo Highway was the scene of horrific fighting and atrocities during the Civil War. It is now a main artery in the road network. Njala University Campus is thriving with young students furthering their education.

NOTE: SIERRA LEONE 1970 TO 1973

Ref: Bradt Travel Guide, Sierra Leone, Edition 1
Authors: Katrina Manson & James Knight, May, 2009

NIGERIA:
1957 TO 1958 & 1959 TO 1963 & 1973 TO 1976

Tin Mining in Nigeria now appears to be an occupation of the past. 10,000 tons were produced in the 1970's falling to 300 tons in the late 1990's and Jos was once the largest producer of tin in the world.

NOTE: NIGERIA 1957 TO 1958 & 1959 TO 1963

The Highway from Lagos Murtala Mohammed International Airport appears to be as busy and chaotic as it was many years ago. The Airport reviews are now favourable, suggesting that the Airport is apparently free form corruption and strife with modernisation in 2007. Lagos lost its capitol city status in 1991 with this honour going to Abuja.

NOTE: NIGERIA 1973 TO 1976

Nigeria has had a turbulent history since Independence in 1960 with crisis years in 1962 and 1964. 1966 brought a coup with assassinations. 1967 to 1970 were the Biafran War Years with the civilian population being most affected. 1980 saw religious riots in Kano and there were riots in Jos during 2001. There followed clashes in Port Harcourt in 2004.

Ref: *Bradt Travel Guide*, Nigeria, Edition 2
Author: Lizzie Williams, 2008

MALAWI
(PREVIOUSLY NYASALAND UNTIL
FULL INDEPENDENCE ON 6/7/64)

Zomba is no longer the capital, having been replaced by Lilongwe in 1975 after massive re-development.

The Lakeshore Road has opened-up the country to tourism as intended and is now referred to as the M1. Ntcheu (on the Mozambique border), our first Road Development Unit posting, is now a location on the M1.

We knew (and enjoyed a holiday) at the lakeshore resort of Fort Johnson, now known as Mangochi.

Karonga has unbelievably developed as Malawi's seventh largest town with the country's largest and most modern

Museum, and is now the largest port town anywhere on the shore of Lake Malawi. Karonga was an outpost until 1981; it now boasts several hotels, an airport, the Cultural & Museum Centre and in 1988 a Uranium Mine came into operation.

NOTE: MALAWI 1963 TO 1966

Ref:

Bradt Travel Guide, Malawi, Edition 5
Author: Philip Briggs, April, 2010

TANZANIA

(PREVIOUSLY TANGANYIKA UNTIL FULL INDEPENDENCE ON 9/12/61)

At Williamson diamonds I mention telegrams (a form of quick delivery, short, expensive message) and it should be remembered that Mobile Phones were unheard of at that time.

NOTE: TANZANIA 1966 to 1969 & 1981 to 1984

RETIREMENT

As I journeyed from Heathrow in our new Metro Saloon my thoughts drifted back to thirty-two years spent overseas where I seemed to be in constant battle with British dealerships whose after-sales service left much to be desired—and even now was following me into retirement as I travelled in my Targa Red vehicle which should have been 'Chocolate Brown.' My blood boiled as I reasoned why I should be satisfied with my second colour choice after paying them £5,000 plus and why should there be mention of 'second choice colour' on their order forms when these amounts are being paid for their products? Second choice should not enter into the deal.

The dealership contacted me some days after I returned home to ask if I was happy and satisfied with the car. I assured them that everything was running smoothly, but voicing my opinion on 'second choice' appeared to leave them baffled and mystified at this trifling complaint. I was not surprised, and this is only one of the reasons we now see German, French and Japanese vehicles dominating the roads of Africa. Actually I don't give a damn about the colour and neither does Jean and, excuse me while I give the car another coat of polish, this Targa Red comes up very nicely.

As stated previously, Jean and I had ordered our bungalow and plot a year before and the Agent had informed us that it would be a year before completion. It was ready a few weeks early and Jean had sold our house in Narborough without any difficulty and had been anxious to move to Long Sutton. Mark had been on hand to assist with the move so Jean and our dog Sherry had been in residence for about three weeks and were already enjoying their retirement when I arrived home.

During my years spent working for two companies in Saudi Arabia I contributed to the Saudi social insurance scheme and this money was to be refunded on leaving the country. Several years had elapsed after my departure from Saudi when I heard from an organisation who said they were in a position to release my money without further delay; it was obviously a scam and I refused to have any further dealings with them. I did not want to see expatriates being exploited and contacted my local MP Sir Richard Body who came to our bungalow accompanied by his Agent. When informed of my misgivings regarding these developments he assured me that he would notify the Police and make further enquiries.

Following this visit I was contacted by the *Daily Telegraph* who asked if they may send a photographer and use the photograph in a forthcoming financial article. The photographer duly arrived and proceeded to take shots of Jean and myself from all different angles and what I assumed would be a session completed in thirty minutes was stretching into several hours. I have never had so many photographs taken of myself in two hours than in the previous sixty-one years. Still not satisfied with his endeavours, he had us pose in the hallway, kitchen, living-room; Jean relaxed in a chair with me alongside perched on the arm of the chair and followed by me relaxed in a chair with Jean perched alongside on the arm, etc. The photograph that finally appeared in the newspaper was his final effort. He eventually departed with enough photographs to fill a large portfolio.

It was an unusual experience, but amusing and we had a few laughs during the encounter.

Jean's parents visited often and we always enjoyed their times with us in Long Sutton. Many hours were still spent planning various visits to places that would interest them. With their 60th wedding anniversary approaching the family were intending to feature their life together with an article in the local Sheffield newspaper and discussions were held over the appropriate wording that should appear. I reminded Polly and Joe that the reporter always asked for the secret of long marriages; the answer did not appear to be readily forthcoming, therefore I suggested: "We might have a few words in bed but we never fall out." It was never used!

Jean often joined her parents for a week's caravan holiday at Cleethorpes. I would take her down in the car and return home to Long Sutton where our dog Sherry and I would spend the week together decorating. It was always my suggestion that whenever decorating needed to be done and furniture needed to be moved, with the ensuing upheaval this caused, that Jean should disappear and have a holiday. I have never had any great interest in cooking and have always regarded the kitchen as a convenient room to pass through on your way to the conservatory or back-garden. My years in Africa with Cooks and Houseboys doing the necessary work indulged this way of thinking. When left with the task of feeding myself I am perhaps one step-up from useless and usually when left to cater for myself would rustle up a salad for lunch (which I enjoy immensely) and never seem to tire of. Dinner would probably be something on toast.

Turning to Sherry, who always watched intently from the kitchen door having often been warned by Jean "Don't get under my feet", I would say, "It's sardines on toast tonight!" Her tail

Expats queue up for Saudi tax rebates

Riyadh is refunding British workers who paid into salary-based insurance schemes

Retired construction worker Ron Bradley: waited two years for cheques to arrive

THOUSANDS of British people who worked in Saudi Arabia between 1973 and 1987, including many who returned to this country last summer when Iraq invaded Kuwait, are entitled to claim large tax refunds from the Saudi Arabian government.

Information about the refunds is hard to obtain and long delays are being experienced, although people with claims should make them as soon as possible.

The refunds result from the decision of the Saudi government in 1969 to introduce a system of social insurance. The scheme began in 1973 and provided generous retirement pensions and other benefits. It was funded by compulsory deductions from salary of 5 p.c. from the employee and 8 p.c. from the employer.

Both contributions were collected by the employer and forwarded to the Saudi General Organisation for Social Insurance (GOSI). The scheme was not compulsory for employers with fewer than 20 employees.

In 1987, the Saudi government decided that the scheme was proving too cumbersome and costly for people who came from abroad to work in Saudi Arabia, as they usually stayed for only a short period of time. A decree was issued on March 10, 1987 to end the scheme for non-Saudi nationals.

The Saudi government decided that those who had paid into the scheme between 1973 and 1987 would have their contributions refunded. Currently, the Saudi government is refunding only the 5 p.c. deduction. Reports in the Saudi press that the 8 p.c. will also be refunded have been denied by the Saudis.

Even if it was refunded, it is not clear whether employer or employee would get it. The amount of the refund is the straight 5 p.c. deduction without interest or allowance for inflation. But it is still not easy to estimate its value. The refund is made in United States dollars by a cheque drawn on the Saudi American Bank. The original contributions made in Saudi riyals are converted into dollars for the refund to be made and into sterling to pay into a British bank.

Because of relative exchange rates, the final total may be disappointing. In 1988, the Saudi government advertised the availability of the repayments and claims began to come in. However, with an estimated 3·8m foreign workers who had paid into the scheme, the refunds are inevitably taking a long time to make. Some people have been waiting for years.

Ronald Bradley is a retired construction worker who has worked abroad for most of his life. He spent four and a half years in Saudi Arabia, leaving in 1986. "A couple of years ago I saw adverts in The Daily Telegraph offering to act on behalf of ex-Saudi workers. One was from GOSI and I wrote and got the special form and sent copies of my GOSI card and other details.

"The Saudis said there were so many that they could not do it all at once, so I waited. They are an honourable people and I was content to wait."

He received two cheques for over £1,000 each in January this year representing the periods he had worked for two employers in Saudi Arabia.

Peter Gartland, editor of The International, a British-based publication read by many expatriates, has found a wide range of responses from the Saudi authorities.

"Some readers have applied and have not even had an acknowledgment after a year; others have had a cheque back within a few weeks," he said. "There seems to be little rhyme or reason to it, though it may depend on how the claim is presented and whether it is straightforward or not."

Because of the delays, a number of intermediaries have set up in business claiming to deal directly with the Saudi authorities and speed up the process in exchange for a percentage of the refund.

However, it seems unlikely that they can do this. An Embassy spokeswoman said: "We know nothing of these third party organisations. The Saudi Government expects people to deal directly with the GOSI office in Riyadh."

Mr Gartland urges potential claimants to act quickly. "Because of the costs of the war, the Saudi Government has had to borrow money for the first time. So it is possible that it will decide at some point that this whole exercise is too costly and issue a decree to stop the repayments. I must stress that there is no evidence that this is likely, but it is a point worth considering."

In order to make a claim, people who worked in Saudi Arabia between February 1973 and March 1987 and who paid the social insurance contributions should write to the Director General, Overseas Benefit Department, General Organisation of Social Insurance, PO Box 2963, Riyadh 11462, Kingdom of Saudi Arabia, and ask for the relevant claim form which can be completed in English.

Proof of payment into GOSI will normally be required. The GOSI card is the ideal proof. The Embassy warns "Not having a card is a disadvantage."

DAILY TELEGRAPH

MARCH, 1991

Expats queue up for Saudi tax rebates

would wag vigorously as she was partial to sardines on toast. The second evening was similar to the first: "Sardines on toast!" I cried. Sherry's tail wagged but not with the same fervour. The third night I remarked: "Sardines on toast tonight!" Sherry's tail did not move and she looked at me with a lack of enthusiasm and a face that said, "Is that all you can manage?" Sherry died a few years later after thirteen years with us.

Jean had joined the Women's Institute in Long Sutton and spent time attending meetings and assisting with various functions. Eventually she was elected President and served in this capacity for several terms until standing down and suggesting that someone younger should take her place. In her capacity as President she organised many local outings and coach trips further afield to places of interest.

We were also keen members of the Long Sutton Indoor Bowls Club which had opened in the same year that we retired. Starting with one game each week it soon became addictive and we found ourselves in various leagues, singles, double and foursomes.

Jean was an avid reader and regularly purchased books to add to her collection of favourite authors. Various libraries supplemented her insatiable appetite for reading material, and our own Long Sutton Library soon lost its appeal as it failed to keep up with her demands, so journeys further afield around Lincolnshire were required. Spalding had an excellent library and a regular weekly visit was soon on the agenda, as were intermittent visits to Boston Library.

A visit to Lincoln was a favourite day out as she pursued her favourite pastime of visiting the city's many second-hand bookshops around the Cathedral area. Everywhere she went she carried a meticulously-recorded notebook containing information regarding authors and their long out-of-print editions. She would extract it from her handbag and we would begin our expedition, with me taking up my usual supermarket, clothes and book-shopping position and following behind like a spare part, uttering the occasional 'Yes dear' or 'No dear' as demanded. There were no Kindles of course at this time.

I suppose roles were reversed as I searched for my vinyl records and tape cassettes in earlier years and I would not have appreciated the idea of downloading music, preferring to see my records stacked neatly on shelves with musicians and recording dates in chronological order. Taking a record down from the shelf, reading the information on the sleeve and placing the vinyl on the record deck before playing it gave me immense satisfaction. I suppose owning a much-loved book and taking it down from the bookshelf to read had the same effect with Jean. She also read the daily newspaper from cover to cover and always left me amazed by how quickly she did it. I would often question her thoroughness, but she would recount the articles in great detail; there was no doubt that she absorbed everything.

Polly died after we had been retired for some years and Joe moved into sheltered accommodation. his two daughters and two sons, all living in sheffield, visited regularly and there was always someone in the family to do his daily shopping, etc. Jean and I visited as often as we could. The accommodation, facilities and social life were good but he obviously missed Polly greatly. Joe died shortly afterwards. We asked the family what caused his death and they all agreed that he just gave up and grew tired of living—especially without Polly.

Liam, my cousin retired a few years after me and on his visits with wife Lynne we were able to show them the merits of Long Sutton together with property for sale. It must have been a good sales pitch as they moved from Leicester to a bungalow on our estate just around the corner from us.

Our very happy and contented retirement had commenced in June 1987, and it was now July 2000, thirteen years of extreme fulfilment later; we had achieved everything we had planned along the way and were 'enjoying life to the full', as they say.

Jean was suffering from frequent stomach pains and we visited our local Doctor who arranged for a hospital visit and thorough check. We had no reason to be alarmed as the Doctor said it would only entail an overnight stay. I still remember the morning the ambulance arrived at 58 Woodlands vividly. Jean was smiling and happy as I stood with her. The ambulance men said they had to travel to nearby villages to pick-up other patients on their way to Pilgrim Hospital near Boston. It was no inconvenience as far as Jean was concerned; she was relaxed, free of pain, and I promised to collect her the following day. We waved to each other, the ambulance moved away and I watched as it disappeared around the corner.

The following day I visited the hospital and learned that further tests were needed, therefore she would stay in hospital. The following two weeks entailed afternoon visits where we talked and she recounted her hospital experiences; on other days I sat at her bedside throughout the visiting hours, she being sedated with eyes closed and silent while I indulged in a kaleidoscope of memories formed over 40 years spent with this marvellous woman, the mother of my two sons, the bedrock of our marriage. Visiting hours would end and I would drive back to our bungalow in Long Sutton with growing apprehension.

My daily visits to Jean in Pilgrim Hospital, Boston, consisted of individual days of elation followed by dark despondency and a growing fear that all was not well. I cannot recall now when actual events happened but it was probably during the second week on entering the Ward and greeting Jean that she calmly informed me that the Doctor (or Surgeon?) wished to see me. I entered the room and the Doctor was accompanied by a Nurse. The Doctor said Jean had Disseminated Carcinoma of the Stomach (Stomach Cancer) and did I understand what he was saying? I replied that I did and asked him, "How long?" He replied by saying it was uncertain and could be six months or longer.

Returning to Jean who was calm and smiling, I embraced her and sat beside the bed. Through misty eyes I could see curtains being drawn around us to offer some privacy. With my head resting in her lap I cried uncontrollably while she ran her fingers through my hair and consoled me. We spoke little and later were brought meals by the nurses. Eventually I returned home and telephoned Jean's sister in Sheffield. "I'm running scared," I informed her and asked that she contact the other siblings for me and advise them to visit urgently; they reacted immediately and we were able to visit Jean together.

Twenty-four hours have elapsed since I wrote the previous chapters. I was affected so much by recounting and recalling those events that I found it difficult to control my emotions; the dark despair enveloped me once again as it did on that occasion. Reaching this point of my story was the time I was dreading and I was undecided how to approach and write about such a personal matter.

On my next visit to Jean a Macmillan Nurse was in attendance, who gave us assurance and explained how we would receive assistance when Jean returned home. Once again I was in awe of Jean who was already planning and sorting-out our future. Paul and Mark had visited whenever they could and brought their wives and children on visits. It was approaching two weeks since

Jean entered hospital and I had visited her every afternoon, when I received an early morning telephone call from the nurse who advised me to attend as Jean's condition was deteriorating; she had already contacted Paul and Mark. We virtually all arrived at the Ward together and spent the day there with a heavily sedated Jean.

During the day my crown tooth dropped-out. I tucked it into my pocket and was annoyed that it should happen at this particular time. We sat by Jean's bedside and darkness fell. The boys went out for some refreshment and I stayed on. "She doesn't want to go," said the nurse and continued on her duties. She was silent as I held her hand—and suddenly she was gone. I rang for the nurse and she came accompanied by the boys.

I found myself in the corridor sitting on a lone chair. How I had come to be there I cannot remember but I expect someone had led me there to keep me out of the way whilst they were occupied with other things. No one seemed to be about; all was quiet but the lights were too bright. I craved the darkness and a corner position; this was a long, bright, empty corridor. A man in a white coat approached and stopped momentarily; touching me on the shoulder he remarked, "I'm sorry," before continuing out of sight. Where was the darkness I longed for? Where were the boys? I hoped they would soon appear from whatever business they were required to do. My thoughts drifted back to Williamson Diamonds in Tanzania, hearing of my mother's death. The lone chair in the darkened bedroom. I had lost the two most important women in my life to cancer. Jean would not be bringing any cups of tea tonight—who would console me in my grief? The boys appeared and led me into the darkness.

Paul returned to his family in Leicester and Mark returned to Long Sutton with me and stayed overnight before attending to necessary arrangements the following day. The year 2000 saw a shortage of Dentists around the British Isles and many Spanish, Portuguese Dentists filled these vacancies. My dental practice in Long Sutton was no exception and had interviewed many graduates unsuccessfully over many weeks; the shortage meant they could pick and choose areas of employment and as my Dentist explained to me, very few young people would choose sleepy Long Sutton and preferred a large town or city with vibrant night-life to practice their dental skills.

My long-term Dentist was moving from Long Sutton Surgery to a practise in Holbeach a few miles away and contacted his regular customers regarding the move and asked whether they were prepared to move with him. I was happy to go along with this suggestion and had already paid two visits there over the last year, and as stated previously my crown tooth had dropped out at the hospital; therefore I visited his surgery in Holbeach where he fixed my tooth and afterwards informed me he was retiring in a few days. I would need to re-register for further dental treatment which left me in a quandary as my previous Long Sutton surgery was full to capacity, with a shortage of Dentists and unable to accept further patients. I was informed that Grantham (thirty miles away) was probably the nearest surgery accepting patients.

Since jean's death a few days previously I had suffered a noticeable lack of confidence and even the short journey in the car to Holbeach had placed me in a "what if?" situation where I imagined a breakdown on the road which led to a tyre pressure check, battery, oil, fan-belt, etc., prior to this journey and every trip even on the same day. This dental business also preyed on my mind and I found myself constantly worried about toothache, the inevitable search and journey to a dentist with the result that I cleaned my teeth immediately after anything had entered my mouth—the "what if I get toothache?" syndrome. Also at that time the fuel Tanker Drivers commenced strike action; there was a nationwide shortage of petrol with long lines of motorists queuing at Garages. "What if I get toothache and require petrol to travel long distances to locate a Dentist?" etc., etc.

Every night before bed I checked smoke-alarms to ensure they were working, and so it went on. I visited my Doctor because I was not sleeping; he would not prescribe any tablets as they could be habit forming and he assured me I would sleep eventually. I sat in front of the television like a zombie; little was of interest and did nothing to speed up those long, dreary, desolate hours. I was desperately lonely and often tempted to step outside the door onto that empty, quiet street and shout, "I'm here, I'm here!" Liam and Lynne lived just around the corner and I found myself telephoning them quite often. "Can I come round this afternoon for a chat?" The answer was always yes. Whenever I left their bungalow I dreaded returning to my own. My neighbour would invite me round to watch the 'Monday Night Football' with him while his wife attended her 'Bingo Session'—I appreciated that very much. My interest in cooking was 'nil' and I arranged with Wiltshire Farm Foods for a weekly selection of meals which were delivered to the door and were excellent value. I could just manage the presentation of a salad for lunch. And so the days passed on until after five months it was arranged that I sell my bungalow and move to Kettering where I could live with Mark, Donna and son Scott.

Shortly after Jean's death I told myself that I should make an effort and continue to socialise. The Indoor Bowling Club appeared to be the ideal venue to put this into practice. It proved to be a disaster! I was a loner amongst couples and I missed seeing the joy on Jean's face as her bowl nestled against the jack and I was reminded of the blues singer B.B. King and his mournful lament 'The Thrill is Gone'. I took our bowls, bowls bags and bowls paraphernalia along to the Club, placed them side by side in the office and requested that they find them a new home "My bowling days are over," I announced and departed the scene.

I gazed at the television and thought that this must be the first stage towards being a recluse. The day dragged slowly and relentlessly on.

The inevitable had to be confronted, and although I had been resisting the task, I knew it had to be faced some time soon. So sorting out Jean's belongings began in earnest.

My intention was to have an initial check and forward many items to a charity shop before inviting the boys and their wives to take any remaining items that might be of use to them. In suitcases I was surprised to discover that Jean had kept every single letter I had written to her. They were all neatly tied in date order, together with birthday and Valentine cards received whenever we had been apart, from my first letter posted from Nigeria to my last, posted in Lesotho. "As long as you write every week you will be in the clear" she always reminded me, and I dutifully carried out her instructions - the proof was all there. I had not known those letters existed. I suddenly felt unworthy of her.

Slowly I read each one, and the memories came flooding back. They were not going to be for public consumption, I decided, to be pored over and discussed with great interest by all and sundry. This was private correspondence relating to our dreams and aspirations.

The letters were shredded and placed in bin liners, which I tied securely. The memories spread over the last forty years which they contained had been noted and transferred safely to my mind, where I hoped to recall them frequently in quiet moments down the years ahead, unless the dark shadow of Alzheimer's disease descended to rob me of this pleasure.

My story has now run its course. The tales have been told and the memory bank is about to close. Nothing exciting has happened to me since the 8th August, 2000. I no longer travel or take holidays, no longer attend jazz concerts. All these things would afford little pleasure without Jean at my side and observing her smiles of joy and pleasure. 'The Thrill is Gone.'

I have made no secret of the fact that I am sure moving from Long Sutton to live with Mark in Kettering saved my life, or to be more specific, my grandchildren Scott and Jade saved my life. I now have something to live for. Scott and I have lived together since he was four years old and I am extremely proud of him at eighteen as he pursues his studies at Keele University. Jade has had me around for all of her life; now she is Fourteen years old. I hope to be around for a few more years until she becomes more independent. I endeavour to assist the family when and where I can; it gives me satisfaction—I can live with that.

For many months I was not able to look at photographs of Jean—it was too upsetting for me. Approximately one year after her death I knew that I wanted a large photograph of her in my room and I knew which one it was to be. I bought a frame and installed it immediately; I suppose that is what people mean when they remark that you are 'ready to move on'.

CONCLUSION

Jean and I always enjoyed a long, brisk walk and this form of exercise I still pursue daily unless the weather is too severe (heavy rain or icy conditions). I detest the ice - at my age if you slip and fall you'll probably break something. An early morning walk from home into and around Kettering town with the return journey covers approximately four miles. Immediately after I begin walking, distances become meaningless as I become engulfed with memories of the past and I refer to it as the 'roulette wheel of my mind' spinning relentlessly and ejecting memories at random.

The park contains several small groups of animated people discussing, stroking and patting their canine companies and relating their latest adventures, illnesses and tricks to anyone willing to listen. Barking dogs chase after balls or sticks thrown vast distances by muscular ladies whose efforts would be worthy of selection to any Olympic discus-throwing team. The arch-backed old man with the long, heavy overcoat and walking-stick approaches; he shuffles along head bowed, his collie dog ambling along a few paces ahead, stopping at intervals to turn his head to check the old man's progress. We often meet around this spot and I used to say "Good Morning" as we passed but I have never received a reply. The collie dog ignores the other dogs as they run across his path chasing and barking around the Park. I wonder if the old man harbours a 'roulette wheel' in his mind and he remembers the time long-ago when he stood tall and erect and enjoyed the attention of many beautiful young ladies.

My Boots prescription has been collected together with other items and I stand in a corner of the shop trying to get myself organised. My coat pockets are rare and small: I no longer carry my wallet because I cannot accommodate its size and I remove any currency and cards required and place them in my pockets before leaving the house. Purchases are completed, small change, notes and receipts are carefully placed in available pockets. I fumble and fret as coins slip form hand to floor. When shopping, Jean would take my wallet and carefully place it in her handbag for safe-keeping until it was required. Life was so easy when Jean was around, I remembered. Looking up I saw the woman approaching, the familiar tartan skirt, the fawn jacket, the grey coiffure hair. I gazed after her as she passed. The music of Herbie Hancock's jazz standard whirled around inside my head while the vocalist repeated his plaintive line, "I thought it was you - I thought it was you."

The shopping centre is coming to life. The elderly couple walking slowly hand-in-hand browse the shop windows as we used to do. How I envy their companionship. Young lovers in the coffee-shop sit at their window table with cups of Cappuccino, gazing at each other and smiling while sharing some confidence as we used to do. Will this be a meeting they extract from the memory bank in future years?

I return home to a quiet house. The family have departed for work or school. I enter my room and switch on the television. I miss Jean so much, the long conversations and idle gossip. The mid-morning breaks with tea and biscuits. I miss her smile and I miss her laughter. All these are long gone and I am left viewing

'Homes under the Hammer' and 'Cash in the Attic'.

Personal maintenance becomes an ever increasing problem as the years take their toll; the engine and airframe require constant attention with the daily schedule consisting of:

BENDROFLUMETHIAZIDE 2.5MG
TABLET FOR BLOOD PRESSURE - EVERY MORNING

SIMVASTATIN 40MG
TABLET FOR CHOLESTEROL - EVERY NIGHT

BI-ANNUAL INSPECTIONS INCLUDE:
BLOOD PRESSURE CHECK
HEIGHT & WEIGHT (BODY MASS INDEX) CHECK
DENTAL CHECK

ANNUAL CHECK:-
EYE TEST
FLU JAB

My ears require syringing to clear them of wax at least once a year.

I am rapidly losing my hair.

My right lower eyelid decided to droop alarmingly overnight, which entailed a visit to the hospital Ophthalmology Department for a skin graft and stitching operation.

Maybe the time has come to conclude these ramblings of an old-timer, carefully close the blue frayed-edged cover of my FORM 700 and consign it to a dark, dusty shelf—marked 'ANCIENT HISTORY'.

However, if I could keep my engine ticking-over for a few more stolen years I may be fortunate enough to witness more joyful family occasions such as coming of age, engagements, weddings, births and great grandchildren.

R. Bradley 2016

ND - #0438 - 270225 - C20 - 229/152/25 - PB - 9781861510211 - Matt Lamination